TELEVISION AND WOMEN'S CULTURE

COMMUNICATION AND HUMAN VALUES

Series editors

Robert A. White, Editor, Centre for the Study of Communication and Culture, London, UK

Michael Traber, Associate Editor, World Association for Christian Communication, London, UK

International editorial advisory board

Binod C. Agrawal, Development and Educational Communication, Space Applications Centre, Ahmedabad, India

Luis Ramiro Beltrán, International Development Research Centre, Bogotá, Colombia

Kwame Boafo, African Council on Communication Education, Nairobi, Kenya

James W. Carey, University of Illinois, USA

Marlene Cuthbert, University of Windsor, Canada

William F. Fore, Yale Divinity School, USA

George Gerbner, University of Pennsylvania, USA

James D. Halloran, University of Leicester, UK

Cees Hamelink, Institute of Social Studies, The Hague, The Netherlands

Neville D. Jayaweera, World Association for Christian Communication, London, UK

Emile G. McAnany, University of Texas, USA

Walter J. Ong, St Louis University, USA

Breda Pavlic, Culture and Communication Sector, Unesco, Paris

Miquel de Moragas Spa, Autonomous University of Barcelona, Spain

TELEVISION AND WOMEN'S CULTURE

The Politics of the Popular

edited by Mary Ellen Brown

SAGE Publications
London · Newbury Park · New Delhi

First published 1990

Introduction, Motley Moments, Conclusion © Mary Ellen
Brown 1986, 1989, *Women as Audiences* © Virginia
Nightingale 1988, *For Television Centred Criticism* ©
Caren J. Deming 1986, *Women Audiences and the
Workplace* © Dorothy Hobson 1989, *Melodramatic
Identifications* © Ien Ang 1989, *Consumer Girl Culture* ©
Lisa A Lewis 1987, *Rock Video* © Sally Stockbridge 1989,
Cagney & Lacey © Danae Clark 1989, *Women and Quiz
Shows* © John Fiske 1989, *Male Gazing* © Beverley
Poynton and John Hartley 1989, *Class Gender and the
Female Viewer* © Andrea L. Press 1989.

This edition is not for sale in Australia or New Zealand.

Sage Publications Ltd
28 Banner Street
London EC1Y 8QE

Sage Publications Inc
2111 West Hillcrest Drive
Newbury Park, California 91320

Sage Publications India Pvt Ltd
32, M-Block Market
Greater Kailash – 1
New Delhi 110 048

British Library Cataloguing in Publication data

Television and women's culture: the politics of the popular.
 – (Communication and human values)
I. Women. Influence on television programmes
I. Brown, Mary Ellen II. Series
305.4

ISBN 0–8039–8228–3
ISBN 0–8039–8229–1 Pbk

Library of Congress catalog card number 89–063638

Typeset and printed in Australia by
Southwood Press, Sydney.

For Kevin, Colin, Sean and Chris

Contents

Conclusion

Acknowledgements

I began teaching classes about women and media in 1975. At that time, women teaching in newly formed Women's Studies Programs were self-educated. We had experienced the 1970's women's movement and subsequently applied its principles to our own areas of expertise. There were no textbooks, few articles and particularly none from the point of view expressed in this volume. I have subsequently used the work of this group of critics in teaching about women and popular culture to women's studies students and to media studies students, and I have found it to be an approach which not only rewards their scholarship in the present, but also gives them tools of analysis which are of continuing value.

Virginia Nightingale's chapter, *Women as Audience*, was presented to the 1988 International Television Studies Conference, London. Portions of *For Television-Centred Television Criticism: Lessons from Feminism* were delivered at the Iowa Symposium and Conference on Television Criticism in Iowa City, Iowa in 1986, and the International Communication Association Annual Conference in Montreal, Canada in 1986. A longer version of this chapter has appeared in *Communication Yearbook II*, edited by James A. Anderson, copyright 1988 by Sage Publications, Inc. The excerpts are reprinted by permission.

A version of *Consumer Girl Culture*, by Lisa A. Lewis, first appeared in *OneTwoThreeFour*, Number 5: Special Issue on Music Video (Spring 1987). A shortened version of *Motley Moments: Soap Operas, Carnival, Gossip and the Power of the Utterance* by Mary Ellen Brown was presented at the International Communication Association Annual Conference, in Montreal, Canada, 1986.

I wish to thank John Wood and Channel Seven in Australia for permission to reprint the still photograph from *Rafferty's Rules*; Joan Collins and Linda Evans for permission to use the off-air images from *Dynasty*; the British Broadcasting Company and Alan Chapman for the still from *40 Minutes*; Columbia Broadcasting Company for stills from *Cagney & Lacey*; the West Australian Newspapers for stills of Warwick Capper and the Sydney Swans;

Grundy Organisation of Australia for *Perfect Match*; Mary Leunig for the use of the cartoon from her book *There's No Place Like Home* Penguin Books, Australia.

I am grateful to Linda Barwick for sharing her knowledge and insight about women's oral culture from the conception through the writing of *Motley Moments*, and my thanks to all the contributors, to the women and men who talked to us about television; to Katharine Brisbane and Sandra Gorman, the editors at Currency Press; and to Robert White and Steve Barr, the editors at Sage Publications. I am also grateful to the various feminist support groups that I have been a part of over the years, but in particular my thanks go to Maxine Hatcher, Marilyn Myerson, Etta Breit, Robyn Quin, Hilaire Natt, and John Fiske for their encouragement, support and practical advice.

Special thanks to Chad Skaggs for his invaluable help in proof reading the final manuscript, to Deb Westerberg who word processed my parts of the manuscript in Australia, to the Department of Media Studies and Women's Studies at the Western Australian College of Advanced Education in Perth, and to Vicky Willis, Terry Collins, and Loretta Lonnen who word processed parts of the final version and to the Department of Communication and the Women's Studies Program at the State University of New York, Brockport.

INTRODUCTION

1

Introduction: Feminist Cultural Television Criticism — Culture, Theory and Practice

Mary Ellen Brown

The perspectives on television criticism in the following chapters are grounded in theory from several streams and from the women's movement of the 1970s. In this introduction, I would like to summarise and contextualise these theoretical perspectives in the hope that this will enhance and clarify the reader's understanding and use of the book.

The evolution of the feminist television criticism in this volume was encouraged by the women's movement in general and mediated by several strands of critical thought. Primary in its evolution are two ideas, one is the use of theory and the other is the close, fresh and specific examination of television programmes and audiences.

The theory, which can be loosely labelled post-structuralist, makes clear but limited use of structuralist thinking while recognising its social construction. The works of Sigmund Freud, Jacques Lacan, and Claude Lévi-Strauss apply here. In discerning what meaning is and how meaning is made, the theories of Ferdinand de Saussure, Umberto Eco, and Roland Barthes provide the semiotic underpinnings. Its Marxist social and philosophical position evolves out of the work of Louis Althusser in France, Raymond Williams and Stuart Hall in England and Antonio Gramsci in Italy. Feminist theoretical underpinnings are harder to pinpoint.

The French feminist thinkers, Hélène Cixous, Julia Kristeva, Catherine Clément, Luce Irigaray, Michèle Montrelay and Monique Wittig, mostly gathered around the publishing house *des femmes*, are an influence because the French feminists have been willing to conceptualise a level of writing, *écriture feminine*, which speaks directly and uniquely to women. The British feminist film theorists, centered around *Screen* and *Screen Education*, the journals which brought to English-speaking cultures the French Marxist political film critique of *Cahiers du Cinéma*, began the serious feminist critique of Hollywood cinema — critics and theorists like Claire Johnston, Laura Mulvey, Annette Kuhn and Pam Cook. This critique, psychoanalytic in bent, is carried on in America by the *Camera Obscura* collective. The feminist psychoanalytic film critique remains a major, if not the major, strand of film theory in the United States. Theorists like Kaja Silverman and Teresa de Lauretis have attempted to combine psychoanalysis and semiotics in recent works. It is, however, to the women in the British culturalist critique of popular culture that the criticism presented here is most indebted.

Feminist Culturalist Television Criticism

In this introductory section of *Television and Women's Culture: The Politics of the Popular*, I shall attempt to delineate how the streams of theoretical and critical work which I have mentioned have come together to form what I am calling feminist culturalist television criticism. A similar and often overlapping theoretical approach has been called resistance theory.

Resistance theory comprises a body of work which addresses the issue of how ordinary people and subcultural groups can resist hegemonic, or dominant pressures, and consequently obtain pleasure from what the political, social and/or cultural system offers, despite that system's contradictory position in their lives. Recently, studies of audiences' conversations about television have been labelled 'reading reception theory' or 'reception and response criticism'. Much of the work in this volume falls into such a classification. Reception and response criticism uses a combination of interviews, participant observation and conversation analyses to determine how audiences respond to various textual practices on television. The critics who have written for this volume are concerned particularly with considering how gendered audiences relate to and use television in their lives.

While the British cultural studies movement redefined working class culture, feminist writers/ethnographers working at the Birmingham Centre for Contemporary and Cultural Studies (CCCS) stood their ground for an investigation as well as a redefinition of the invisible 'other' in working-class culture — its girls and women. Out of their collective work evolved publications such as *Women Take Issue* and the work of authors like Charlotte Brunsdon, Marion Jordon, Dorothy Hobson, Christine Geraghty and Angela McRobbie.[1] These authors re-examined our commonsense assumptions about media using both ethnographic methodology and theoretical perspectives which assume that audiences have a great deal of control over their reading practices.

Concurrent with these events, some American feminists had begun to use content analysis to describe women's presence on television. The first assumption behind content analysis is that broadcast television has a moral obligation to serve (and therefore to represent) all of a country's citizens. The political argument here assumes that equality can, as a practical matter, be achieved within patriarchal capitalism. The major problem with such an approach is that content analysis is only descriptive and fails to critique the discursive construction of women within representational systems like television. A second assumption behind content analysis is psychological/ideological; and has to do with modelling behaviour. The notion is that people's perceptions of themselves hinge on seeing other people, like themselves, acting out particular roles. Content analysis takes for granted that women's 'real lives' are a given unproblematic and naturalised concept — an idea that most feminist culturalists would question.

While early feminist television studies in the United States centred on content analysis and film criticism centred on psychoanalysis, feminist literary and art criticism concentrated on restructuring the canon of the great writers and artists. This restructuring involved the re-writing of art and literary history to include the women, and the re-evaluating of what is classified as 'great art' or 'great literature'. Patchwork quilts and diaries, for example, have had their status elevated in the process. Attention has also been paid to the role of institutions like the gallery system and the academic system, as well as to the social context in which girls and women are culturally subordinated, to show how the meaning of the term 'high art' has been constructed to exclude women's work.

The British cultural studies movement, on the other hand, has seen it as essential to accept a redefined meaning of the term 'culture' as all that we do, say and believe, that is the practice of everyday living — a definition which has virtually eliminated the high/low distinction in terms of the analysis of cultural practices and artifacts. Cultural studies, of which feminist culturalist television criticism is a part, replace aesthetic criteria based on a notion of culture as the 'best' that has been thought and created in the world as defined by T.S. Eliot and Matthew Arnold, for instance. Instead, cultural studies offer an analysis of how ideology is produced and functions within television products and practices and how audiences use and interact with television in their lives. It involves textual, contextual, theoretical and anthropological analysis. Its aim is understanding and empowerment.

The feminist movement of the 1970s in its radical forms relied on consciousness-raising as a tactic. Consciousness-raising is the systematic attempt to break through ideological assumptions. It is from this technique that the feminist construction of the personal as political evolved at the grass-roots level and that the concept of non-hierarchical and revolving leadership developed. Unlike most other political movements, there was no discrete organisation involved in the feminist movement; and because of the unique position of women in the class and economic structure, 'membership' in the women's movement was ideological rather than structural. Although politically liberal women's groups which had actual membership lists sought changes within existing systems in order to benefit women, such groups sometimes failed to make the primary ideological connection which distinguished the grass-roots radical feminists from their liberal counterparts.

Like ideology itself, the grass-roots women's movement eluded the simple classifications that capitalist and patriarchal press analysis was prone to make. Thus the expression 'the personal is political', which has several levels of meaning, in this case functioned to identify an ideological stance which bound women together in positions for which current social myths about women had no set position, i.e. loyalty to other women could replace jealousy over men or aggressiveness in women could exist alongside tenderness. These women developed the idea of a woman's culture based on theory and practice which cut across existing constructions of the feminine. A major concern within the academic, critical and research aspects of the women's movement has to do with a preference for theory rather than for practice since practice is considered the essence of a political movement. I would argue that the development of theory is a type of practice and that in feminist television criticism one can apply feminist theories to the process of deconstructing ideology, an aspect of the 1970s women's movement that has been essential to its politics since the beginning.

Feminist Practice and Television Criticism

What then are the terms of feminist practice within current television criticism? Since language is the medium in which feminist television criticism operates, the evolution and meanings of the terms 'female' and 'male', their various derivatives and the ways in which they are used, are of primary importance. The terms 'feminine' and 'masculine' are used to define social constructions of woman and man as opposed to biological, essential, and/or natural, inherited properties of men and women. This is not to ignore completely biological differences between women and men, but to see the influence of biological differences and indeed sexuality itself, as constructed over time through discourse. Discourse is here used in the Foucauldian sense, as a network of possible ways of speaking or being spoken, being, belonging, empowering, and consequently socially and physically enforcing normalcy. In other words, the ways that people can live, their social practices, are 'constructed' by the way these practices can be spoken about or conceptualised in language.

Another way of looking at language in this context is semiotically, as a system of codes and signs, non-linguistic as well as linguistic, which construct meaning. A sign is anything that stands for something else. Signs also acquire meaning from the things that they fail to stand for, that is the other possible meanings available to us the audience (or subject), and from their position in social myths that we already understand. The television criticism in this volume looks at the myths and conventions which shape the way we perceive television and ourselves in cultural, economic, political, historical, social, racial and sexual contexts. Television's languages and texts are seen as polysemic sites for potential ideological meaning generation. Television texts are not, however, isolated in their generation of meanings. They gain meaning by interacting with other media and cultural forms and, in addition, audiences composed of differing social and cultural groups can use television texts for their own purposes and in different ways from each other.

As feminist practice, these approaches — the re-evaluation of language, discourse and signifiers and the consideration of audiences not as masses but as unique, shifting, and respected groups — coincide with other similar feminist notions which relate to research practices.

The first of these is that past histories and research approaches have been constructed according to ideological, social, and political needs based on power relationships. Thus, research methodologies are structured by the power relationships of the people who construct them. Feminist researchers, theorists and critics favour research methods which empower the subjects, which are often non-quantitative and which avoid hierarchies.

Secondly, the idea of looking at audiences as unique and specific allows for the fact that women and men and sub-groups of both may see things differently because of their position in society. They may construct meanings in terms of class, gender, race or any number of variables, and texts may be constructed to these positions. Such research also tries to place the researcher *with* the audiences, not above and/or apart from them. Like consciousness-raising, it respects each person's personal experience while recognising her or his construction ideologically in society and language.

The Audience/Spectator and Feminist Criticism

It is clear then that the conceptualisation of 'the audience' is crucial to our reading of televisual texts. The pivotal feminist inquiry into the nature of the audience or spectator in film criticism is Laura Mulvey's 'Visual Pleasure and Narrative Cinema'.[2] Her article argues that the spectator, controlled by the economy of the gaze and involved with the psychoanalytical concepts of voyeurism, scopophillia and fetishism, is constructed as masculine. This conceptualisation presents a problem for feminist critics as long as the text is considered to have the power to construct its reader as masculine. Mulvey's insights into the construction of certain narrative forms, with their cause and effect relationships and ultimate resolution as masculine, generated an interest in looking at the form of a work as possibly gender-related and thus shaped, at least in part, by its intended audience.

Once film criticism had begun to use psychoanalysis as a theoretical tool, the idea of difference (particularly sexual difference) became important. Feminist critics then began to use the psychoanalytic theories of Freud and Lacan to analyse the patriarchial cultural and psychoanalytical implications of Hollywood narrative ideology. Their analysis was textual in that its emphasis was on the power of the text to create its subject.

Like the British culturalists they relied at least partially on the reinterpretation of cultural Marxism by Althusser, along with the use of Lacan's theory that the unconscious is structured like a language. Psychoanalysis was coupled with Althusser's notions of 'hailing' and 'interpellation', implying that particular audience positions (or subject positions) are created through the audience's acknowledgement of a place created for them by a text. This implied a theory of subjectivity in which the text was theorised as being more or less allpowerful. Since much of the work using the type of psychoanalytic theory briefly described here was published in the British film journal, *Screen*, it is often referred to as *Screen* theory. The television criticism in this volume reacts against this strong textual emphasis in favour of a more polysemic view of television audiences.

Broadcast television, although it incorporates traditional narrative form (usually referred to as classical Hollywood realism or sometimes simply as realism), is essentially segmented. Audiences incorporate it into their lives differently from the way audiences incorporate film, or for that matter, radio or reading. Audiences *use* it much more freely than many other media forms. Television's segmented, serial and series forms are different from classical Hollywood narratives. What this difference is and how it works are important to feminist culturalist television criticism. Therefore this type of criticism incorporates both the semiotic analysis of textual form and content and the context and uses made of television by its audiences in the practice of viewing and in the incorporation of television into other cultural practices, like gossip networks.

To summarise briefly, the feminist television criticism included in this volume has developed from three sources. The first is British cultural studies criticism, which developed in the 1970s at the Birmingham University's (CCCS) under Stuart Hall and which was influenced by the work of Raymond Williams. The second major influence on feminist television criticism is feminist psychoanalytic film criticism. The third influence is the women's movement of the 1970s itself and the social-cultural critique which the movement encouraged.

Television Criticism and Ideology

Television is a powerful fictional medium in contemporary society. It is produced by a combination of technological, industrial, political and ideological events in society and as part of what Althusser would classify as Ideological State Apparatuses (ISA's).[3] According to Althusser, there are seemingly unconnected social institutions like the family, religion, language, the media or the political system which operate as overlapping or 'overdetermined' ideological influences which develop in people a tendency to behave and think in socially acceptable ways.

The repetition of similar perspectives over these multiple social institutions within a community of people is used to reinforce and perpetuate the ideology of the dominant group. However, Gramsci had previously advanced the idea that these ideological positions are not static but have to be consciously accepted by people before they become part of the cultural practice of various groups and subgroups within society, even though the particular ideological position in question may go against their interests.[4] His position is that people have to be continually won and rewon to any ideological position. It follows that such ISA's as the media, particularly television with its constant accessibility, has to continually convince and reconvince its subjects or audiences, through various types of repetition.

The work of ideology, however, is rendered invisible because it is so overdetermined or comes from so many different sources that it seems like commonsense. It seems 'natural'. This is the reason, in part, as Fiske and Hartley point out, that television is so hard to read:

> after all, everybody *knows* what it is like to watch television. Certainly; and it is television's familiarity, its centrality to our culture, that makes it so important, so fascinating, and so difficult to analyse. It is rather like the language we speak: taken for granted, but both complex and vital to an understanding of the way human beings have created their world.[5]

They maintain that the television message is forced by its own constraints and internal contradictions to accord a 'freedom of perception to all its viewers.'[6] In other words, television is inherently polysemic. This view, means that television contains within it the contradictions which enable viewers to understand the play of ideology; it is crucial to the reading of television texts and practices presented here.

Some of the diverse ways in which women have integrated television into their cultural perspectives are presented here as an amplification of the struggle over the meanings of 'women' produced by television and the relationship of these meanings to specific audiences and to the structures of social power and control in which women and girls live their lives and experience pleasure. The meaning of the term 'popular culture' resides in the fact that people choose particular items over others. How and why people use popular culture in particular ways is important to the politics of feminism and to women's struggle to construct meanings of their own.

Television and Women's Culture

This book makes no attempt to cover the entire context and development of feminism and feminist criticism. Rather I have tried, as editor, to gather works which exemplify a specific strand of feminist television criticism which I call feminist culturalist television criticism. I have also tried in the first part of the introduction to explain how this strand of criticism evolved. As women, our interaction with television is complex and involves a number of aspects of critical thought as well as a large group of reading, textual, and contextual practices.

This book is arranged to first acquaint the reader with the critical perspective in the Introduction. Then, in Part One, to look at ways to conceptualise audiences and criticism. This is followed, in Part Two, by the analysis of fantasy, reading practices and 'structures of feeling'. Part Three looks at either specific television genres or a specific television series. The conclusion deals with the notion of audience empowerment. The twelve contributors to this volume deal with issues related to women as television users, audiences, and critics. The following chapters map out some of the possibilities for feminine consumption and analysis of that ubiquitous cultural form raging out of control in our lounge rooms, living rooms and kitchens.

Virginia Nightingale, in an Australian context, analyses the assumptions made by programmers about audiences. While women's patronage of media products supposedly is keenly sought, only a narrow range of women's genres exist. This chapter links the ways that television executives talk about their desire for women audiences with the ways this desire is expressed in the marketplace. The theme is compared with Rachel Bowlby's discussion of the ways women were addressed and constructed as shoppers by the department store entrepreneurs of the 1850s.[7] Emphasis is placed on the ways television has co-opted the family into re-structuring notions of women as both shoppers and audiences to better match the selling strategies of the modern shopping world.

Dorothy Hobson looks at how television and work are integrated in women's stories in the workplace. She and Jacqui, her informant, tell the story of how the women in Jacqui's office negotiate their space and time around their conversations about television. The interview reveals the complex relationship between the pleasures of talking, particularly about television, and the requirements of the job.

Caren Deming locates the problem of the absence of represented female experience and vision in dominant narrative forms as a part of a sex-gender system which works to marginalise the status of women and their ideas. Television and its criticism have been similarly marginalised by various discursive formations used to critique the medium, the notion of 'realism' in particular. What critics should be asking, she says, is 'Whose fictions are these? What culture(s) do they serve?'. Television critics can, in her view, also acknowledge the openings for oppositional readings in television's products and practices and thereby help to create such openings.

Ien Ang, using letters from Dutch women, analyses the specific sorts of pleasures that women get from watching *Dallas*. These pleasures connect with readings that construct, among other aspects, what Ang calls 'tragic structures of feeling'. Ang here reflects on the meanings of this type of pleasure, its relation to fantasy, women's lives, and feminist politics. Most important to her premise is the acknowledgment that pleasure should not be explained by referring to the 'real' social lives of women, but to the — relatively independent — dimension of fantasy life.

Lisa Lewis' essay analyses the connection between girls' cultural lives and the music videos and star styles of female musicians. She makes the argument that the video and star texts of Cyndi Lauper and Madonna address girl audiences by symbolically referencing consumer girl culture, a type of gendered cultural experience engaged in by American middle-class girls. Girls, in turn, confirm and respond to the address through female fan practices, most notably, style imitation.

Sally Stockbridge examines the possibilities for female appropriations of television by focusing on current music video programmes and the subject positions they make possible. Starting from the position that femininity and masculinity, and differences between them, are constructed within discourse, both audio-visual and theoretical, her essay argues that sexuality and the appropriations available in video clips are multiple and therefore give rise to polyphonic readings and pleasures.

Danae Clark looks at female spectatorship in relation to television's *Cagney & Lacey*. She spotlights the negotiation that occurs between the subject positions that the text constructs and the social positions that female spectators rely upon to complete meaning construction. She maintains that *Cagney & Lacey* is a program that explicitly addresses issues of interest to women and refuses relations of male voyeurism and fetishism, thus redefining how women 'look' in terms of textual characterisation and spectatorial point of view. *Cagney & Lacey*'s feminine discourse opens up a space for understanding how women speak to one another within patriarchy.

John Fiske contends that quiz and game shows, watched by a predominantly female audience and played mainly by women, occupy a problematic position in women's culture. While they clearly position women as consumers, and they are under the masculine control of questionmaster, a feminine counter-test exists. In quiz shows, Fiske maintains, the domestic is made public and masculine, factual, educational knowledge is challenged by the feminine knowledges of intuition or of the collective consensus. Women's skills at shopping, bargain hunting and understanding people form the basis of many games while the segmentation of quiz shows allows for interrupted viewing which enables them to fit with the domestic routine. The more 'educational' ones are often shared by mother and children together. The shows which Fiske analyses are *The Price is Right*, *Family Feud* and *Perfect Match*. The first show recognises women's skills as shoppers; in the second, women are in charge of the families engaged in the contest, and in the last, women are allowed to have fun and express their sexuality without guilt or punishment.

Beverley Poynton and John Hartley examine the discourse of masculinity and how women negotiate positions from which to read that discourse using the example of sport on television. They offer an analysis of Aussie Rules football from a partially feminine point of view. The writers contend that the television coverage of Aussie Rules football is homoerotic if sublimated and that the voice-over narration helps to cover the erotic content of the images. They also offer a socio-economic analysis of the role of football in the development of capitalism in Australia. Feminine and masculine voices struggle for space in this essay.

Andrea Press interviews women of different classes regarding their reactions to and interpretations of the television show *Dynasty*. She discusses how working-class women and middle-class women view and talk about television shows and characters differently. Working-class women respond to the female characters as primarily women, while middle-class women see them as primarily upper-class. Working-class women also see *Dynasty* as more realistic than middle-class women. Even though the middle-class women in her study are somewhat cynical about *Dynasty's* fantastic setting they, at the same time, relate to the fact that the show deals with issues in their own lives. The problem of assigning class designations to women who have been, in much research, assigned the class of their husband or fathers is also discussed in this essay.

In Chapter 12, I use Bakhtin's idea of the carnivalesque to analyse how women use soap operas to integrate a parodic critique of patriarchal traditions into their daily lives. I contend that women play with the social and cultural rules by which they live in the process of enjoying both the soap operas themselves and the oral and performance networks that surround them. A number of similarities between television soap operas and women's traditional oral narratives are illustrated. The parallels operate on various levels, from the process of production (which is more responsive to the audience than is usual in written forms), to the subject matter (which concerns, above all, women's intimate personal relationships), to the formal aspects of plot and characterisation. The chapter relates these similarities to the temporal dimension in which both forms are experienced by the audience. The open and decentred narrative, the labile nature of plot and character formation and the responsiveness of the producers to the audience are all indices of a non-literary mode of production, rather than weaknesses in the genre. Thus the literary bias of accepted aesthetic values in terms of evaluating soap operas is called into question.

In the Conclusion I attempt to isolate the problem of finding a feminine way of speaking that acknowledges subordination and yet empowers women, not necessarily to change the world, but to develop an image of ourselves as powerful.

PART ONE

Women as Audiences and Critics

Chapter 2. John Wood as Michael Aloysius Rafferty in
Rafferty's Rules.

Chapter 4. 40 Minutes: 'If you love him, let him go'
Photo: Alan Chapman.

2

Women as Audiences

Virginia Nightingale*

The pedagogic relation expects her as 'authority' to have a 'truth', a
'theory' which would allow her to 'simply' answer. She would then
'answer for woman', speak for her not as her. Woman would be the
subject-matter, the material of her discourse. She would trade woman,
just as woman have always been 'merchandise' in a commerce between
men.

Jane Gallop[1]

The experience of reading about women as audiences is reminiscent
of reading anthropology. 'Women' are objectifiable, somehow a
unified whole, a group. The qualities that divide women, like class,
ethnicity, age, education, are always of less significance than the
unifying qualities attributed to women, such as the inability to know
or say what they want, the preoccupation with romance and relationships, the ability to care for, to nurture, others. It seems as though
research is about 'other women' not 'me', other cultures, not mine.
The certainty of generalisation about women seems to assume
mythic proportions − most usually the Oedipus myth, a myth
which leaves nothing to explain about men, and everything unex-
plained about women. When writing about women as audiences, this

* This chapter was presented as a paper at the International Television Studies
Conference, London, 1988.

problem has become my problem. The gap between myself and other women, between my world of experiences and that of other women, stretches out before me like an uncharted sea, dotted with islands of unexpected similarities but mostly resembling a vast incomprehensible marshy wilderness which denies any possibility of serious generalisation. Here I want to wade through the marshes towards some of the nearest islands, the firmer ground, trying to map one or two certainties. I have drifted towards examples of the ways women are talked about as audiences, and tried to link them to the ways women talk about their own experiences and interests in regard to television viewing.

I shall begin by examining a newspaper article which appeared in the Sydney, Australia, press in February 1987.[2] The reporter, Michael Visontay, had managed to encourage television executives responsible for programming, from each of the five Sydney channels, to discuss the programming formats their channels had adopted for 1987. The article forces a consideration of how 'women as audiences' are seen by the industry, especially the three commercial channels, and of the interests the industry has in maintaining this vision. The symbiotic relationship between women as audiences and women as purchaser/consumer produces complex implications for the nature of women's viewing styles, and the possibilities for women's culture.

My overall concern here is not to provide a definitive statement about women as audiences. I do not believe that is possible. I am concerned more particularly to provoke discussion about the assumptions and contradictions inherent in some of the writing about women as audiences; to reconsider the shared socio-cultural experiences of twentieth century post-capitalist society, particularly those in which women are audiences; those experiences which continue to shape cultural ideas about the nature of women, about me as a woman, about other women, about my thinking about other women. The main focus is on the way the family is used to define women and women's culture, in limiting what texts women are offered while at the same time provoking action and activities which can legitimately be called women's culture.

> We want more women viewers and we're trying to get them, subtly. We would like more women but it's very hard to get them, especially when you're broadcasting Rugby League two nights a week.
>
> John Stevens, Channel Ten, Sydney.[3]

At the beginning of 1987 two commercial television channels broadcasting to the Sydney market were quoted in the *Sydney*

Morning Herald as intending to improve their overall ratings by 'targetting women'. Channel Seven intended to target women aged 25-39 by providing more 'family' viewing;

> The family aspect attracts more female viewers, and also, kids bring their mums along. Dads are lighter television watchers.
>
> Glen Kinging, Channel Seven[4]

Channel Ten intended to target women aged 18-39 by broadcasting films with a bigger attraction to women, and by featuring 'personality-oriented comedy and magazine shows' in the 7.30 pm slot.

These strategies were based not on knowledge of actual women as audiences, but on beliefs and hopes about how to get women to watch television. Beliefs and hopes based on ratings research. Beliefs and hopes tied, apparently, to a cult of male personality, since Don Lane, Richard Neville and Jack Absalom, along with 'the American comedy, *Cheers*' were the line-up Channel Ten expected to attract women. The titles of programs mentioned mystify the situation even further. The series and serial titles included *Rafferty's Rules* (about a suburban male magistrate); *Hey Dad* (about a single father, an architect, with a dotty secretary, two daughters and a son); *A Country Practice* (initially about two male country doctors, and now about a heterosexual couple)[5] and *Sons and Daughters*. The films mentioned were *The Big Chill* (crisis of male identity) and *The Man Who Loved Women* (confessions of a Casanova). The programs believed capable of delivering women audiences predominantly featured or were about men.

Needless to say, the strategies failed. In the end Channel Nine remained the ratings winner for 1987. Channel Nine's strategy, as articulated by its vice-president of programming, Vicki Jones, had been

> We have found the trend now is to 'actuality' television, but the public demonstrated last year that they were also very fond of 30-minute laughs.[6]

The main age group for Nine's strategy is quoted as being targetted at 18-44 year olds, 'especially women'. The words were chosen to explain the change, but the programs presented vary minimally. In a line-up of strategies which is remarkable for its uniformity, Nine's format succeeded, it seems, because Nine's 'news/current affairs have an appeal which cuts right across the demographic board'. Nine won the ratings battle by appealing to everyone and making no attempt to single out women.

Several important questions are raised by the way these strategies single out women as a desired audience, yet offer programs to attract women which seem to directly address men or children. The statements assume some knowledge about women as audiences, some understanding of the nature of women and what women want. But the strategies point to a very limited commitment to women as audiences, and to a narrow, even claustrophobic, definition of woman as audience. Women as audiences, women as housewives, women as mothers; the same themes appear and reappear in newspaper and research discourse alike. When reading about women as audiences in these statements it is possible to believe that no other possibilities exist. Especially when the medium is television.

Glen Kinging's definition of the interests of women as audiences ('the family aspect attracts more female viewers, and also, kids bring their mums along.') is articulated both directly and indirectly in the newspaper article. But what is this family aspect? On what basis can it be said to exist in a television program? The series *Rafferty's Rules*, which Channel Seven hoped would be capable of attracting women, managed to establish itself as a viable series during 1987. In a newspaper review of the program[7] the reviewer endorses the need for such a program by reference to the successive allegations of corruption and graft within the judicial and political establishment in New South Wales.

> The obvious thing about *Rafferty's Rules* is that it has emerged at a time when the judicial system in NSW needs help in recovering from the flogging it has taken lately.

The reviewer's hope seems to be that the program will restore faith in the legal profession, in a way that the British series *Rumpole* is unable to do because, from an Australian perspective, Rumpole's 'windmill tiltings' seem 'too far away' and 'too few'. Rafferty himself is obviously designed to encourage recognition and affection if not identification from the average Australian male.

> He's an unassuming, knockabout bloke — amiable and informal with the shrewd attitude of a country publican. But that's not to say you immediately know all about him. Far from it.[8]

The only clues to the program's expected power to attract women audiences come from the sub-heading, stating that the series 'reveals a human side to the law', and a statement of the Rafferty enigma:

His ambiguity of impartiality, heightened by various personal crises occurring in his private life, makes it hard for Rafferty to maintain even-handedness and difficult to conduct relationships on a variety of levels with his colleagues.[9]

His most important colleague is Pauline Gray, the Public Solicitor (attorney). Rafferty's availability for, and reluctance to engage with, romance are secured: Rafferty is separated from his wife and children. Any similarities with *Hill Street Blues* end here. The family aspect: for men — the good bloke struggling to do his job; for children — anticipatory socialisation about the law and how to stay out of trouble; for women — complex relationships and the prospect of romance.

It is obvious in the choice of *Rafferty's Rules* as a family show, that the Channel Seven executives expect women to watch because another member of the family, child or dad, chooses it. It is equally obvious that once watching, mum's attention is believed to be held by the way human issues are dealt with. The particular human issues in this case are the enigma of the male psyche, the conduct of relationships and the social dramas which result in people appearing before a magistrate. The strategy is very similar to that of another high-rating Channel Seven series, *A Country Practice*, in which the conduct of relationships and a wide range of health and social problems have successfully attracted high ratings over the last five years.[10]

'Love' is entangled with the question of woman's complicity; it may be the bribe which has persuaded her to agree to her own exclusion.[11]

Women are considered obsessed by the family and caught in its web of emotions — emotions spun by a male psyche, dominated by the enigmas of a masculine imagination. For the television executive, the context 'family' defines woman, her interests and her concerns, as well as her continuing subordinate status within the family; a subordinate status which is believed to be chosen by women. Women are implicated in their own exploitation through love, through the desire to first please their husbands, fathers and children. Faced with a vacuum of ideas and knowledge about what women as audiences want, the Channel father constructs woman as he would like her — in his own image — interested in the family aspect, interested in him as he goes about being himself, and takes enough care of her interests to keep the television family together.

When it comes to scheduling television programs, these constructed characteristics become the information or data, the facts which inform a dominant masculine rational decision-making about the most cost-effective way of attracting more women viewers while holding onto other family members. According to such a logic, the program, the vehicle for attracting that attention, need never resemble anything real women might say they want to watch. The program is always both a calculation and a guess: a calculation about how to build up the ratings and a guess about the unknowable — women as audiences.

It is strange that echoes of the beliefs about women's interests held by television executives can be heard in feminist writing. Angela McRobbie has said that 'feminism is about being who you want to be — and finding out who you are in the first place'.[12] We have tended to do this by looking inwards, using psychoanalysis to help us to understand the invisible psychical obstacles in our way, clinging to the desire to be, and to be acknowledged as a person in our own right. The project of sixties feminism was that

> issues of direct relevance to women's lives — the family, sexuality, the private or domestic sphere, interpersonal relations — were to be included, in some instances for the first time, as a relevant and worthy object of intellectual concern.[13]

There is a sense in which it is possible to see the culmination of this project in the inclusion of women's concerns within mainstream programming on television rather than in specifically labelled 'women's programming'. This certainty seems to have happened in American series such as *Golden Girls*. Yet there remains a deep-seated ambiguity about the status of the role of the woman television viewer. Does recognition of the importance of the domestic realm and human interests in broadcast television confirm the lower status of women, or affirm the equal importance of these interests with those of men? Have women been 'caught' again, implicated in their own subordination, again? Women 'see' their interests displayed in prime time. The industry 'sees' the means to attract the woman viewer, and perpetuates existing patterns of family subordination of women, of existing stereotyping.

These family-based definitions of women mask another aspect of women's culture which is of vital concern to the television industry. The desire for women as audiences is motivated by women's role as prime domestic consumer/purchaser. Television channels desire women audiences not in their own right, but for their attraction to advertisers. And advertisers want women not as women but as consumers, and even more as purchasers for other consumers (i.e. the rest of the family). The place of shopping in women's culture is affirmed by television's definitions of women.

The introduction of television coincided with the development and intensification of shopping trends which, in Australia, began with the price-cutting wars in the grocery trade in the late 1940s. The price-cutting wars dramatically changed the nature of the relationship between the grocer and his customer. The traditional grocer fostered a paternalistic relationship with his customers. He looked after their interests and offered advice about their purchasing, he took phone orders and delivered free of charge. This contrasted with the actions of the rapacious price-cutter who cared nothing for the needs of his customers, being interested only in turnover and money-making. Commercial television allowed the extension of an advertising trend which had begun in the days of radio. The cut prices were advertised in the press, particularly the afternoon and Sunday tabloids but the meaningfulness of these cuts depended on knowledge of the meaning of brands. The inculcation of this knowledge was, and is carried out by broadcast brand advertising on radio, and subsequently on television. So the broadcast media became established as a site for brand advertising and the press dealt with prices. A separation of products from prices and a link between prices and corporation/store name were established. Stores are responsible for prices; manufacturers for product quality and product image.

Television broadcasting began in Australia in 1956. In 1958 the first shopping complex, Chadstone, was opened in Melbourne. Roselands, in Sydney, opened in the early sixties. The shopping complex allows an even greater amassing of goods than occurred with the introduction of the department store in the mid-1850s. Television is even better than radio for brand advertising. Brand status and brand image quickly became important factors in the price-cutting game. And goods not previously sold as branded commodities became them. The distinctions between the department store and the supermarket were blurred and finally abolished. One hundred years' experience of the power relations of shopping were generalised to the expectations of television programming.

The responsibility for purchasing passed to women when mass production of goods made domestic labour redundant. The time formerly spent on domestic labour was replaced by time spent shopping. The development of the department store in the 1850s confirmed and institutionalised the role as a feminine one. The department store became a temptation. In her analysis of commerce and femininity, Rachel Bowlby points out that the use of 'grandiose architecture and theatrical forms of lighting and display' in the construction of the department store created an environment where

> people could now come and go, to look and dream, perchance to buy, and shopping became a new bourgeois leisure activity — a way of pleasantly passing the time, like going to a play or visiting a museum. [14]

The department store constituted a site for the seduction of the purchaser, a place of temptation and indulgence, an arena for a 'masculine appeal to women'. [15]

> The essential point is that the making of willing consumers readily fitted into the available sociological paradigm of a seduction of women by men, in which women would be addressed as yielding objects to the powerful male subject forming, and informing them, of their desires. [16]

The development of the department store signalled a basic change in the concerns of industry, a change from concern with manufacture to the development of strategies for selling. The department store is itself a strategy for selling goods, as are supermarkets and shopping complexes. The techniques used included the abolition of specialities and the unification of all goods as 'things for sale'; the free-entry fixed-price policy abolished the sense of obligation to buy formerly associated with entering a store, but also abolished the conventions of bargaining; the institutionalisation of the 'impulse buy', encouraging unplanned purchasing by customers on their way from one department to another; the blurring of the boundaries between looking and having, by encouraging shoppers, free from the obligation to buy, to spend time in the fantasy world of unlimited buying power created by the accumulation and display of merchandise. Such techniques were part of a 'rigorously rational entrepreneurial scheme' to sell more, but as Bowlby points out, such techniques also involve the 'manufacture of minds disposed to buy them'. [17] This involved the acceptance as 'natural' of the irrationality of shopping, of the nature of women as superfluous and frivolous, narcissistically absorbed in the beautification of themselves and their houses. It involved persuading women shoppers to accept the view of themselves as reflections of the style presented inside the display window — the entrepreneur's most desirable object, and to believe that there she saw 'what she wants and what she wants to be'. [18]

The trends begun with the establishment of the department store have continued into the age of the suburban shopping complex. But suburban location, with its demands for frequent visiting, and the agglomeration of goods provided, have demanded changes in the ways of addressing and appealing to the purchaser. My mother and my grandmother wore hats and gloves and furs. They bought commodities they could use to construct themselves as versions of the shop window. They dressed in style on smaller incomes than mine. They dressed up to go shopping in department stores not daily or weekly, but three or four times a year. They saved up for the luxury of 'going to town'. They embroidered tablecloths or practised haberdashery and millinery skills which have been lost in my generation. They knew how to sew velvet, taffeta, silk and satin. They could make hats. Boxes of knitting needles and crochet hooks, bias binding and buttons, left-over lace, braids and ribbons languish in my linen cupboard. Their world contained commodities I no longer have words to describe, no longer have skills to use. Shopping and the modes of consumption have changed. I watch television and engage imaginatively with brand names or corporations. I shop in 'centres' and 'complexes'. I no longer encounter Anthony Hordern, David Jones or the Farmer Bros. I experience the Westfield Corporation or the Woolworths Empire. The sex has gone out of shopping. Dreiser's *Sister Carrie* has given birth to *Mrs Brady*.[19]

Commercial television is an integral part of the modern shopping world. In this age of image advertising, it is from television that the meanings of brands are learned. If women learned to shop in the nineteenth century, they had to be taught to shop for others in the twentieth. The unpredictable woman of the nineteenth century had to be transformed into predictable, programmable 'Mum' one hundred years later. The branding of food commodities and the establishment of television as an efficient system of brand information assisted a change in the mode of address of the shopping world to women purchasers. In the cut-price world of the 50s and 60s seduction was out and value was in. In a shopping world of comparable brands, Mum has to learn not only the meaning, the lifestyle connotations of branded products from television advertising, but their meanings for the members of the family destined to consume her purchases.

It is because of the relationship between advertising and television that watching television is work.[20] Watching television is a leisure activity in the pursuit of which viewers are asked to lose themselves, to blur the distinctions between reality and fantasy. They are asked to forget that watching television is also work, to see television advertisements not as a continual reminder of the work of purchasing, but as entertainment. They are asked to believe that what they see on television is what they want to see, specially selected to please them. It is in such a context that the 'distracted' viewing characteristic of women as audiences can be seen to serve the needs of advertisers.[21]

The fiction that television viewing is not work could be difficult for the viewer to sustain without the help offered by the structures of broadcast television, which actively assist the viewer not to notice the work of viewing. The television program has become a virtual display case for things for sale. Television programs display advertising. Stories are structured around advertising breaks to minimise viewer loss from the program while ensuring greater viewer attention to advertisements. The cheapness of program sets helps to focus viewer attention on the high cost glitz of advertisements. Programs themselves can serve as display cases for advertised goods. Quiz shows, for example, present catalogues of glittering prizes which establish a hierarchy of commodity values attached to brands and objects; at times contestants even compete in price-guessing games, putting their shopping skills to the test. Children's cartoons help establish at an early age knowledge of the symbiotic relationship between programs and advertised products − sometimes the toy commodity follows the cartoon (*Voltron*), sometimes the cartoon brings already existing commodities to life (*Winnie the Pooh*). All television programs offer exposure to commodity goods, albeit in varying degrees. *Dallas* hairstyles were the rage for a while in certain yuppie Sydney hairdressing salons.

Television and the family go together. The liaison is not the product of technological determinism. It is the result of entrepreneurial strategy, of rational decision making. A convenient social institution, the family, the site of most consumption, and a medium of mass communication suitable for addressing the domestic realm, have become 'commercial television' − a medium where 'advertising uses television as a system of reference; returning the favour, programming uses advertising as its framework, and sometimes as its exemplar'.[22] Broadcast television, as a cultural form, presents the outside world inside the family,[23] but it also sets up differential roles within the family for its viewers, different possibilities for experiencing that televisual outside world. Moreover, these different viewing roles, with their strong articulation of women as family-oriented and consumption-oriented people, reflect the gender-based differentiation of personhood in Western society.

I have suggested that the incorporation of women's interests into prime-time television programming is part of a strategy to attract women viewers as mothers and shoppers. The paradox is that within a system where women should or could be seen to hold some power, programming decisions are consistently made to address men or children before a direct attempt is made to discover what real viewing interests women might have. This too is part of the strategy. John Hartley's 'paedocratic regime' of television describes a viewing situation where the relatively powerless viewer is treated as a child, as the object of paternal concern from the channels. Within such a system men identify with the power of the channels. In the very moment they appoint themselves managers or guardians of family viewing they are co-opted to set up a situation in which television can talk to women on male terms.[24] The family acts to extend the regime of television. Women's interests are relegated to the background, to be videotaped and viewed in moments stolen from the busy domestic schedule.

In describing the specifically feminine readership of the romance novel in the 1980s, A.R. Jones points out that continued readership is a product not only of cultural habit, but also of a concerted program of market research, mass publication and multi-media advertising.[25] Television matches mass publication with never-ending serials, and is equipped with even better multi-media advertising and public relations strategies. Its promotion and construction of its own audiences lessens the possibility for genre subversion. The opportunities for experimentation with television production are considerably less than for other media because of the high cost of drama production and the differentiation of work practices within production teams.

The strategy of incorporating women's interests within prime-time programming could work to establish an equality between women's interests and those of men and children, but it could equally work to ensure women's continued subordination within the home as well as outside it. It can also be seen as an attempt to co-opt women into managing their own viewing on male terms.

It is difficult with television to separate text from medium. The small amount of work that has been done to analyse the pleasure of particular television programs for women audiences provides considerable information about the women's enjoyment of and knowledge about those programs.[26] They are less successful at demonstrating the power of these texts to live in and through their audiences, in the way for example that Valerie Walkerdine demonstrates the power of the video *Rocky II* to 'live' in the Cole family, to explain and justify the family dynamic.[27]

The tendency for women's genres to be enjoyed privately by women[28] is very similar to the patterns of consumption described by women readers of romance fiction.[29] There is a sense of carnival about the organisation of such illicit reading and video-viewing sessions. The session becomes a metasocial rite, performed in an everyday space hallowed for the time allocated.[30] The usually-denigrated programs are elevated to pride of place. The family is in some cases replaced by an audience sure to be appreciative of the woman's choices — her own friends. Indulgence in excesses of emotion can be enjoyed. A few tears can be shed. But as Victor Turner points out, ritual and carnival owe their hold over their participants to the 'degree to which the participants identify themselves to the traditional scenario'.[31] The ritual is most meaningful to women most committed to traditional patterns of self-fulfilment.

This perspective corroborates observation that television soap operas do not provide the viewer with opportunities for escapism, but are a way of understanding and coping with problems shared with other women.[32] One of those shared problems is the experience of exploitation within the family. The very existence of this sort of program allows women opportunities to subvert that power structure at the same time that family viewing patterns intensify the sense of oppression. However, the drawing of more and more women back into the workforce seems likely to produce more and more television programming designed to keep women viewing on male terms, on terms which leave the rationality of shopping and the subordination of women within the family unquestioned.

3

For Television-Centred Television Criticism: Lessons from Feminism

Caren J. Deming

We can now understand why there should be so many common features in the indictments drawn up against woman, from the Greeks to our times. Her condition has remained the same through superficial changes, and it is this condition that determines what is called the 'character' of woman: she 'revels in immanence,' she is contrary, she is prudent and petty, she has no sense of fact or accuracy, she lacks morality, she is contemptibly utilitarian, she is false, theatrical, self-seeking, and so on. There is an element of truth in all this. But we must only note that the varieties of behaviour reported are not dictated to woman by her hormones nor predetermined in the structure of the female brain: they are shaped as in a mould by her situation.

Simone De Beauvoir, *The Second Sex*

No influx of talented directors or writers can offset the technical limits of the medium itself. No matter who is in control, the medium remains confined to its cold, narrow culverts of hyperactive information. Nothing and no one can change this, nor can anyone change how television's technical limits confine awareness. As the person who gazes at streams becomes streamlike, so as we watch television we inexorably evolve into creatures whose bodies and minds become television-like.

Jerry Mander, *Four Arguments for the Elimination of Television*

The history of women's art is a history of exclusion and confinement dating back to the emergence of patriarchy. When men wrested economic and political power from women, it was logical that they also would appropriate fantasy and creativity; for women's stories were incomprehensible and fearsome. The Greeks excluded women (and slaves) from attendance (as either actors or audience) at their tragedies ostensibly because the presence of either inferior group threatened to debase the ethical and aesthetic character of the drama. Christa Wolf summarises the interrelated developments that brought women and their goddesses under male control:

> This whole earthy-fruitful hodgepodge, this undisciplined tendency to merge and change into each other, this thing which it was hard to put a name to, this throng of women, mothers and goddesses which it was hard to classify and to count, was brought under control, along with the right of male inheritance and private property, after what appear to have been long, difficult centuries, which now are described as 'dark' and have been forgotten.[1]

Out of the public sphere, really until the present century, women and their art were relegated to the domestic and the decorative, the sensual and the trivial.

As a case in point, women writers long were demeaned for being preoccupied with domestic problems and the emotions attending them. Such 'frivolous' themes condemned stories about them to 'hopeless mediocrity'. The overwhelming need for liberation from such thinking was voiced by De Beauvoir:

> How could one expect [woman] to show audacity, ardour, disinterestedness, grandeur? These qualities appear only when a free being strikes forward through an open future, emerging far beyond all given actuality. Woman is shut up in a kitchen or in a boudoir, and astonishment is expressed that her horizon is limited. Her wings are clipped, and it is found deplorable that she cannot fly. Let but the future be opened to her, and she will no longer be compelled to linger in the present.[2]

Some twenty-five years earlier, Virginia Woolf saw independence as the prime necessity if women's literature was to flourish. She implored young women 'to earn money and have a room of your own, . . . to live in the presence of reality'.[3] She saw the woman writer as a looking glass 'possessing the magic and delicious power of reflecting the figure of man at twice its natural size'.[4] Lacking the self-confidence to explore their own experience intellectually or artistically, women writers were distracted by criticism of their moral vision and accompanying values; and, with few exceptions, they altered their values 'in deference to the opinion of others'. Woolf saw the lack of integrity as 'the flaw in the centre that had rotted [their novels].' She marvelled at the courage it must have taken Jane Austen, Emily Bronte, and George Eliot to have written 'as women write'.[5]

Feminist critics locate the problem in the inherent androcentricity, or male-centredness, of dominant artistic forms and the inability of those forms to convey an experience that women recognise as congruent with their own. Rachel DuPlessis links the problem in narrative to gender simply and powerfully: 'All forms of dominant narrative, but especially romance, [represent] the sex-gender system as a whole'.[6] Although the connection between the problem posed for all women by the dominant androcentric ideology and the specific problems that ideology poses for artists and writers was made early by Woolf and others, contemporary feminist critics identify the relationship between narrative and ideology as explicitly hegemonic, circumscribing the creation and interpretation processes.[7] The absence of represented female experience and vision in dominant narrative forms thus conspires with the sex-gender system at large to maintain the marginal status of women, their ideas, and their art:

> Women's absence from the hallowed chambers to which they were denied entry is now presented as evidence of their extraordinary lack of ability. The recourse to nature for the substantiation of uniquely 'sexual' characteristics postulated *a priori* certitude and guaranteed agreement.[8]

The first principle of feminist criticism is the subversion of that reasoning.

For critics, a woman-centred analysis is one that is 'thoroughly genderised,' to use Gisela Ecker's phrase. This means that the gender of both artist and critic 'including their relations to gender-values in their institutions and within the theories they apply' must be taken into account.[9] Implicit in the feminist critical agenda, then, is the Utopian myth of woman as authentic (not second) sex, woman seeing and experiencing herself as autonomous (not deviant) and complete (not lacking male traits).[10]

Encouraged by the work of Woolf and (now) long lines of feminist critics, novelists, and poets, women have found the courage to write the stuff of women as women write. The result is a vast women's literature whose development parallels the incremental recognition of the validity of a distinct woman's vision in a wide range of disciplines. What have women's history and the history of women's literature to do with television criticism? My purpose in exploring some comparisons between feminism and television criticism is to articulate some lessons all television critics might learn from feminist writers, who turned so much negative force to energy for good by discovering and then promulgating the merits of their own thoughts and expressions. Ultimately, I will advance the thesis that feminist modes of thinking may be applied productively to television.

Before we turn to the subject of television, however, a few words about terminology are in order. In this essay, *feminism* refers to 'an analysis of women's subordination for the purpose of figuring out how to change it'.[11] Feminist criticism is by definition overtly political whether or not specific critical works also include a program of action for effecting change. *Feminine* is a term eschewed by many feminists because of its association with socially and culturally prescribed behaviours that subordinate women. To this writer, *feminine* is not necessarily pejorative. I use the term to refer to behaviours and attitudes commonly adopted by women, most of which are socially constructed, and some small (although undefinable) parts of which may be related to biology. Obviously, a feminine way of thinking or behaving is not necessarily feminist; however, it may not necessarily be entirely regressive either. My point is to have use of the word as an adjectival form of *female*. This usage acknowledges the extensive influence of patriarchy on the construction of gender but stops short of throwing out the baby with the bathwater. Feminist writers need access to a fuller, not a narrower, lexicon than other writers have at their disposal; and redefining and reclaiming terms are as appropriate to the feminist agenda as coining new ones.

The Predicament of Television Criticism

That writing television criticism still is regarded in some quarters to be a futile, if not deadly, exercise is not news to communication scholars. Like the pots and potsherds of women novelists, television is too prosaic and mundane to engender valuable thoughts. The subject is so unworthy, in fact, that some academicians find themselves in the delicate position of uttering high-sounding statements about the meaning of television in one breath and adamantly denying they watch the cursed thing in the next. It was inevitable that the wet blanket thrown by literary elitists upon the study of all popular culture phenomena would extend to the critical study of television.

As history would have it, however, television was born in the heyday of scientism. Like the introduction of pool to River City, the introduction of television to the American home spelled trouble. The

American love affair with its 'idiot box' was a social problem. Thus, the critical study of television (at least in America) was not merely irrelevant (as was the study of comic books or popular Westerns), but it was entirely inappropriate. As its social and psychological effects were what we had to discover, the tools of the social scientist were most appropriate for understanding the impact of television. Anyone foolish enough to look upon television as art, by any definition, was in double jeopardy.

To this day, aesthetically oriented analyses of television and television programs are easy targets. One must acknowledge that some criticism is merely descriptive and even that some critics are starstruck. As De Beauvoir said of women's faults, 'There is an element of truth in all this'.[12] Even critics who are properly sceptical, however, and those who surpass description to advance arguments (*see* Brockreide) are vulnerable if they find admirable qualities in television.

The Reality Criterion

There are several reasons for this state of affairs. One reason is related to the historical dominance of the idea that television is a social problem. In the light of television's ubiquity, popularity, and power as an information medium, it seemed natural to use social reality criteria for judging it. Seen from within, however, the medium was driven by economic and, yes, artistic values, as well as by social values. Thus, it was also natural that television would be found wanting in social realism, at best an ambiguous mirror (*see* Loevenger), at worst a cheap and distorting reflector.

Ien Ang has identified two major flaws in the use of what she calls 'empiricist realism' as a criterion for evaluating television programs, in this case, *Dallas*.[13] Firstly, no text can be a direct, immediate reproduction or reflection of an outside world, the problematical nature of such a concept notwithstanding. Secondly, Ang found that Dutch fans of *Dallas* experience the series as realistic in some ways, even though they recognise that it is not empirically realistic. In other words, Ang's fans experience genuineness of characterisation and effect in *Dallas* even though they are well aware of the fiction's constructedness.

Feminist literary critics also have rejected the social reality criterion. Toril Moi's critique starts from the failure of demands for faithful reproduction of a world outside the fictive to consider the constructed nature of any reality. Her critique proceeds to the inability of 'extreme reflectionism' to

> accommodate notions of formal and generic constraints on textual production, since to acknowledge such constraints is equivalent to accepting the inherent impossibility of ever achieving a total reproduction of reality in fiction. [14]

Focusing attention on the fictive nature, or constructedness, of so-called reality programs (news, documentary, talk, games) yields a more productive line of inquiry than demanding empirical realism from television fictions. Popular fictions, even preliterate ones, always have claimed to tell 'the true story' of 'what really happened'. In retrospect, such claims mark the mythic overtones of the narrative. Instead of, How realistic is television? critics need to ask, Whose fictions are these? What culture(s) do they serve? Framing the issues surrounding realism this way leads not to a dead end but to a higher level of analysis — more sophisticated models of balance and fairness, as well as of the audience's interpretive behaviour. The critic's conception of the television audience was affected by other factors, which I will take up shortly.

The Bardic Trap

Of course, not all television critics succumbed to the reality criterion's inevitable condemnation of the medium. However, even critics who could see a positive role for television fettered it with circumscribed expectations. Fiske and Hartley's notion of bardic television illustrates this point. Characterising television as a bard, those authors see its role as:

1. To *articulate* the main lines of the established cultural consensus about the nature of reality.
2. To *implicate* the individual members of the culture into its dominant value-systems.
3. To *celebrate*, explain, interpret and justify the doings of the culture's individual representatives in the world out-there.
4. To *assure* the culture at large of its practical adequacy in the world by affirming and confirming its ideologies/mythologies in active engagement with the practical and potentially unpredictable world.
5. To *expose*, conversely, any practical inadequacies in the culture's sense of itself which might result from changed conditions in the

world out-there, or from pressure within the culture for a re-orientation in favour of a new ideological stance.

6. To *convince* the audience that their status and identity as individuals is guaranteed by the culture as a whole.
7. To *transmit* by these means a sense of cultural membership.[15]

Fiske and Hartley's list of functions is more comprehensive and more positively cast than most descriptions that preceded it. Yet, at least two implications of the bardic view of television are problematical. First, as the authors state, 'these seven functions are performed *in all message sequences of the television discourse* . . .' (my emphasis).[16] That statement implies that television is by definition anti-literate, and just like a woman, generically mediocre. Invoking Barthes, the authors compare bardic television to the ethnographic society's 'mediator, shaman or relator whose "performance" — the mastery of the narrative code — may possibly be admired but never his "genius"'.[17] By precluding genius from being found on television, they have set a bardic trap for the television critic.

A second reason for the view that anyone who praises television must be an inferior critic, is television's proclivity for melodrama. For good reason, as I will argue later, the marriage of television and melodrama is a natural one. To those who take the narrow view of melodrama, however, all those cop shows and soap operas are just so much evidence of television's depravity.

A third, and related, reason that critics are predisposed to negative criticism of television is the existential paralysis that derives from the absence of an appropriate artistic and critical tradition. Woolf described what she saw as the greatest difficulty facing early nineteenth-century women novelists:

> . . . They had no tradition behind them, or one so short and partial that it was of little help. For we think back through our mothers if we are women. It is useless to go to the great men writers for help, however much one may go to them for pleasure. Lamb, Browne, Thackeray, Newman, Sterne, Dickens, DeQuincey — whoever it may be — never helped a woman yet, though she may have learnt a few tricks of them and adapted them to her use.[18]

Television's lack of place in the critical canon stunted the early growth of television criticism. I am not referring here merely to the paucity of places to publish critical essays on television or of secure places in which the academic could practice television criticism. The problem runs deeper than that.

The Missing Auteur

Television is a medium that cannot be read in the strictly literary sense. The bardic voice, as Fiske and Hartley assert, is oral as opposed to literate. It easily avoids the 'vast and wide-ranging . . . cultural repertoire not appropriate to transmission by television'.[19] This is a profound insight that is not without truth. However, it also has a profoundly deleterious impact on the validity of television criticism as an endeavour. Based on a vision of the individual author seeking individualised expression in an idiosyncratic text, literacy by definition devalues the expressions of the collective, and by implication, a medium preoccupied with such expressions.

So far, this discussion reiterates the idea of the bardic trap. The point I wish to make here is that the conception of the artist as a lone individual is inappropriate to a medium in which artifacts are produced by groups under the direct control of powerful economic institutions. The preoccupation with literacy and its standards of value (including the preference for individualised characters over stereotypes)[20] forestalls the attempt to develop standards appropriate to a collaborative art. Unlike film critics, who could salvage a remnant of literary tradition in auteurism, television critics have not found true auteurs there, the efforts of Horace Newcomb and Robert Alley notwithstanding.[21]

Most television programs only get made with the approval of powerful gatekeepers within the networks and production companies that service them. Television production is simply too expensive to be done speculatively. Once in production, programs evolve with the contributions of actors and technical staff. In series production, time constraints are so severe that programs are polished to a limited perfection. Network censors, who approve every moment broadcast by a network, have the power to delete the most carefully crafted scene on the basis of an objectionable word or image.

Ultimately, the author of most television programs is the culture *as perceived by television's gatekeepers*. Critics need to develop and to apply standards derived from an understanding of the contingencies under which programs are produced. Such standards would recognise the influence of the culture at large as well as the culture of the industry and the particular organisation from which a program emerges. Individual achievements should not be overvalued by ignoring the cultural context, nor should they be undervalued by insisting that only idiosyncratic works are significant.

The Problem of Closure

In addition to the practical problems created by applying aesthetic criteria inappropriate to the works under study, dedication to traditional literary standards presupposes the completeness of the 'text' and, by implication, the passivity of the 'reader'. As Moi argues, the traditional humanism underlying the demand for unity and idiosyncrasy is part of patriarchal ideology and

> constructed on the model of the self-contained powerful phallus. Gloriously autonomous, it banishes from itself all conflict, contradiction and ambiguity. In this humanist ideology the self is the *sole author* of history and of the literary text: the humanist creator is potent, phallic and male — God in relation to his world, the author in relation to his text. History or the text become[s] nothing but the 'expression' of this unique individual: all art becomes autobiography, a mere window on to the self and the world, with no reality of its own. The text is reduced to a passive, 'feminine' reflection of an unproblematically 'given', 'masculine' world or self.[22]

Aesthetic standards derived from such a conception of art and artists inevitably generate negative judgements of works created in an atmosphere of compromise, as well as those created by women.

These standards also interpose themselves between television critics and their subject by valorising closure in the conceptualisation of narrative;[23] to wit, stories are well-formed when they end unequivocally (without any loose ends such as unresolved story lines or themes). Television's preference for serial and series forms, which require more tentative endings, demands a kind of analysis different from that appropriate to the novel or poem. In one sense, the problem is to define the unit of analysis apropos of a particular critical question. Those who have been quick to pronounce a discontinuous or indeterminate television text shallow and monolithic, most often are those whose narrow definition of it precludes any other judgement.[24] In another sense, however, the problem is to define narrative in a fashion that depends less on traditional ideas of closure and adequately takes into account television's ongoing nature.

Viewer Autonomy

Finally, the traditional dominance of textuality and the autonomous author conspired with the social reality criterion to cloud the role of the audience in making meaning from programs. Despite overwhelming empirical evidence that the 'hypodermic' theory of mass communication grossly underestimates the autonomy of the viewer, critics have been slow to abandon the theory in fact.[25] The assumption that watching television makes one television-like undergirds much of what has been written. Whether the issue is violence, role-modelling, agenda-setting, or attitude formation, television critics often leave simplistic assumptions of effects unstated even when whole arguments depend upon them. When stated, assumptions about effects rarely have been qualified carefully enough. The result is criticism that unravels all too easily.

Television criticism needs to be informed by more sophisticated views of the televisual text and the audiences for television programs. Fortunately, groundwork has been laid by advocates of readership theories, post-structuralist and deconstructive theories (the varied descendants of semiotics), and their Marxist cousins. However, little direct application or extension of these approaches to American television has occurred. It remains for television critics to advance and refine these theories in relation to the medium they know best.

To summarise, the maturation of television criticism has been impeded by devalued status in the academy born of cultural elitism, by the dominance of empiricism (and especially behaviourism) co-incident with the rise of television, by the resultant precedence of a social reality criterion of judgement, by the lack of a critical tradition generative of appropriate aesthetic criteria, and simplistic views of television production and reception. In the face of odds so great as these — not to mention the fact that the medium has existed as a mass phenomenon for less than a generation — the current immaturity of television criticism is more natural than astonishing.

Liberating Television Criticism

If the foregoing description of the 'problem' of television criticism is at all accurate, indeed the discipline is in need of liberation. It must be liberated from limitations imposed by critics themselves as well as from those imposed by tradition and circumstance. It is here that the experience of women and the struggle for emancipation by women artists is most instructive. As they began stripping away the elements of 'women's condition' in society on the way to self-discovery, that effort produced a burgeoning women's culture — literature, art, and science. The keys to that development are increased recognition that gender is socially, culturally, and politically constructed (and, thereby, susceptible to opposition) and increased confidence in women's own experience and vision.

Similarly, the keys to a powerful new generation of television criticism are increased recognition of the cultural, political, and economic constructedness of television programs of all types (including commercials and continuity) and exposition of the ways in which television is susceptible to opposition and development. Critics have an important role to play in that development.

Feminist writers have politicised not only criticism but artistic creation itself. Their subversion of established critical judgements abets the growth of a new television criticism. Feminists have exposed the constricting biologism that has kept women in 'their place.' The lesson for television critics is that 'TV biologism' must be rooted out and criticism politicised along more constructive lines. If more critics were to assume, as some clearly do, that television and, more importantly, television viewing, are not by nature depraved, more good television criticism would be written. Beyond that, if television-centredness became a tenet of critical practice, a new world of discovery would be at hand. By television-centred I mean criticism grounded in thorough understanding and appreciation for the cultural, economic, and political milieu that frames the construction of televisual messages *and* specific, detailed analysis of the aesthetics (selection and arrangement of visual and temporal elements) of television programs, with an eye toward identifying potential for change.

Repetition as Virtue

The following paragraphs constitute an agenda of sorts for achieving a more productive, television-centred television criticism.

Firstly, we need to recognise that the mundanity and repetitiveness of television are necessary to its functioning. If we understand and accept the mythic and ritualistic functions of television, we can see its conventionality as the affirmation of an implicit dominant vision essential to popular forms. Repetition may thus be seen as something like having to be pregnant − with the tedium, discomfort, pain − as a prerequisite to giving birth. Critics, such as Fiske and Hartley, who have adopted such a view of television (if not the simile) have found fertile ground to till.

If we are to avoid the bardic trap, however, it is not enough to see television as empty ritual. We must understand that originality cannot exist without repetition. Repetition is the background (a set of occurrences) that makes originality (one event) visible. As Edward Said puts it, 'originality is the difference between primordial vacancy and temporal, sustained repetition'.[26] In any medium of expression the familiar moments outnumber the original ones, as artistic production is a complicated process of 'conquering and reclaiming, appropriating and formulating, as well as forgetting and subverting'.[27] The obligation of the critic is to understand television's repetition in such a way as to remain sensitive to its potential for originality, even for genius.

As feminist researchers discovered the near impossibility (and political undesirability) of delineating uniquely feminine language or aesthetic conventions, they began to advocate the close scrutiny of individual texts as those texts relate to ideology, psychology, politics, and other texts.[28] Television criticism, too, would benefit from a greater emphasis on individual programs, series, and even episodes. Working out from the particular (rather than applying ready-formed analytical systems) gets critics closer to the subject *before* deciding which analytical systems are appropriate and with what limitations. Psychoanalytic and semiotic analyses of television, for example, easily become exercises in the use of arcane terminology devised for literary analysis when they emphasise the system of analysis at the expense of greater understanding of the object of analysis. The danger in not having a large body of television-centred analysis to work from, is production of criticism that at best is able to see only the most obviously repetitive features, missing the rest, and that at worst misunderstands those same repetitive features.

What is more, repetition is not always tedious. Ang's analysis of letters from *Dallas* viewers reveals that they derive pleasure from recognising familiar patterns of behaviour common to popular forms. Further, the letters reveal that such conventions are not taken by these viewers to be referential but rather to be metaphors for problems and stresses of modern life. Speaking of Sue Ellen Ewing's alcoholism, for example, Ang asserts that

> Such a metaphor derives its strength from a lack of originality and uniqueness: precisely because it constantly recurs in all sorts of popular narratives, it takes on for viewers a direct comprehensibility and recognisability.

It is this sort of insight that is likely to be

> missed by the intellectual who only watches a soap opera now and then with a mistrustful attitude and seeks to evaluate the narrative only on the basis of its literary value.[29]

Critics always need to be vigilant for condemnations resulting from failure to comprehend either the detail or the context of particular works. The lesson of feminism here is clear: male critics, failing to comprehend women's creativity, also failed to recognise that failure as a shortcoming of their criticism. Instead, they projected the shortcoming onto women and called it the 'eternal feminine mystique'.[30] Only through careful work by analysts intimate with the subject was the mystique dispelled.

The Incomplete Text

In addition to appreciating television's fondness for repetition, a second related task is to look upon television programs as inherently incomplete, or heteronomous texts rather than as autonomous causers of effects.[31] This is a logical approach to textuality in a medium in which authorship is dispersed across collaborative teams and institutions. A deconstructive stance toward textuality argues that 'the meaning of a text is diverse, multiple, unstable'[32] and finally produced by a reader. The text manifests a system of reconstruction-inviting structures that sometimes are referred to as constituting an implied reader.[33]

The implied reader, as a manifestation of the text, is discrete from real audience members, whose highly variable responses to television have been demonstrated in the empirical literature. Out of respect for the variability in their sense-making, *auditors* is preferable to *viewers* (a term implying too much passivity) and to *readers* (for obvious reasons) when referring to television's audience. Auditors, in sum, are actively involved in listening (sound dominates picture in television), examining, checking, and adjusting content to suit their experiences of the world.

The auditing process is not arbitrary. If it were, there would be no basis for linking audience responses to texts at all. However, the research of Ang, Modleski, and Radway, for example, demonstrates that the matter of audience response to popular media is far more complex and variable than usually has been recognised. Recent feminist inquiry on this topic raises the issue of why women attend to books or films or television programs that are alien to women's experience or that even are misogynist. Gertrud Koch, whose article is entitled Why Women Go to Men's Films, poses the likelihood of a film subhistory not entirely dictated by the male gaze, which gives minimal scope to female projections.[34] Such an hypothesis opens the inquiry not only into why women use male media, but also to why any auditor uses any medium or program and, importantly, what auditors do in the 'reading' process. There is little certainty about these matters either in the empirical literature or in the critical literature.

Film scholars, Koch among them, assert that television is an impoverished medium, far less able than film to provide interpretive opportunities. Literary critics, of course, made the same assertion about films until television came along to free film to be art. There is no reason why television critics should accept this judgement. The history of film criticism and recent audience research argue for just the opposite stance. Television-centred criticism, together with what we may now call audience-centred criticism, promises to show us the openings in texts that auditors use to transform those texts to suit their various purposes.

An added advantage of the attitude toward textuality expressed above, which by now should be obvious, is its amenability to interaction with the analytical schemata of empirical research. For example, critics may find useful the research into the parasocial relationships that television auditors build with television personalities. M.S. Piccirillo employs the concept of parasocial closure to argue for the utility of a critical perspective that takes everyday televisual experience into account in analysing television as art. Ang uses *Dallas* fans' and foes' own accounts of pleasures derived from auditing the series as a basis for her reinterpretation of the text. Tentative and limited in scope as such efforts are, they point in a promising direction.

Only barely tapped is the enormous potential for insight generated by the critic's willingness to engage with the empiricist's growing data on such topics as the physiology and psychology of perception (the ultimate locus of aesthetics), demographics, and attention-direction, as well as qualitative data from ethnographic studies. To suggest that empiricists too might benefit from interaction with critics working along these lines is not immodest. With some practice, the deconstructive critic would be well-suited to teasing out the implicit assumptions in a set of questions or responses.

So much for modesty. The critic is well advised to be extremely wary of taking existing data about audiences at face value, that is, without first deconstructing the research that produced them. Marketing and demographic studies are notorious for employing assumptions biased in terms of gender, class, and race. As Koch observes of that administrative research,

> Flicking through these studies is like looking at a nineteenth-century atlas. They are spotted with blank patches, unexplored areas, which

nevertheless already bear the names of the colonisers: the routes are known; who owns what has already been agreed.[35]

Although Koch's analogy may be extreme if extended to academic research, female respondents have appeared as mystifying deviants often enough for vigilance to be appropriate there too.

The Invitation to Interpret

There are other gains more intrinsic to criticism to be made by thinking of the televisual text as incomplete. Though not noted for the production of texts that highlight contradictions, television nonetheless produces programs that invite rather than discourage interpretation. *All in the Family* and *Hill Street Blues* are examples that readily come to mind. However, the greatest critical advantage occurs when we approach the more typical television text, the slick, hermetically sealed narratives that vituperative critics have discarded as hopelessly consumerist.

As Frank Kermode has pointed out so graciously, even the most well-formed narratives have their secrets, even though they do not advertise them. Narrative secrets are those elements of plot that 'form associations of their own, nonsequential, secret invitations to interpretation rather than appeals to a consensus'.[36] Thinking of all texts as to some degree incomplete, if even cynically so, challenges the critic to action; for some secrets of the text may not be manifest in the text.

The Critic's Invention

It is the television critic's job — perhaps in concert with the audience researcher and surely in concert with the audience — to identify the unspoken or unenacted in a text. Whether we call this work decentering, deconstructing, or simply, thinking critically, it is the critic's responsibility, regardless of the pretensions of the text: 'The critic is responsible to a degree for articulating those voices dominated, displaced, or silenced by the textuality of texts'.[37] The responsible critic is, then, 'frankly inventive':

> In producing knowledge of the text criticism actively transforms what is given. As a scientific practice it is not a process of recognition but work to produce meaning. No longer the accomplice of ideology, no longer parasitic on an already given literary text, criticism constructs its object, produces the work. In consequence the author loses all authority over the work.[38]

The heteronomous televisual text (whose 'author', ironically, we failed to find) enjoins critics to exercise their interpretive freedom, as auditors have done all along. Acknowledging the creativity of the critical endeavour enhances rather than obviates the critic's obligation to be systematic in approaching texts. No matter how systematic the analysis, however, the inventive elements of criticism are certain to distress the empiricist. I would argue nonetheless that television critics have not been inventive enough, and not just in Said's sense. That is, they have not been able or willing to spend much effort imagining how concepts of empirical research might be adapted to the critical project; nor have many been willing to look as patiently at television as literary critics have looked at literature. As a result, few of television's secrets have been revealed.

Series Television

Appreciating the value of repetition and accepting the incompleteness of the televisual text pave the way for achieving a third task in the liberation of television criticism. That task is to turn attention away from literary criticism's traditional emphasis on narrative closure in favour of something that fits televisual discourse better. Series television is resistant to narrative resolution. John Ellis suggests that the news update is a more appropriate fictive model than the well-made story for series television:

> The TV [sic] series repeats a problematic. It therefore provides no resolution of the problematic at the end of each episode, nor, often, even at the end of the run of the series. Fundamentally, the series implies the form of the dilemma rather than that of resolution and closure. This perhaps is the central contribution that broadcast TV has made to the long history of narrative forms and narrativised perception of the world.[39]

Although television resolves particular incidents, the underlying problematic of the series must remain. Here, then, is television's genetic link to melodrama, a form that expunges particular villains but does not offer redemption. Adding the notion that auditors establish ongoing parasocial relationships with television personalities, who shamelessly trample the borders between representation and presentation, it becomes clear that new conceptions of narrative and of closure are in order.

Melodrama is a natural focus for rethinking television narratives.

That idea is not entirely new.[40] The purpose of the second half of this essay is to incorporate implications of recent feminist research into that critical agenda. Specifically, this analysis is intended to demonstrate the potential for liberating television criticism through the application of feminist principles by exploring the particular case of television melodrama.

Television and Melodrama

Two contemporary works of feminist literary criticism provide insight into the problems posed by the romance genre to women writers and readers: Rachel DuPlessis' *Writing Beyond the Ending* and Janice Radway's *Reading the Romance*. Duplessis analyses the works of several twentieth-century writers selected for their 'critical approach to the production and maintenance of gender categories' and subsequent reworkings of the romance plot and related narrative conventions so as to make 'alternative statements about gender and its institutions'. The techniques for reworking the romance are what DuPlessis refers to as 'writing beyond the ending.'

Where DuPlessis' focus is writers of so-called serious fiction, Radway tackles the contemporary popular romance. Radway's analysis includes a historical survey of popular publishing and extensive ethnographically oriented work among a group of romance fans. Her discussion of genre thus incorporates elements of text, institutional forces, and readership.

Against the background provided by the insightful treatments of the romance by DuPlessis and Radway, my purpose is to explore television melodrama to identify some points at which melodrama seems especially vulnerable to oppositional readings by audiences and critics and to form-breaking reworkings by television creators. My thesis is that by its very definition television melodrama is amenable to feminist opposition and, by implication, other types of opposition as well. After a discussion of key elements of the melodramatic form, I will apply those ideas to soap operas and primetime crime dramas for purposes of illustration. My purpose is not to devise an analytical system that works in all varieties of television melodrama. Rather, it is to show that the form is more open than the romance and, therefore, hegemonically more 'leaky' than the hermetically sealed romance. Recognition of melodrama's oppositional potential thus is central to the liberation of television criticism.

Like the popular romance, which Radway characterizes as 'a myth in the guise of the truly possible,' melodrama shrouds its mythic structure in topicality.[41] Unlike the romance, however, melodrama is at its heart a modern form, an artistic response to the shattering of myth and loss of tragic vision which Peter Brooks traces to the French Revolution. Having abandoned the likelihood of the absolute triumph of virtue, melodrama rehearses the confrontation with its enemies (clearly labelled as villains), expunging them over and over again. The drama 'represents both the urge toward resacralization and the impossibility of conceiving sacralization other than in personal terms'.

According to Brooks, melodrama is a theatrical substratum found in works of low art (those which attempt little, risk little and are, therefore, conventional and unselfconscious) as well as high (ambitious works whose conception and mode of representation constitute 'the very process of reaching a fundamental drama of the moral life and finding terms to express it'). Melodrama polarises good and evil and shows them operating as real forces in the world. It uses 'heightened dramatic utterance and gesture' to demonstrate the moral drama in ordinary, private life. It assumes that 'the quotidian life, properly viewed, will live up to the expectations of the moral imagination'. Finally, it posits good and evil as moral feelings, thus asserting that emotion is the realm of morality.[42]

Melodrama thus resists evaluation according to empiricist conceptions of realism.[43] Its realm is affect. As Ang points out about *Dallas*, melodrama evokes what Raymond Williams has called a 'structure of feeling'.[44] More precisely, what Ang's viewers recognise is an authentically tragic structure of feeling, 'tragic because of the idea that happiness can never last forever [as it can in romance] but, quite the contrary, is precarious'.[45] Melodrama's tragic universe is not that of great suffering, the traditional domain of romance and patriarchal heroes, but of 'what is usually not acknowledged as tragic at all and for that reason is so difficult to communicate . . . the ordinary pain of living of ordinary people in the modern welfare state'.[46] To Ang, Brooks's melodramatic imagination is a normal aspect of modern life, a way of seeing ordinary suffering as special and meaningful. Watching melodramas — with their extravagant feelings and incidents at the expense of characterisation — is therefore not compensation for or escape from the reality of daily life but a dimension of it.

Melodrama's emphasis on affiliation, as opposed to individualism (its preference for moral order over glorification of the individual hero), not to mention its fascination with the ordinary, points to the form's attraction to feminine conceptions of morality. As Carol Gilligan has demonstrated, women conceive of morality as a construct quite different from the construct formed by men. While men tend to see moral problems as the result of conflicting *rights*, women tend to see moral problems as arising from conflicting *responsibilities*:

In this conception, the moral problem arises from conflicting responsibilities rather than from competing rights and requires for its resolution a mode of thinking that is contextual and narrative rather than formal and abstract. This conception of morality as concerned with the activity of care centres moral development [upon] the understanding of responsibility and relationships, just as the conception of morality as fairness ties moral development to the understanding of rights and rules.[47]

In the light of these gender differences, it is no wonder that daytime melodrama — with its endless talk of relationships and responsibilities — is attractive to so many women auditors and despised by so many men. More importantly, however, placing Gilligan's conception of morality next to Brooks's conception of melodrama as representing the urge toward resacralisation in terms of personal responsibility and emotion suggests a link between the two that may help to explain why both women and melodrama have been despised categorically as primitive or trivial. Furthermore, in the restoration of melodrama as a valid form, we may valorise feminine moral thought as distinct from that of males.

Moreover, melodrama came to television gendered, with contrasting female-oriented and male-oriented species already evolved. Early night-time melodramas — most notably crime dramas and Westerns — inherited radio's penchant for adolescent fictions. There, white-hatted heroes fought black-hatted villains, and women were kept at a distance. Wives and potential wives, if not anathema, were as irrelevant to the Lone Ranger and Joe Friday as to Kojak and the A-Team.

Daytime Melodramas

Yet television also inherited the soap opera, a species of melodrama that from its inception was peopled by women and — as often as not — produced by women for a predominantly female audience. Despite recent forays into terrorism and thievery of ancient artifacts, the primary concern of soaps is affiliation: familial, romantic, and social.[48] Compared to popular romances — whose affiliative goal is the heroine's developed self-in-relation to one whose principal preoccupation is elsewhere in the world[49] — the soap opera is preoccupied with the web of relations within a community whose members (predominantly white, middle-class professionals) bear similar characteristics and talk to each other *a lot*.

In addition, as Robert Allen points out in an intriguing discussion of the relative indeterminacy of the soap opera text, the form depends more heavily than less open forms on the auditor's creative participation: 'The soap opera privileges that ever-changing moment [when] the reader comes to the text once again' after an absence as short as a commercial break or as long as several years. Drawing heavily from Tania Modleski, Allen contrasts the formal characteristics of the soap opera to those of the male-oriented narrative. The dominant form favours

> action over dialogue and ruthlessly reduces indeterminacies in order to arrive at a single moment of closure, solution, and knowledge. The soap opera makes the consequences of actions more important than action itself, introduces complications at every opportunity, and denies the desire for ultimate control by assuming its own immortality. In the male narrative dialogue is motored by plot and serves to explain, clarify, and simplify. In the soap opera, dialogue increases indeterminacy and retards resolution.[50]

Thus, the moment of narrative closure in soap operas is more like a pause for breath.[51] Closure in a soap always threatens to come unstuck, as indeed it sometimes does.

This is not to say that soap operas do not serve the sex-gender system; they are intensely conservative. However, unlike the romance's polar outcomes for the heroine — euphoric (marriage) or dysphoric (death) — soap opera's outcomes are layered with potentialities for further development. In soaps, neither marriage nor death is final. Resistance to narrative closure provides an opening for speculation by auditors as well as by creators as to how the case itself may be reopened. That opening is not insignificant. Like an unsealed letter, soap operas' unsealed narratives may be easier to open than we might have suspected.

Next to its focus on female characters, soap opera's preoccupation with process (as reflected in its resistance to closure and emphasis on the personal ramifications of actions) may explain more than any other factor the form's attraction to female audiences. In a sense, soaps' creators are always 'writing beyond the ending', DuPlessis' term for a group of techniques subversive of the finality of narrative closure in the romance. Finally, soap operas may be the best of a bad deal for female television auditors. Like Radway's subjects, who view their romance-reading as a mild form of protest to a system they cannot change, soap opera fans may be getting from daytime melodrama the best that television has to offer them. More importantly, auditors of soap operas may be finding *in the form* something resonant with their experience as women. Even though the predictability of traditional romantic closure has an important compensatory function, Radway's readers describe their fascination with the process of bringing heroine and hero together, a process which varies from novel to novel.[52] The soap opera's preoccupation with developing (and dissolving) relationships, for better or for worse, is a female-oriented narrative convention.

This is not to say that the convention is unique to television or to soap operas. Every narrative faces a paradox: it must ensure that it will be understood (and so employs familiar, intelligible conventions); and it must delay comprehension

> so as to ensure its own survival. To this end, it will introduce unfamiliar elements, it will multiply difficulties of one kind or another . . ., or simply delay the presentation of expected, interesting items.[53]

Soap operas exploit this paradox, some critics would say, to excess. Rather than to dwell on matters of taste, however, the point is to understand in meticulous detail the operation of the text in the televisual context (television-centred analysis) and to discover with equal sophistication what auditors do with the textual invitations and secrets identified (audience-centred analysis). This is a tall order; for what we do not know about soap operas from these perspectives is far greater than what we know.

Primetime Melodramas

Primetime melodramas would seem to speak less ably than daytime melodramas to women's experience. Nonetheless they too provide evidence that melodrama is a leakier form than romance. This is especially true of television melodrama by virtue of the fact that television dramas are performed. David Thorburn has called attention to the sophistication of television acting, in which the required obedience to formulaic plots and characterisation challenges the performer

> to recover from within himself and from his broadly stereotyped assign-

ment nuances of gesture, inflection, and movement that will at least hint at individual or idiosyncratic qualities.[54]

Thorburn's masculine pronouns suggest (as do his exclusively male illustrations) that his point refers to male performers.

Although it is true that primetime melodramas have been male territory traditionally, some contemporary crime dramas explicitly explore the gender differences that come to light when women invade that turf. Even such phallocentric series as *Policewoman* and *Charlie's Angels* contained moments when female actors were able to use their performances (if not often the script) to enter what Edwin Ardener called 'the zone of difference,' that tiny space created by the mismatch of dominant visions with muted ones.[55] In contemporary series such as *Cagney & Lacey* and *Hill Street Blues*, the zone of difference remains small (dominant vision still prevails); but the zone of difference is entered more often and much less covertly than was the case in the past.

The very presence of female protagonists in crime dramas affords writers and actors opportunities to 'break the sentence', to use Virginia Woolf's term for writing (or speaking) with rhythm, pace, flow, and expression that are authentically and unmutedly female.[56] Even though the context of dialogue may be unquestionably male, the performer may inject a female voice or glance that indicates, however subtly, that she is unafraid of making gender an issue. With series longevity, relationships between characters can take on increasing significance. Judine Mayerle in her study of *Cagney & Lacey* has demonstrated how characterisation has assumed ascendancy over traditional generic elements of crime drama. The series' increasing concern for Cagney and Lacey's relationship and for the effects of their work on their personal lives and families is an instance of what Charlotte Brunsdon has observed as characteristic of soap operas: that they '[*colonise*] the public masculine sphere, representing it from the point of view of the personal'.[57]

Such a narrative strategy suggests that 'breaking the sequence', Woolf's term for rupturing the expected order of events in a narrative to break their hegemonic inevitability, is also possible in television.[58] Here the movement of television drama away from narrative closure and toward an emphasis on process (in some cases, the experimentation with high melodrama) is extremely significant. Moving the site of struggle away from *action* in the streets toward *conversation* in the precinct house or even the boudoir or delivery room moves it in the direction of the mind, where all things are possible.

Conclusion

At minimum, television critics need to understand televisual aesthetics as they are applied; to understand the implications of production processes (as opposed to emphasising standards of judgement developed for finished works created by individuals); to understand the role of compromise and the impact of institutional and regulatory restraints; and to understand the role of affiliative themes and serial forms in shaping television discourse. Furthermore, television critics need to recognise and to document the variety of forms that constitutes the televisual text. This requires a willingness sometimes to study programs or series or commercials one at a time, starting with their concrete particularity. It means resisting, or at least suspending, the manly inclination to argue deductively from principles assumed to apply to all television equally. It also means being open to the possibility that televisual texts may manifest opposition under a glossy surface of consumerist or patriarchal values.

In short, I am advocating criticism that is unquestionably programmatic, whose aim is to increase the political, economic, cultural, aesthetic understanding, appreciation, and critique of television. However, I am at the same time advocating criticism in which the absence of critical orthodoxy is a virtue, criticism that does not replace an old literary or filmic canon with a new television one. Rather, we need to amass detailed analytical work on television programs and the industries that produce them to use as the springboard to more general theoretical work. Without that work in hand, our arguments will continue to be more moral and ethical than intellectual in the best sense.

In closing, it is appropriate to comment upon the audience for television-centred television criticism. To whom should it be addressed? First, television critics should write for one another in order to develop a body of knowledge worthy of anyone else's attention. That is, we need to write criticism that, like traditional literary criticism, assumes a reader who is 'educated, responsive to the text, [and] attentive' in order to advance our own knowledge agenda. However, this reader is not necessarily the 'masculine [reader who is assumed to be] in command of and fully engaged by the high culture of the Anglo-American elite' typical of literary criticism.[59] Television critics arise from a variety of backgrounds, a fortunate situation that inhibits the development of canonical hierarchies and requires the utmost precision and specificity in the application of terminologies and analytical methods.

Television critics should write also for more general audiences. As a group, television critics perhaps are most aware of the need for the general population to understand the social and cultural power of a medium so ubiquitous as television. The criticism that appears in the press and popular periodicals is scattered and mostly superficial; and media literacy is not yet a common goal of public school curricula in America, although it is elsewhere. If not writing for the popular press themselves, academic critics should be teaching courses required of journalism majors, at the very least, and advocating the inclusion of critical approaches to television in general education.

Finally, critics should work to cultivate an audience for television criticism among television's creators and gatekeepers. Unlike literature, a field in which creation and criticism are allied occupations, television writing and production reside in a universe far removed from criticism. Unlike drama and art critics, however, television critics are not regarded with hostility either. They more often are thought of as benignly ignorant, a situation that could change if more television-centred criticism were written. The audience of practitioners and regulators is important if critics do not wish to abandon the Utopian goal of having significant influence on television itself someday.

For those critics who hope that by their efforts television will go away, let me pose one last parallel to feminism. The feminist agenda requires women to develop a new relationship to other women, an objective that sometimes requires women to neglect their relationship to men. The liberation of television criticism requires critics to develop a new relationship to television (what I am calling television-centredness). Developing that relationship calls for ignoring some predispositions and suspending some old habits, healthy academic exercises undertaken to produce television criticism that is both wise and salutary.

4

Women Audiences and the Workplace
Dorothy Hobson

DH: When you were at work how much did you talk about the job and how much did you talk about things which were not to do with work?

JW: Because of the kind of job that we did, although you worked as a team you looked after your own particular area. Unless you'd got a particular problem or something you thought might be interesting, or something funny happened on the telephone, then you did not often discuss work unless you needed help. But there was always general chatter going around about where you'd all been the night before, what you'd been doing, if you'd seen a video, or what's happened with some program on the telly, or what's happened with the latest boyfriend and things like that. And although you all sat at your own desks there were little groups talking and because your job was talking and it was highly motivated, it would be OK for the noise level to be high.

Jacqui, aged 20, Telephone Sales Representative
Pharmaceutical and Feminine Hygiene Company

For many women the pleasures of paid work are as much connected with the culture of their workfriends as with the satisfaction which they get from their job and, of course, from the wage which they earn. Talking and 'having a laugh' can bring extra job satisfaction because it can create a much more attractive working environment than one where there is little opportunity to talk to co-workers. Some jobs provide little or no opportunity for talking; but in those jobs where conversation is permissible and even essential, the ways that women talk and discuss their own lives, the state of the world and the cultural artefacts which they read and watch, and the interweaving of all these aspects of everyday life, can give interesting and incisive accounts of the way that women manage their lives and incorporate disparate influences into their discussions.

Television is a part of the everyday life of its audience. The way that women manage their time to fit their viewing into their domestic work has been discussed in many texts but there is much less information about the way that television comes into discussions outside the home and particularly in the workplace. This chapter begins to look at the way that a group of women talked about television in their general conversation at work. But it tells much more than that, for in talking about television these women reveal the way that their discussions are wide-ranging and the whole question of the way that women bring their feminine characteristics to their work situation, to augment their jobs, is revealed in their accounts of how they work and at the same time talk about everything. The thesis of this chapter is that women use television programs as part of their general discourse on their own lives, the lives of their families and friends and to add interest to their working lives. It adds to the critique of audiences as passive viewers by putting forward the hypothesis that it is the discussion after television programs have been viewed which completes the process of communication and locates television programs as part of popular culture.

The article is based on an account which one young woman — Jacqui, who worked as a telephone sales manager for an internationally-known pharmaceutical and feminine hygiene company — gave of the way that the women in her office spent their working day, selling, talking and as she terms it 'putting the world to rights'. The women are graphically described in the following comment by Jacqui:

> The eldest was Audrey who was 56, two children, both gone to university, husband has a good job, staying there till she retires, quite quiet, just talks about curtains and things like that, but will contribute to discussions. The youngest person, who is the office junior, is little Tracey, who gets a black eye from her boyfriend every 5 weeks or whatever — 17 and very young in her ways. And then you've got all the ages in between and all the different marital statuses and all the different backgrounds, different cultures and classes which were just mingled together. Which was so nice

because it was so different but they all came together in one unit and discussed openly different issues and topics, which were sometimes, but not necessarily triggered off by television.

Although this chapter is based on the account of one telephone sales office it is part of a larger study of the way that women talk about television in the workplace. Although the amount of talking which can be done differs according to the occupation, there are general features which are similar in many of the accounts which women have given.

The amount of talking which can be carried out during working times is largely determined by the type of job and the control which is exercised in the workplace. Sales is one of the careers which attracts the most gregarious and voluble and sales offices are renowned for the high decibels which emanate from their staff. But not all the talk that goes on is selling. When Jacqui told me of the way that the women with whom she works spend their days, it was a tale of interweaving of personal interests, current affairs, social and philosophical debates and media events. Work was fitted in, around conversations which were sometimes triggered by television programs or newspaper articles; sometimes the conversations led on to discussions about the media. The office where she worked consisted of 17 women, 'the girls in the office'. Jacqui begins by telling of the way that they organise their work.

> Well you'd all got your own little units which consisted of two filing cabinets, a desk a bookshelf which had your computer, your telephone and everything else. And there were 17 of us and the manager. And if you went out to another office you'd notice the change 'cos in our office it would be all bubbly and somebody messing about, and laughter and everything. And if you walked next door into the clerical office it was very quiet more like an exam really, you felt you were going into a time warp.

With 17 girls in one office not every conversation included everyone, but there were often little groups talking. However, there were topics which drew in the whole office. They would plan to go out on pay day and everyone would join in the decisions about where to go and whether they would go out straight from work. Television was also a topic which drew in the whole of the group in conversation:

> Somebody would say something like 'Who saw *Coronation Street* last night?', and Anita would say, 'Oh, I saw it!', and you'd sort of have Mary sitting there going 'Oh, my God!', and making comments about *Coronation Street* and doing some stupid impression beneath the desk and you'd say 'Shut up Mary, shut up!' and everybody would go 'Ssh, ssh,

Anita, tell us what happened . . .' It would depend on who was telling the story as to how much detail they would go into but if it was Anita she would go into great detail about what had happened and the expressions on the faces of the actors and everybody would sit and listen and if you'd seen it the night before and she missed any bits out you'd say 'Er, wait a minute, he wasn't very happy about that', or whatever.

Once the people in the office were talking about a television program, they quickly adapted the conversation to include topics which were about their own lives and interests. After the initial catching up on storylines, the women who worked in this office would extend the stories of what had already happened in the serials to speculating as to what was likely to happen next. The next phase was to extend the conversation to discuss what they would do if they were in the same circumstances as the characters:

As I was saying you might be talking about an episode of *Coronation Street* or *Eastenders* and after you had said 'What happened?', then you would say 'What do you think is going to happen next?' 'Well, I think Angie's going to run off'. (She did.) 'No she won't', 'Well, I think she will'. It's all a bit of a laugh really, a bit of gossip, nobody really takes it seriously but then you might move on to talk about Kath and Willmott-Brown and someone will say 'I think Kath is going to go off with Willmott-Brown' and then they would start putting things in relating it to themselves, but doing it in a joking way. Like saying, 'Well, if my Alan was as vile as Pete, I think I'd go off with Willmott-Brown!'.

The comments about whether they would actually have an affair if their husband behaved as the character in the television serial, are offered only in a joking manner. For some of the women who had difficult lives, the events in the serials were close to their own lives and they did not comment as to what they would do in similar circumstances. One particular woman revealed not only her interest in soap operas but also what Jacqui terms 'her own particular domestic hell'.

Vicky, who hardly ever contributed to discussions, if you talked about soap operas then she was at the forefront of the conversation. She lived in this sort of domestic hell with this bloke who was not her husband. She'd never been married and she lived with this bloke and it was his house and her philosophy was that she had to do what he said because he could throw her out because it was his house. She used to say she loved all the soap operas, 'I watch them all, *Coronation Street*, *Crossroads*, *East-enders*, *Dallas*, I watch them all and I love them.' But if Brian came in she could not watch them. She used to say, 'Brian hates them and if I'm watching them he'll come in and turn them off and I'm not allowed to watch them. He turns the telly off and I'm not allowed to watch them, I have to go and get his tea'.

Vicky is not alone in not being allowed to watch soap operas on television. Many other women have told me that they are restricted in what they are allowed to watch, and this is a point that differs from the one of the man having control of the remote-control. But Jacqui continued to explain that although Vicky never prophesied as to what she would do if she were in the position of someone in a television drama, it did provide a means for her to talk about the way that she experienced her own life.

Using an event which had happened in a television program to talk about events in their own lives was a common practice amongst the group. I asked directly if they moved from topics or situations that were seen on television, to talking about how those events might figure in their own lives or lives of their acquaintances. Jacqui responded:

> Well, it would be quite funny actually, what would happen would be somebody would talk about something that had happened in a program. The hypothetical situation that they might be in is that their husband had been unfaithful and they found out. And they would be coming out with this and that of what they would do. 'Well, I'd pack his bags, send him off, put him outside, wouldn't have him back!' And there would be all this big palaver going on. And then you would have people who it had actually happened to or it was happening to and they would begin to talk in the abstract, as in, 'But what if you loved him? But what if he said?'. They would try to get the reactions from the other girls. I suppose it was a way to assess their own feelings and situations.

The use of events within fiction to explore experiences which were perhaps too personal or painful to talk about to a complete work group is a beneficial and creative way of extending the value of the program into their own lives. Fiction was not the only televisual genre which acted as a trigger for further discussion. Documentaries also had this effect and could result in long, detailed discussions on their subject.

> If they'd watched a documentary which had moved them they would talk about it all day. There would be a general conversation and in the hub-bub someone would pipe up, 'Did you see *40 Minutes* last night, the documentary about handicapped people?' And it would usually be something that they didn't really know about before they'd watched it and it really moved them and they'd start to discuss it. And somebody might

know something about it from their own personal experience of somebody they knew who's handicapped. And they would perhaps agree with
the program, and the whole office would be enlightened by this one program that had moved them. And it might only be one person who had
actually seen it.

It would seem that a documentary did not have to have been seen
by everyone for it to become the topic of conversation in the office.
One interested viewer could spread the information which would
provide the trigger for the whole conversation. The program would
work in conjunction with any knowledge or experience other people
in the office had about its subject and they would impart their
knowledge to the others and the whole subject would become a topic
for open discussion and debate. These accounts disprove the theory
that watching television is a mindless, passive event in the lives of the
viewers. On the contrary, the events and subjects covered in television
programs often acted as the catalyst for wide-ranging and open discussions. The communication was extended far beyond the moment
of viewing.

One of the most interesting aspects of the way that work groups
affect the viewing habits of their colleague was revealed when Jacqui
talked about *Moonlighting*. When some of the women in the office
had talked about the program their discussions had been so intriguing to the other people in the office that they were enticed to watch
the program so that they could join in the talk. Mary and Jacqui led
the group into viewing *Moonlighting* and extended the cult nature of
the program to the way that they talked about it. Talking about
Moonlighting became a cult within the office and to take part you
had to watch the program. Mary was not an avid television viewer, in
fact she rather looked down on those members of the office who
watched a lot of television, particularly soap operas. She professed
to prefer documentaries. However, she did love *Moonlighting*.

The one program which Mary did watch and was like a religious follower
of, and it would be taped if they were going out, and tragic if she missed
it, and anything that was in a magazine to do with it she would read —
was *Moonlighting*. I watched it as well if I was in. I wouldn't make a habit
of staying in to watch it but I would watch it and enjoy it if it was on. And
she would shout across the office, 'Did you see *Moonlighting* last night? I
can't believe Maddie's doing this to him. Poor Bruce!' Bruce Willis was
always Bruce but Maddie is always Maddie. Maddie was always the
character but Bruce Willis is Bruce Willis and it is always on a personal
level and she'd talk about them and she'd say, 'Did you see that look on
his face when he told her?' And we would be shouting across the office

and there would be so much emphasis on how wonderful it was and we'd be raving on about it all day and the conversation could go on for hours. And someone would say, 'What is this program *Moonlighting*?' And we'd say, 'Haven't you ever seen *Moonlighting*?' As if to say, this girl hasn't lived! And it went on like that and eventually they all started watching it.

The power of one person being drawn into watching a program because it was a topic of conversation among other women at work is familiar. This is often because the culture of work includes talking about programs and if a number of people in the group are talking about a program then others will not wish to be left out. In the above comment, from Jacqui, she illustrates not only the necessity to have watched the program but also to know the significance of the use of character or performers' names when talking about last night's episode. David and Maddie are partners in a firm of private detectives; they are played by Bruce Willis and Cybil Shepherd. When Jacqui reports that Mary refers to Maddie as the character and Bruce as the actor it is not a confusion of fiction and reality, but rather an indication that Mary is more interested in Bruce Willis the man, as well as the character he plays. The comment assumes a shared knowledge with me, not only about the program but about the way that some women audiences view Bruce Willis. Talking about the program in the office required this shared knowledge if everyone were to be able to join in the discussions.

In this case it was the power of enthusiasm of two members of a group of 17 who got the majority of the office to watch the program. (Remember this is a telephone sales office — enthusiasm and persuasion are crucial as professional skills.) However, once they had persuaded everyone to watch the program there were many differing responses from the women in the office. Once they were all watching it different discussions ensued.

> Someone would come in and say, 'I watched *Moonlighting* and it was very good, I really enjoyed it and can you tell me why?' And they'd try to catch up on the storyline that they had missed. Other people because of the way it sort of went off into surrealism at points during the episodes — when the actors would be prancing around in leotards when they would be trying to portray Maddie's feelings, or something like that — Some people, like Debbie, who is a real down-to-earth person, who loves *Cell Block H*, she wouldn't like these flights of fantasy. She would say 'I think it's bloody stupid prancing around in a leotard, criminals running away . . .'. And you would try to explain but she wouldn't have it she just thought it was a stupid program.

The different perception of the program by different members of the office added to the nature of the discussions which they had the next day. While Debbie rejected the program and defined it as stupid, others struggled to catch up with the storyline or to understand the underlying joke of the program. The day after transmission the program dominated discussions.

> Everytime you mentioned the program there would be Debbie saying it was rubbish. There'd be Susie or Janet who'd be trying to catch up, saying, 'But I don't understand why Bruce is with Maddie in the first place'. And then there would be Mary raving about it. I'd join in and there would be like a war going on that could go on for the whole of the day. Not all the time, but little comments all through the day. Somebody would say, 'Oh, don't ask Mary she likes *Moonlighting*, she's hardly likely to know is she?' And there would be little jibes attached to the programs which you watched, that sort of thing.

The talk about the programs extended into jokes about the type of program you watched and liked and this became part of the cultural perception of both the program and those who liked it. Of course, the perceptions changed depending on who was making the observations. For Debbie, *Moonlighting* was weird and Mary, as a fan of the program, was not to be trusted to have sensible opinions on other matters.

The notion that you are defined by your cultural preferences is not a new one but it is often seen as defining the cultural elite. Cultural choices, however, can work both ways and those who are completely *au fait* with popular culture can see themselves as superior to those who do not watch popular programs. To be aware of the worst programs on television is as necessary as to watch those which are perceived as being worthy or important. For this group of women their choice of television viewing was catholic. As well as soap operas, dramas, films, documentaries and American series, they needed to watch what was generally seen as the worst program on television — the Australian soap opera set in a women's prison, *Prisoner Cell Block H*. The reasons for the popularity of this series came out unsolicited when Jacqui was replying to a question as to whether they were interested in the technical aspects of the productions or the content. Although she says that they are only interested in content, she goes on to state that they make comments on the acting and the way that *Prisoner* is put together:

> JW: Oh, it would be content all the time. The way that it had been directed or produced or the sets or the location was not important to

the discussions. If it was a factual program then it would be the issue that they were discussing — the content. If it were fiction then it would be the storyline, how much gossip they had got into it, how it related to people's own experiences and things like that. Occasionally, if something was really gross like *Cell Block H* or some sloppy mini-series where the acting was absolutely atrocious, somebody might make a comment about it and then perhaps somebody might pop up and do a quick impression.

DH: If people thought *Cell Block H* was atrocious why did they watch it?

JW: Because it's hilarious and you watch it and you can't believe the storylines are so outrageously ridiculous and the acting is so atrocious, so that the whole thing put together is so hilarious so that people who are up at that sort of time, they just watch it and it would be like a cult. Some people would say 'Well why do you watch it?' And the answer would be, 'Well it's brilliant, I love it!' And they'd love it for a different reason from why they would love something that had been tremendously well made or with fantastic acting. They would love it for a different reason. They'd enjoy it because it was so awful really and they'd discuss the storyline and it would be all taken with a pinch of salt and enjoyed for what it is which is appalling but funny. And they would watch it in disbelief to see whether it could possibly get any worse.

Cell Block H was seen as the best of the worst and so it was in good taste to watch it, but other programs had a certain stigma attached to them. This was seen as light-hearted but, as Jacqui said, 'There were certain programs you could not admit that you watched'. These were mainly the other soap operas and Mary seemed to be instrumental in attaching social class to watching soap operas. If anyone admitted to watching *Crossroads*, then they were defined as of limited intellectual capacity. To be teased and defined as a *Coronation Street* watcher, *Sun* reader, social club goer!' may be meant as a joke — but even in the context of inter-office joking, to be described as a *Sun* reader is not funny.

The converse of being socially defined as a *Sun* reader, in Britain, might be being seen as a Channel 4 viewer. Britain's newest television channel began transmission in November 1982 and it was charged by Parliament to cater for tastes and interests not generally catered for by Britain's other commercial channel, ITV. In the early days both the channel and its viewers were perceived by some as being socially aware, opinionated, arty and different. Channel 4 and its viewers were seen as being 'caring people'. This image was one which prevailed in the office. If someone mentioned a program which was seen as out of the ordinary, others in the office would ask, 'Was it on

Channel 4?' This notion of being a Channel 4 viewer was one which was attached to Jacqui by the other women in the office.

> Because I'm so opinionated about certain things and stand up for certain views, they would say, 'You have to be careful, don't make a racist comment or Jacqui will be on her soap box.' And if there had been a program on say for instance about South Africa, they would say, 'Did you see that program, you should have watched it because you're interested in that sort of thing.' And that would really be because they wanted me to have seen it and to have enjoyed it as much as they did . . . And we would have a bit of a discussion. They might say, 'When that man was talking last night I thought that was a bit one-sided, what do you think?' And we would have a discussion not only about the program but about the topic in general.

It became clear during the course of this interview and our discussions that this working group had used television to its and their best advantage, to advance their understanding of themselves and the world in which they lived. The myth that people who watch television are not using their time to the full is demolished by the range of views which these women expressed and explored through their use of television. The office seemed never to be silent and conversation was the dynamism which fuelled their work and social intercourse.

> We have touched on every single subject from AIDS, the *Network* film on homosexuals and some people would say, 'I think that it is disgusting', and somebody else said, 'Do you mind, my brother's gay.' And somebody would make a joke about it and then you would talk about it. We have talked about every single thing, racism, people's experience, why certain people are prejudiced. Some people would freely admit they were prejudiced and try to justify the reasons behind it because they lived in an area which was populated mainly by black people and they would say they were trying to understand their prejudice. And that was OK because they were trying to go one step towards not being prejudiced and to judge everyone when they met them. We touched on everything in the office and each girl would have a different opinion and conflicting view but we all talked about what we felt.

They were a group who were open about their feelings and views and it was often a topic set forth in a television program that triggered the discussions.

Considering the amount of talking that went on, it might be asked when they managed to do any actual selling and the notion of fitting discussions around the tasks of their work day took on a different perspective with this group. When I spoke to a group of women who worked in a local authority, they told how they stopped the communal conversations when anyone had to take a telephone call from outside. In this group (the telephone sales group) the women so regulated their own work that if they had an outside call which interrupted their conversations, they did not stop talking but returned the call when their discussions had finished. They planned their own days and as long as they reached their sales targets they had full control of their leisure time within work. An amusing story clarifies the importance of their own culture within their working time.

> Your time was basically your own and when you went in in the morning you could decide what you were going to do. If you had a fantastic morning and you'd done £3,000 that day then you knew you didn't have to do much in the afternoon. So then, if you were having a major discussion and were just about to put the world right on what you thought about Nicaragua and somebody says, 'Jacqui, I've got Neil from Blackwoods on the telephone', You'd say, 'tell him I'll ring him back'. And you'd finish the discussion and then you would ring him back and deal with him. He wasn't about to complain to anybody, he was probably ringing to complain about something anyway, so you would wait until you had finished the conversation and then ring him back to sort out his problem.

Presumably, Neil from Blackwoods never knew that a discussion about Nicaragua was in progress when he phoned and doubtless he was happy when his problem was sorted out.

It is clear from the way that these women managed the professional requirements of their paid work, and from the range of personal, philosophical and political discussions which they explored together, that they were skilled in bringing their culture into their workplace and combining many aspects of their lives. Television was one of the many experiences which they shared and which they used to expand their discussions. Jacqui was a particularly articulate storyteller of their working lives and the way that they experienced them together. I have let her words predominate here because it is these women's experience that she is relating — her narrative of their narratives within their working days. Earlier she told how it was the content, the storyline or the topic, which they found of most interest in the television programs which they watched. It is the interweaving of the narratives of fiction with the narratives of their reality that formed the basis for sharing their experiences and opinions and creating their own culture within their workplace.

Chapter 6. Madonna in shopping mall, Austin, Texas.
Photo: Lisa Lewis.

Chapter 9. Greg Evans and Kerrie Friend celebrate her
500th appearance as hostess of 'Perfect Match'.
Photo: Grundy Organisation.

PART TWO

Representation and Fantasy: The Structuring of Feminine Reading Positions

Chapter 11. Dynasty: Joan Collins as Alexis Carrington.

Chapter 11. Dynasty: Linda Evans as Krystle Carrington.

5

Melodramatic Identifications: Television Fiction and Women's Fantasy

Ien Ang

Contemporary popular television fiction offers an array of strong and independent female heroines, who seem to defy — not without conflicts and contradictions, to be sure — stereotypical definitions of femininity. Heroines such as Maddie Hayes (*Moonlighting*) and Christine Cagney (*Cagney & Lacey*) do not fit into the traditional ways in which female characters have generally been represented in prime-time television fiction: passive and powerless on the one hand, and sexual objects for men on the other.

Christine Cagney, especially, and her partner Mary-Beth Lacey, are the kind of heroines who have mobilized approval from feminists.[1] *Cagney & Lacey* can be called a 'social realist' series, in which the personal and professional dilemmas of modern working women are dealt with in a serious and 'realistic' way. Cagney explicitly resists sexual objectification by her male colleagues, force-fully challenges the male hierarchy at work, and entertains an adult, respectful, and caring friendship with her 'buddy' Lacey.

Maddie Hayes is a little more difficult to evaluate in straight-forward feminist terms. However, while she often has to cope with the all-but-abusive, but ever-so-magnetic machismo of her recal-citrant partner David Addison, *Moonlighting*, as a typical example of post-modernist television self-consciously addresses, enacts, and acknowledges metonymically the pleasures and pains of the ongoing 'battle between the sexes' in the context of the series' characteristic penchant for hilarious absurdism and teasing parody.[2] In that battle, Maddie is neither passive nor always the loser: she fights and gains respect (and love) in the process.

Many women enjoy watching series such as *Cagney & Lacey* and *Moonlighting*, and it is likely that at least part of their pleasure is related to the 'positive' representations of women that both series offer. But this does not mean that other, more traditional television fictions are less pleasurable for large numbers of women. On the contrary, as is well known, soap operas have traditionally been *the* female television genre while prime-time soaps such as *Dallas* and *Dynasty* have always had a significantly larger female audience than a male one.

Personally, I have often been moved by Sue Ellen of *Dallas* as much as I am at times by Christine Cagney. And yet, Sue Ellen is a radically different heroine from Cagney: she displays no (will for) independence whatsoever, she derives her identity almost entirely from being the wife of the unscrupulous and power-obsessed J.R. Ewing, whom she detests because he is never faithful, but whom she does not have the strength to leave.[3] As a consequence, Sue Ellen's life is dominated by constant frustration and suffering – apparently a very negative representation of 'woman' indeed. Despite this, the Sue Ellen character seems to be a source of identification and pleasure for many women viewers of *Dallas*: they seem not so much to love to hate J.R. but to suffer with Sue Ellen.

An indication of this can be derived from the results of a small-scale research that I conducted a few years ago.[4] Through an advertisement in a Dutch weekly magazine, I asked people to send me their views about *Dallas*. From the letters, it was clear that Sue Ellen stood out as a character whom many women viewers were emotionally involved with. One of the respondents wrote:

> . . . I can sit very happy and fascinated watching someone like Sue Ellen. That woman can really get round us, with her problems and troubles. She is really human. I could be someone like her too. In a manner of speaking.

Another wrote:

> Sue Ellen is definitely my favourite. She has a psychologically believable character. As she is, I am myself to a lesser degree ('knocking one's head against a wall once too often') and I want to be (attractive).

It is interesting to note that another *Dallas* character whose structural position in the narrative is similar to Sue Ellen's has not elicited such committed responses at all. Pamela Ewing (married to J.R.'s brother, Bobby) is described rather blandly as 'a nice girl', or is seen as 'too sweet'. In fact, the difference of appeal between the two characters becomes even more pronounced in the light of the findings of a representative Dutch survey conducted in 1982 (around the time that the popularity of *Dallas* was at its height). While 21.7% of female viewers between 15 and 39 years mentioned Sue Ellen as their favourite *Dallas* character (as against only 5.9% of the men), only 5.1% named Pamela as their favourite (and 4.2% of the men).[5]

Clearly Sue Ellen has a special significance for a large number of women viewers. Two things stand out in the quotes above. Not only do these viewers assert that the appeal of Sue Ellen is related to a form of realism (in the sense of psychological believability and recognisability); more importantly, this realism is connected with a somewhat tragic reading of Sue Ellen's life, emphasising her problems and troubles. In other words, the position from which Sue Ellen fans seem to give meaning to, and derive pleasure from, their favourite *Dallas* character seems to be a rather melancholic and sentimental structure of feeling which stresses the down-side of life rather than its happy highlights; frustration, desperation and anger rather than euphoria and cheerfulness.

To interpret this seemingly rather despondent form of female pleasure, I shall examine the position which the Sue Ellen character occupies in the *Dallas* narrative, and unravel the meaning of that position in the context of the specific fictional genre to which *Dallas* belongs: the melodramatic soap opera. The tragic structure of feeling embodied by Sue Ellen as a fictional figure must be understood in the context of the genre characteristics of the *Dallas* drama: just as Christine Cagney is a social-realist heroine and Maddie Hayes a post-modern one, so is Sue Ellen a melodramatic heroine. In other words, articulated and materialised in Sue Ellen's identity is what in 1976 American critic Peter Brooks called a melodramatic imagination.

Of course, fictional characters may be polysemic just as they can take on a plurality of meanings depending on the ways in which diverse viewers read them. Thus, Sue Ellen's melodramatic persona can be interpreted and evaluated in several ways. Whilst her fans tend to empathise with her and live through her problems and troubles vicariously, others stress her bitchiness and take a stance against her. In the words of one *Dallas* viewer:

> Sue Ellen has had bad luck with J.R., but she makes up for it by being a flirt. I don't like her much. And she's too sharp-tongued.

Others have called her a frustrated lady. One of my respondents was especially harsh in her critique:

> Take Sue Ellen. She acts as though she's very brave and can put up a fight, but she daren't make the step of divorce. What I mean is that in spite of her good intentions she lets people walk over her, because (as J.R. wants) for the outside world they have to form a perfect family.

According to Herta Herzog, who interviewed German viewers about *Dallas* in 1987, older viewers tend to see in Sue Ellen the woman ruined by her husband, while younger ones tend to see her as a somewhat unstable person who is her own problem.[6] However, despite the variation in emphasis in the different readings of Sue Ellen, a basic agreement seems to exist that her situation is an extremely contentious and frustrating one, and her personality is rather tormented. This is the core of the melodramatic heroine. But while many viewers are put off by this type of character, some are fascinated, a response evoked not only by the dramatic content of the role, but by the melodramatic style of the actress, Linda Gray. As one fan discloses,

> Sue Ellen (is) just *fantastic*, tremendous how that woman acts, the movements of her mouth, hands, etc. That woman really enters into her role, looking for love, snobbish, in short a real woman.

As a contrast, the same viewer describes Pamela as a Barbie doll with no feelings!

It is not my intention to offer an exhaustive analysis of the Sue Ellen character as melodramatic heroine. Nor do I want to make a sociological examination of which segment of the audience is attracted to characters like her. Rather, I use her as a point of departure to explore women's pleasure in popular fiction in general, and melodramatic fiction in particular. Women who use Sue Ellen as a source of identification while watching *Dallas* do that by taking up, in fantasy, a subject position which inhabits the melodramatic imagination.[7] The pleasure of such imaginary identification can be seen as a form of excess in some women's mode of experiencing everyday life in our culture: the act of surrendering to the melodramatic imagination may signify a recognition of the complexity and conflict fundamental to living in the modern world.

Soap opera and the melodramatic imagination

I now move to summing up some of the structural soap opera characteristics of *Dallas* which contribute to its melodramatic content.[8] It should first be noted, however, that because *Dallas* is a prime-time program, some of its features are different from those of the traditional daytime soaps. Most importantly, because the program must attract a heterogeneous audience it will include a wider range of themes, scenes and plots. For example, male characters, as well as themes, scenes and plots which traditionally are mainly appreciated by male audiences, such as the wheelings and dealings of the oil business, and the cowboy/Western elements of the show, occupy a much more prominent place in the fictional world of *Dallas* than in regular daytime soap. Nevertheless, the general formal characteristics of *Dallas* do remain true to the soap opera genre, and are very important for the construction of melodramatic meanings and feelings in the text.[9]

First of all, as in all melodrama, personal life is the core problematic of the narrative. Personal life must be understood here as constituted by its everyday realisation through personal relationships. In soap operas, the evolution of personal relationships is marked out through the representation of significant family rituals and events such as births, romances, engagements, marriages, divorces, deaths and so on. It is the experience of these rituals and events (and all the attendant complications and disputes) on which soap opera narratives centre. This does not imply that non-personal issues are not addressed. However the way in which they are treated and take on meaning is always from the standpoint of personal life:

> the action of soap opera is not restricted to the familial, or quasi-familial institutions, but everything is told from the point of view of the personal.[10]

Thus, while J.R.'s business intrigues form a focal narrative concern in *Dallas*, they are always shown with an eye to their consequences for the well-being of the Ewing family members, not least his wife Sue Ellen.

A second major melodramatic feature of soap opera is its excessive plot structure. If family life is the main focus of the *Dallas* narrative, the life of the Ewings is presented as one replete with extraordinary conflicts and catastrophes. To the critical outsider this may appear as a purely sensationalist tendency to cliché and exaggeration — a common objection levelled at melodrama since the late nineteenth century. It is important to note, however, that *within* the fictional world of the soap opera all those extreme story lines such as kidnappings, bribery, extramarital affairs, obscure illnesses, and so on, which succeed each other at such a breathtaking pace, are not treated in a sensational manner, but are taken entirely seriously.[11] The parameters of melodrama require that such clichés be regarded and assessed not for their literal, referential value — that is, their realism — but as meaningful in so far as they solicit a highly charged, emotional impact. Their role is metaphorical, and their appeal stems from the enlarged emotional impact they evoke: it is the feelings being mobilised here that matter. An excess of events and intensity of emotions are inextricably intertwined in the melodramatic imagination.

Sue Ellen's recurrent alcoholism is a case in point. Even though she has stayed away from alcohol for a long time loyal viewers are reminded of this dark side of her past every time she is shown refusing a drink. Do we detect a slight moment of hesitation there? Alcoholism is a very effective narrative motif that, in a condensed way, enables the devoted viewer to empathise with her feelings of desperation. She is married to a man she loathes but who has her almost completely in his power. In other words, Sue Ellen's propensity for alcoholism functions as a metaphor for her enduring state of crisis.

Such a state of crisis is not at all exceptional or uncommon in the context of the soap opera genre. On the contrary, crisis can be said to be endemic to it. As a result, Sue Ellen's predicament, as it is constructed, is basically unsolvable unless she leaves the *Dallas* community and disappears from the serial altogether. Here, a third structural characteristic of the soap opera makes its impact: its lack of narrative progress. *Dallas*, like all soap operas, is a never-ending story: contrary to classic narratives, which are typically structured according to the logic of order/disorder/restoration of order, soap opera narratives never reach completion. They represent process without progression and as such do not offer the prospect of a conclusion of final dénouement, in which all problems are solved. Thus, soap operas are fundamentally anti-utopian: an ending, happy or unhappy, is unimaginable. This does not mean, of course, that there are no moments of climax in soap operas. But, as Tania Modleski has observed, 'the "mini-climaxes" of soap opera function to introduce difficulties and to complicate rather than simplify the characters' lives.'[12] Here, a basic melodramatic idea is conveyed: the sense that life is marked by eternal contradiction, by unsolvable emotional and moral conflicts, by the ultimate impossibility, as it were, of reconciling desire and reality. As Laura Mulvey has put it,

> The melodrama recognises this gap by raising problems, known and recognisable, and offering a personal escape similar to that of a daydream: a chance to work through inescapable frustrations by positing an alternative ideal never seen as more than a momentary illusion.[13]

The life of the Sue Ellen character in *Dallas* exemplifies and dramatises this melodramatic scenario. She even expresses an awareness of its painfully contradictory nature. In one dialogue with Pamela, for example, she states:

> The difference [between you and me] is that you're a strong woman, Pam. I used to think I was, but I know differently now. I need Southfork. On my own, I don't amount to much. As much as I hate J.R., I really need to be Mrs J.R. Ewing. And I need him to be the father of John Ross [her son]. So I guess I just have to lead a married life without a husband.

In general then, it could be said that the soap operatic structure of *Dallas* opens up a narrative space in which melodramatic characters can come to life symbolically — characters who ultimately are constructed as victims of forces that lie beyond their control. A heroine like Sue Ellen will never be able to make her own history: no matter how hard she tries, eventually the force of circumstances will be too overwhelming. She lives in the prison of an eternally conflictual present. No wonder that she reacts with frustration, bitterness, resignation and cynical ruthlessness on the rebound. As she neatly summarises her own life philosophy:

> If J.R. seeks sex and affection somewhere else, so why shouldn't I? All Ewing men are the same. And for you to survive you have two choices. You can either get out, or you can play by their rules!

In fact, this frame of mind has led her to give up all attempts to find true happiness for herself: although she has her occasional moments of joy (a new lover, for example), they are futile in the face of her biggest self-imposed passion: to use all the power she has to undermine J.R.'s projects, to ruin his life just as he has ruined hers. She even refuses him a divorce to keep him from marrying another woman (by which he expects to win an extremely advantageous business deal). It is such small victories which make her feel strong at times. But they are ultimately self-destructive and will never allow her to break out of her cage.

Against this background, identifying with Sue Ellen implies a recognition of the fact that Sue Ellen's crisis is a permanent one: there seems to be no real way out. She may experience happy moments, but as viewers we know that those moments are bound to be merely temporary and inevitably followed by new problems and difficulties. At stake, then, must be a rather curious form of pleasure for these viewers. Whereas in other narratives pleasure comes from the assurance and confirmation of a happy end — as with the romantic union of a man and a woman in the formulaic 'they live happily ever after', involvement with a character like Sue Ellen is conditioned by the prior knowledge that no such happy ending will ever occur. Instead, pleasure must come from living through and negotiating with the crisis itself. To put it more precisely, many female Sue Ellen fans tend to identify with a subject position characterised by a sense of entrapment: a sense in which survival is, in the words of television critic Horace Newcomb, 'complicated by ambiguity and blurred with pain even in its most sought-after moments.'[14]

If this is true (and I have already given some indications that this is indeed the case) how do we interpret this kind of identification, this form of pleasure in popular fiction?

Pleasure, fantasy and the negotiation of femininity

One could assert that melodramatic heroines like Sue Ellen should be evaluated negatively because they attest to an outlook on life that stresses resignation and despair. Isn't the melodramatic imagination a particularly damaging way of making sense of life because it affirms tendencies of individualistic fatalism and pessimism? And isn't such an impact especially harmful for women as it reinforces and legitimises masochistic feelings of powerlessness? Wouldn't it be much better for women and girls to choose identification figures that represent strong, powerful and independent women who are able and determined to change and improve their lives, such as Christine Cagney?

Such concerns are, of course, often heard in feminist accounts of popular fiction, but it is important to note here that they are often based upon a theoretical approach — what could be called a role/image approach, or more conventionally, 'images of women' approach — which analyses images of women in the media and in fiction by setting them against real women. Fictional female heroines are then seen as images of women functioning as role models for female audiences.[15] From such a perspective, it is only logical to claim that one should strive to offer positive role models by supplying positive images of women. And from this perspective, feminist common sense would undoubtedly ascribe the Sue Ellen character to the realm of negative images, reflecting a traditional, stereotyped or trivialised model of womanhood.

However, this approach contains both theoretical and political problems. Most importantly here, because it implies a rationalistic view of the relationship between image and viewer (whereby it is assumed that the image is seen by the viewer as a more or less adequate model of reality), it can only account for the popularity of soap operas among women as something irrational. In other words, what the role/image approach tends to overlook is the large *emotional involvement* which is invested in identification with characters of popular fiction.

To counteract this attitude, we first of all need to acknowledge that these characters are products of *fiction*, and that fiction is not a mere set of images to be read referentially, but an ensemble of textual devices for engaging the viewer at the level of fantasy.[16] As a result, female fictional characters such as Sue Ellen Ewing or Christine Cagney cannot be conceptualised as realistic images of women, but as textual constructions of possible *modes of femininity*: as embodying versions of gendered subjectivity endowed with specific forms of psychical and emotional satisfaction and dissatisfaction, and specific ways of dealing with conflicts and dilemmas. In relation to this, they do not function as role models but are symbolic realisations of feminine subject positions with which viewers can identify *in fantasy*.

Fantasy is central here. In line with psychoanalytic theory, fantasy should not be seen as mere illusion, an unreality, but as a reality in itself, a fundamental aspect of human existence: a necessary and unerasable dimension of psychical reality. Fantasy is an imagined scene in which the fantasising subject is the protagonist, and in which alternative scenarios for the subject's real life are evoked. Fantasising obviously affords the subject pleasure, which, according to the psychoanalysts, has to do with the fulfillment of a conscious or unconscious wish. Here I would suggest more generally that the pleasure of fantasy lies in its offering the subject an opportunity to take up positions which she could not do in real life: through fantasy she can move beyond the structural constraints of everyday life and explore other situations, other identities, other lives. It is totally unimportant here whether these are realistic or not. As Lesley Stern has remarked, 'gratification is to be achieved not through acting out the fantasies, but through the activity of fantasising itself'.[17]

Fantasies, and the act of fantasising, are usually a private practice in which we can engage at any time and the content of which we generally keep to ourselves. Fictions, on the other hand, are collective and public fantasies; they are textual elaborations, in narrative form, of fantastic scenarios which, being mass-produced, are offered ready-made to audiences. We are not the originators of the public fantasies offered to us in fiction. This explains, of course, why we are not attracted to all the fictions available to us: most of them are irrelevant. Despite this, the pleasure of consuming fictions that do attract us may still relate to that of fantasy: that is, it still involves the imaginary occupation of other subject positions which are outside the scope of our everyday social and cultural identities.

Implicit in the theoretical perspective I have outlined so far is a post-structuralist theory on subjectivity.[18] Central to this is the idea that subjectivity is not the essence or the source from which the individual acts and thinks and feels; on the contrary, subjectivity should be seen as a product of the society and culture in which we live: it is through the meaning systems or discourses circulating in society and culture that subjectivity is constituted and individual identities are formed. Each individual is the site of a multiplicity of subject positions proposed to her by the discourses with which she is confronted; her identity is the precarious and contradictory result of the specific set of subject positions she inhabits at any moment in history.

Just as the fictional character is not a unitary image of womanhood, then, so is the individual viewer not a person whose identity is something static and coherent. If a woman is a social subject whose identity is at least partially marked out by her being a person of a certain sex, it is by no means certain that she will always inhabit the same mode of feminine subjectivity. On the contrary, many different and sometimes contradictory sets of femininities or feminine subject positions (ways of being a woman) are in principle available to her, although it is likely that she will be drawn to adopt some of those more than others. Certain modes of femininity are culturally more legitimate than others; and every woman knows subject positions she is best able to handle. This does not mean, however, that her identity as a woman is something determined in the process of socialisation. On the contrary, the adoption of a feminine subjectivity is never definitive but always partial and shaky: in other words, being a woman implies a never-ending *process* of becoming a feminine subject: no one subject position can ever cover satisfactorily all the problems and desires an individual woman encounters.

All too often women (and men too, of course, but their relationship to constructions of masculinity is not at issue here) have to negotiate in all sorts of situations in their lives — at home, at work, in relationships, in larger social settings. In this women are constantly confronted with the cultural task of finding out what it means to be a woman, of marking out the boundaries between the feminine and the unfeminine. This task is not a simple one, especially in the case of modern societies where cultural rules and roles are no longer imposed authoritatively, but allow individualistic notions such as autonomy, personal choice, will, responsibility, and rationality. In this context, a framework of living has been created in which every individual woman is faced with the task of actively reinventing and redefining her femininity as required. The emergence of the modern feminist movement has intensified this situation: now women have become much more conscious about their position in society, and consequently are encouraged to take control over their own lives by rejecting the traditional dictum that anatomy is destiny. Being a woman, in other words, can now mean the adoption of many different identities, composed of a whole range of subject positions, not predetermined by immovable definitions of femininity. It would stretch beyond the purpose of this article to explore and explain in more detail how women construct and reconstruct their feminine identities in everyday life. What is important to conclude at this point then is that being a woman involves *work*, work of constant self-(re)construction. (The ever-growing array of different women's magazines is a case in point: in all of them the central problematic is 'how to be a true woman', while the meanings of 'true' are subject to constant negotiation.) At the same time, however, the energy women must put in this fundamental work of self-(re)construction is suppressed: women are expected to find the right identity effortlessly. (Women's magazines always assume an enthusiastic, 'you-can-do-it!' mode of address: work is represented as pleasure.)

It is in this constellation that fantasy and fiction can play a distinctive role. They offer a private and unconstrained space in which socially impossible or unacceptable subject positions, or those which are in some way too dangerous or too risky to be acted out in real life, can be adopted. In real life, the choice for this or that subject position is never without consequences. Contrary to what women's magazines tell us, it is often *not* easy to know what it means to be a 'true' woman. For example, the social display of forms of traditional femininity — dependence, passivity, submissiveness — can have quite detrimental and self-destructive consequences for women when strength, independence or decisiveness are called for. In fantasy and fiction, however, there is no punishment for whatever identity one takes up, no matter how headstrong or destructive: there will be no retribution, no defeat will ensue. Fantasy and fiction then, are the safe spaces of excess in the interstices of ordered social life where one has to keep oneself strategically under control.

From this perspective identification with melodramatic heroines can be viewed in a new way. The position ascribed to Sue Ellen by those identifying with her is one of masochism and powerlessness: a self-destructive mode of femininity which, in social and political terms, could only be rejected as regressive and unproductive. But rather than condemn this identification, it is possible to observe the gratification such imaginary subject positions provide for the women concerned. What can be so pleasurable in imagining a fantastic scenario in which one is a self-destructive and frustrated bitch?

In the context of the discussion above, I can suggest two meanings of melodramatic identifications. On the one hand, sentimental and melancholic feelings of masochism and powerlessness, which are the core of the melodramatic imagination, are an implicit recognition, in their surrender to some power outside the subject, of the fact that one can never have everything under control all the time, and that consequently identity is not a question of free and conscious choice but always acquires its shape under circumstances not of one's own making. Identification with these feelings is connected with a basic, if not articulated, awareness of the weighty pressure of reality on one's subjectivity, one's wishes, one's desires. On the other hand, identification with a melodramatic character like Sue Ellen also validates those feelings by offering women some room to indulge in them, to let go as it were, in a moment of intense, self-centered abandon — a moment of giving up to the force of circumstances, just like Sue Ellen has done, so that the work of self-(re)construction is no longer needed. I would argue that such moments, however fleeting, can be experienced as moments of peace, of truth, of redemption, a moment in which the complexity of the task of being a woman is fully realised and accepted. In short, whilst indulgence in a melodramatic identity in real life will generally only signify pathetic weakness and may have paralysing effects, fantasy and fiction constitute a secure space in which one can be excessively melodramatic without suffering the consequences. No wonder melodrama is often accompanied with tears.

Final remarks

This interpretation of the appeal of melodramatic characters among women must, of course, be contextualised and refined in several ways. First of all, by trying to explain what it means for women to identify with a melodramatic fictional character, I have by no means intended to justify or endorse it. I have tried to make it understandable, in the face of the ridicule and rejection that crying over melodramatic fiction (as if it were irrational) continues to receive. However, my analysis does not extend to any further impact upon the subjects concerned. Whether the release of melodramatic feelings through fantasy or fiction has an empowering or paralysing effect upon the subject is an open question and can probably not be answered without analysing the context of the fantasising.

Secondly, we should not overlook the fact that not all women are attracted to melodrama, and that some men can be moved by melodrama too. If anything, this fact suggests that femininity and masculinity are not positions inhabited inevitably by biological women and men, but that identity is transitory, the temporary result of dynamic identifications. Further research and analysis could give us more insight into the conditions, social, cultural, psychological, under which a surrender to the melodramatic imagination exerts its greatest appeal. Melodrama has been consistently popular among women in the modern period, but this does not have to be explained exclusively in terms of constants. The fundamental chasm between desire and reality, which forms the deepest 'truth' of the melodramatic imagination, may be an eternal aspect of female experience, but how that chasm is bridged symbolically and in practice is historically variable. In fact, there is a fundamentally melodramatic edge to feminism too. After all, are not the suffering and frustration so eminently materialised in melodramatic heroines the basis for the anger conveyed in feminism? And does not feminism stand for the overwhelming desire to transcend reality — which is bound to be a struggle, full of frustrations and moments of despair?

While the melodramatic heroine is someone who is forced to give up, leaving a yawning gap between desire and reality, the feminist is someone who refuses to give up, no matter how hard the struggle to close that gap might be.

Christine Cagney, too, shares more with Sue Ellen than we might expect. Of course, the manifest dramatic content of *Cagney & Lacey* is more in line with feminist ideals and concerns, and as such the Cagney and Lacey characters can provide an outlet for identification with fantasies of liberation for women viewers.[19] Despite the fact that Christine Cagney is an independent career woman who knows where she stands, she too must at times face the unsolvable dilemmas inherent in the lives of modern women: how to combine love and work; how to compete with the boys; how to deal with growing older . . . Often enough, she encounters frustration and displays a kind of cynical bitchiness not unlike Sue Ellen's. I would argue that some of the most moving moments of *Cagney & Lacey* are those in which Cagney gives in to the sense of powerlessness so characteristic of the melodramatic heroine.

6

Consumer Girl Culture: How Music Video Appeals to Girls

Lisa A. Lewis

Cyndi Lauper and Madonna are pop music stars whose appeal among young women has been particularly strong. This essay analyses the connections between a social audience of girls and the two musicians' promotional videos and star styles. Their video and star images, I argue, address girl audiences by textually making reference to consumer girl culture, a gendered cultural experience engaged in by American middle-class girls.

Adolescence binds both boys and girls in an ideology of lifestage, but gender guides them towards separate spheres of cultural experience. In the context of American adolescence, one's relation to school and family life, outlets for sexual expression, modes of leisure and consumption, are structured by assumptions based on a social system of gender inequality. Barbara Hudson, in her study of femininity and adolescence, describes adolescence as a form of discourse which fundamentally incorporates assumptions and definitions of *male* experience, activity, and desire.[1] Adolescence and masculinity, she says, are ideologically united to support male privilege. Behaviour typically associated with adolescence — retreat from parental surveillance and the constrictions of domestic life, aggressive attention to leisure practices and associated peer activities, pursuit of sexual experiences, and experimentation with social roles and norms

— embody the very activities and attitudes which serve boys in the assumption of their position in patriarchy.[2] Towards this end, boys learn to feel comfortable in public space, adjust to competitive pressures, network with male peers, build a familial support system, and prepare for risk-taking in future work endeavours. The social authorisation of such practices is gender specific, and does not fully extend to girls.

Similarly, Angela McRobbie has described the consequences of gender discrimination on youth cultural expression, how it mediates against girl participation in the street culture of boys.[3] Leisure practices engaged in by boys are often deemed inappropriate for girls. Subcultural youth groupings, many of which are allied, in part, by musical preferences, are usually off-limits to girls. Girls are, in effect, excluded from much of the leisure activity, social bonding practice, and subcultural formation that critics of male youth culture identify as important sites for the negotiation of social contradictions. Girl leisure takes different forms as a consequence of gender inequality, or perhaps more aptly stated, as a result of female resourcefulness and will to resist subordination. Social biases constructed around gender difference push girls into less visible interior spaces, into what McRobbie and Garber label, 'bedroom culture'.[4] If subculture critics find girls to be peripheral cultural participants, says McRobbie,[5] it is because they fail to grasp the different, but complementary ways in which girls organise their cultural lives.[6]

This complementary world of female cultural activity is developed into a system of textual address in the video and image constructions of Cyndi Lauper and Madonna. Representations of consumer girl culture and its composite parts of fashion, shopping, and personal style guide female spectators toward recognition of themselves and their common gender experience, and prompt intense and often visible forms of fan response.

Video Texts: The Discovery of Consumer Girl Culture

The targeting of audiences by the television industry is a familiar marketing practice. In the 1970s methods for measuring demographically-specific audience sectors provided the means for identifying and addressing upscale consumers.[7] In the same vein, the American music video channel MTV chose to target a youthful audience noted for its expendable income. In an attempt to create an address to a youth audience, MTV and the record companies who produce the videos MTV airs, adopted imagery designed fundamentally around the discourse of male adolescence. Ideologies of rebelliousness, independence from social authorities, and sexual promiscuity were culled into symbolic representations of street culture, leisure practice, and female conquest.

Unaccommodated by MTV's preferred male address were the rising number of female musicians in need of a vehicle of self-representation and promotion. MTV's semiotic disparagement of female subjectivity left female musicians without a means to position their own gendered subjectivity. In defiance of the channel's dependence on male discourse, a select number of female musicians, among them Cyndi Lauper and Madonna, began to fashion videos predicated on the representation of *female* gender experience. Two interrelated sign systems developed as cornerstones of the new textual system of female address, what I call respectively: *access signs* and *discovery signs.*[8]

Access signs are those in which the privileged experience of boys and men is visually appropriated. The female stars textually enact an entrance into a male domain of activity and signification. In this way, the texts work at providing imagery that challenges assumptions about the boundaries which gender, as a social construct, draws around men and women. The texts visually execute takeovers of male space, the erasure of sex roles, and a demand for parity with male privilege.

Discovery signs reference and celebrate distinctly female modes of cultural expression and experience. They attempt to compensate in mediated form for female cultural marginalisation by drawing pictures of activities in which females tend to engage apart from males. By representing girl practices, the videos set a tone that celebrates female resourcefulness and cultural distinctiveness.

The system of address devised by MTV relied heavily on the representation of male leisure practice. The street, a key symbol, referenced the decidedly male experience of adolescent cameraderie and public space. As McRobbie suggests, leisure, for boys, represents a privileged 'space' for the sowing of wild oats and experimentation with roles and dangers before a lifetime of work.[9] The street is a major site of sociability and escape, of subcultural formation, rebellious play, male bonding, and female pursuit. But herein lies the problem for adolescent girls, for they are subject not only to expectations based on their age, but overwhelmingly by those assigned to their gender.

Streets are dangerous and fearful places for girls and women.

What Rayna Rapp Reiter describes as 'sexual geography' in her study of male and female use of public space in southern France applies to the United States as well. Females are expected to use streets as the route between two interior spaces, be they places of employment or consumption activity. The social consequence of street loitering or strolling is the label, 'prostitute', and the coding of one's body as available to male pursuit. Women's level of comfort on city streets is tenuous at best; rape and harrassment are constant threats structuring their behaviour. Girls learn early the gestures of deference: to avoid making eye contact, to cause one's body to 'shrink' so as to take up as little space as possible.

In female address videos, like those of Lauper and Madonna, the street is a representation appropriated for the production of access signs. Lauper's video *Girls Just Want to Have Fun* and Madonna's *Borderline* video, released on MTV in 1983 and 1984 respectively, both feature scenes of street takeovers. In *Girls Just Want to Have Fun* the bouncing Lauper leads her band of girlfriends through New York city streets in a frenzied snake dance that turns women's experience of foreboding streets upside-down in a carnavalesque display. Their arms reaching out for more and more space, the women push through a group of male construction workers who function as symbols of female harrassment on the street. The lyrical refrain, *Girls Just Want to Have Fun* enacts a powerful cry for access to the privileged realm of male adolescent leisure practice.

In *Borderline*, Madonna portrays a rambunctious teenager immersed in male street-corner culture. She is shown street dancing, spraying graffiti on urban walls, and loitering on a street corner with female peers. She blows kisses and initiates flirtation with street boys, and takes her female companions into the male turf of the pool hall. In short, she appropriates activities and spaces typically associated with male adolescence. Many of the activities in which she engages also place her in the role of the male youth delinquent. She defaces public and private property, loiters in 'bad' neighbourhoods, and hangs out in the pool hall. Such images confuse the iconography of the prostitute suggested by her street corner lingering and flirtation, and obviate the different social standards for male and female transgressions. Building a tension between the two implicitly raises questions about how the visual code of prostitution is elaborated and about how representations of females on the street might be revisioned.

Access signs open out into discovery signs that rejoice in female forms of leisure to which adolescent boys have little access. These are the representations that call forth the allegiance of girls to bedroom and consumer cultures. In *Girls Just Want to Have Fun*, the construction workers, their threatening status alleviated, are brought back to the Lauper character's home to experience female fun: dancing with wild abandon to records in one's bedroom. Fun is visually defined both in terms of doing what boys do: i.e. getting out of the house (and housework) and onto the street, and in terms of the activities and relationships girls devise in their attempts to create a complementary order of female fun.

Borderline moves into discovery signs in its presentation of the female fantasy of becoming a fashion model. In the video, a fashion photographer 'discovers' the character played by Madonna during the first street dance scene. She participates in the excitement and pleasure of wearing glamorous clothes and makeup, until the male photographer begins to assert his authority over her 'look'. Defiantly she grabs back the hat he does not want her to wear. Desiring to manage her own image, she returns to participate with boys in street culture. Later Madonna videos rely on discovery signs to a greater extent, dwelling on the recognition that fashion and madeup faces achieve for women. In *Material Girl*, a peak performance by Madonna, draped in furs and male attendants, rewrites the tragic Marilyn Monroe image she references, into a decidedly female image of recognition and power.[10]

Star Texts: Style and Female Adolescence

From birth, the imposing of a gendered appearance by parents, largely in the form of clothes, signals the social recognition of gender difference and becomes the first step in the construction of a gender identity. Dressing up in Mother's clothes is an encouraged socialisation activity for little girls, one that develops their self-conception as female-identified. Girls have been shown to engage in dress-up play to a greater extent than boys and to develop a higher level of clothes awareness.[11] Boys are considered by one study to be disadvantaged by their lack of participation in dress up play. Dressing up in commercially-designed costumes instead of their father's clothes has consequences for male sexual identity, according to Stone's study. Another interpretation might be that boys are under less pressure socially to identify with the role of father, whereas, the role of mother is central to female identity. Its internalisation, in the form of dress imitation, must be ensured.

The girl practice of dressing alike also has roots in female socialisation and cultural expression, not just in the form of adherence to a regime of feminine attire, but as a symbolic system that signifies female solidarity and female bonding. Mother-daughter dresses are signs of matrilineal identification and represent one of the few permissible expressions of mother-daughter love within the hegemony of the Oedipal construct. Dressing alike is frequently part of the signification system of girl friendships at the time in a woman's life before heterosexual desire is rigidly channelled. Christine Griffin describes the rich texture of girl friendships and its reliance on the manipulation of consumer items:

> These best friendships were typified by young women going everywhere together, walking along arm in arm, wearing *exactly* the same clothes, shoes, hairstyles, even jewelry.[12]

Purchasing and dressing up in feminine clothes accompanies every major event in a girl's life from confirmation to prom night, until the arrival of the most fussed–over ritual, the wedding, with its expensive and rigidly defined attire. It is the regimen of dress codes and restrictions on hairstyle and application of makeup that often first exposes girls to gender contradictions. Girls learn that buying and wearing particular clothes is a highly-charged activity that situates one's own desires against a host of social approval ideologies. The desire to dress like a boy is an early form of resistance to the physical and mental restraints that gender definitions seek to impose on girls. As girls age and experience physical body changes, they discover relationships between modes of displaying the body and social response.

Barbara Hudson, a British writer, describes clothing and appearance manipulation by girls as a reaction to their conflicted status as female adolescents. As she describes it, adolescence is unproblematic as a masculine construct, but becomes the source of contradictory expectations when applied to female adolescents who are subject to conflicting gender discourses, most notably the discourse of femininity.[13] The femininity discourse exists as a set of expectations that attempts to restrict girls' behaviour and choices especially at the time of adolescence. Girls, during this phase of life, are required to display a driving independence at the same time they prepare for a social role predicated on an acceptance of dependency. The authorities they come in contact with expect them to simultaneously demonstrate political and career interests, and develop a 'personality style of caring for others, looking after children, being gentle and unassertive'.[14]

Susan Brownmiller has written an exegesis of the femininity discourse in an American context. Recalling her own experience of female adolescence, she paints a picture of the contradictory impulses which propelled her into gender conflicts as an adult.

As I passed through a stormy adolescence to a stormy maturity, femininity increasingly became an exasperation, a brilliant, subtle aesthetic that was bafflingly inconsistent at the same time that it was minutely, demandingly concrete, a rigid code of appearance and behaviour defined by do's and don't-do's that went against my rebellious grain. Femininity was a challenge thrown down to the female sex, a challenge no proud, self-respecting young woman could afford to ignore, particularly one with enormous ambition that she nursed in secret, alternately feeding or starving its inchoate life in tremendous confusion.[15]

Hudson describes the two discourses of adolescence and femininity as subversive of one another and argues that they are manipulated to this effect by girls through a symbolic alignment with modes of self-presentation. The femininity pigeonhole is opposed symbolically in two usual ways:

1) through affecting an appearance and behaviour based on the male adolescence discourse, or

2) through exaggeration of the codes of feminine appearance and mannerisms that frequently crosses over into sexual display.

Interviews with Madonna and Cyndi Lauper in the popular press suggest a certain familiarity with and adoption of strategies of subversive self-presentation in the stars' own youth. In one interview conducted by Harry Dean Stanton, Madonna describes how she and a best girlfriend developed a sexual persona in order to subvert their parents' authority, an image which, interestingly, was inspired by their identification with a female musician:

M: . . . it was a private joke between my girlfriend and me, that we were floozies, because she used to get it from her mother all the time, too . . .

S: So somewhere you did like the floozy look?

M: Only because we knew that our parents didn't like it. We thought it was fun. We got dressed to the nines. We got bras and stuffed them so our breasts were over-large and wore really tight sweaters — we were sweater-girl floozies. We wore tons of lipstick and really badly applied makeup and huge beauty marks and did our hair up like Tammy Wynette.[16]

Hudson's fieldwork suggests how overtly sexual dress by girls, the kind Madonna develops into an image for her videos, can send school authorities reeling:

> . . . teachers respond positively to 'feminine' girls, whilst they like to encourage the development of feminine traits; nevertheless, the school is not regarded as an appropriate arena for the display of unbounded femininity. The idea that femininity can be taken on and off by changing clothes explains a form of behaviour that is common amongst teachers; if femininity is bestowed by dress then teachers can keep displays of femininity within bounds by insisting on a plain, deindividualised dress.[17]

In *People Magazine* and *Newsweek* Cyndi Lauper describes an alienated adolescence filled with quests for independence, rebellious behaviour, and an appearance set against the conventions of femininity:

> In high school I fell out of step. Everything became unreal for me. I felt there just wasn't any room for me in this world . . . I didn't fit in, didn't have nobody to do things with that I liked. I did them by myself.[18]
>
> *People Magazine*

> I was an oddball . . . No matter how hard I tried to look normal there was always something that wasn't right.[19]
>
> *Newsweek*

Whether or not Cyndi Lauper and Madonna draw directly on their own personal experiences of female adolescence to construct their images, the enacting of subversive styles and roles in their video performances can be interpreted by female readers as textual strategies of opposition.

Madonna's visual style engages with and hyperbolises the discourse of femininity. She combines contradictory accoutrements of a feminine presentation with the affected attitude of a cinematic vamp. Bleached blonde hair proudly displays its dark roots. Glamour eye makeup and lipstick create a look that is likened to Marilyn Monroe's, but a cocky demeanour exudes a self-assuredness and independence to counter the outdated, naive image. Skin-tight, lacy undergarments and crucifixes add up to a blasphemous, 'bad girl' affectation, particularly in a woman who, we are told in the promotional press, hated the uniforms at her own Catholic school.

Lauper's image is more an ode to the adolescence discourse and incorporates a rebellious, anti-feminine, 'she's so unusual' address. It is this sense of bucking the norm that *Ms.* magazine applauded by awarding Lauper a Woman of the Year citation in 1985. In explanatory notes, *Ms.* characterised her rebellious style as a feminist stance. Lauper's display of odd color combinations in dress and hair, her wearing of gaudy fake jewelry, application of striped and sequined eye makeup, mock socially appropriate modes of female attire and behaviour. Thrift store and boutique renditions recirculate fashions from the past, calling attention to the circularity of consumption and pointing out ways to construct personal style on a budget and to exercise control over the terms of prevailing fashion.

Whether tied to femininity or adolescent discourses, both Madonna and Lauper styles grow out of and address the investment of girls and women in fashion and consumer culture. They both depend on an articulation of the tensions between conforming and resisting codes of gendered appearance, between marketplace dictates and consumer innovation of fashion. The proliferation of consumer items at shopping venues constitute the raw material out of which their styles are constructed, and from which symbolic negotiation and textual communication is made possible.

Fan Response and the Marketplace

I have suggested ways that Lauper and Madonna videos incorporate style and appearance manipulation and its many meaningful intersections with girl culture. Style is also a mode through which girls formulate their response to the videos and associated stars. By imitating the dress and performance codes of their favoured musician, girl fans demonstrate their identification with the star and with female address, represent their extensive knowledge of textual nuances, and display their association with a community of fans.

Use value is demonstrated most spectacularly by Lauper 'dress-alike' and Madonna 'wanna-be' fans. Their efforts to reproduce the look of the star extends the status of best friend to the stars they mimic, conjuring up the cult of female friendship. The fans' imitation of the stars' affected modes of appearance re-enacts the stars' subversive stance against the femininity discourse and the privileging of male adolescence. Many of the female audience members have undoubtedly discovered all by themselves the subversive potential of an aberrant personal style, and may already have been practising such behaviour in isolation. The video and star texts of Lauper and Madonna affirm this individual and private response, but additionally, they enable a girl to organise with other girls into an interpretive community to participate in struggles over meaning in a public arena.

The style imitation practices of intense Lauper and Madonna fans signal their membership in a group identity in a form that resembles the subcultural organisations that British critics have described primarily as a male youth activity. Reproducing the stars' styles and performance codes encompasses the three interconnected features Michael Brake identifies as features of subculture:

1) image, the projection of an identity through costuming, makeup and other visual material;

2) demeanour, the mode of stance, pose, performance, in effect, the way the image is worn; and

3) argot, a special vocabulary and delivery style.

Although the Lauper dress-alike and Madonna wanna-be fans manifest typical subculture behaviours, they do not conform to many of the underlying assumptions in the subculture literature.[20]

Much of the work on subculture, primarily under the purview of British cultural criticism, places theoretical emphasis on class as the determining social structure dictating subcultural form. Yet the female fan's response derives primarily from an association with gender and female expressions of culture. Likewise, a focus on authenticity in the subculture literature devalues the diffusion of subcultural style into mass media representations and marketplace reproductions. But, in the case of Lauper and Madonna fans, their spectacular response arises directly out of member interaction with mass media texts. There is a correspondence between the video address and its reception as manifested by its use. This demonstrates, more generally, the dynamic relationship between mediated texts and social practice, something subculture critics have tended to overlook. The fan response also integrally involves the marketplace as a point of reference as if to assert shopping and fashion as an authentic arena of female culture.

Culture critics' expressed aversion to dominant culture forms, their coding of the marketplace as the antithesis of authentic cultural expression (as essentially a mechanism of capitalist reproduction), has created an obstacle to the analytical consideration of consumer girl culture. Such assumptions operate to portray girl participation in consumer culture as a kind of false consciousness, useful only as a means of preparing girls for social roles that support the economic status quo. Erica Carter, developing McRobbie's critique of male bias in the work of British theorists of youth subculture, cites certain critics' alignment of commercialism with female gender and the disdain for both that permeates much of their work:

> Like the phenomena which they examine, the analyses themselves are founded on a number of unspoken oppositions: conformity and resistance, harmony and rupture, passivity and activity, consumption and appropriation, femininity and masculinity.[21]

Close analysis of the overlap between consumption practice and female gender reveals far more complicated patterns of use and considerable activity between the opposed characteristics that Carter identifies in the assumptions of the critics.

Part of the structural/cultural experience of female gender in the United States is women's participation in and relation to consumption practice.[22] The domestic division of labour has long positioned women as the primary consumption workers in American society. The consumption of products and services by unpaid women is, indeed, crucial to recreating and maintaining a productive cycle that functions to support the capitalist economy. In this respect, consumption activity has served to promote both gender and economic stratified forms of exploitation. But, wherever exploited labour plays a key role in economic relations, hegemonic struggle is implied.[23] The fact that consumption work has been largely framed by Marxists as non-productive labour does not negate the potential that exists for its mobilisation for resistance practices.

William Leach links the historical rise of consumption culture in the late nineteenth century to a transformative effect on women. Centralised sites of consumption, in the form of department stores, offered middle-class women a socially acceptable way to escape the confines of their houses and provided a richly imaginative culture in which to explore social possibilities. He suggests that modern advertising methods and store display prompted suffragettes of the time to adopt colourful, graphic forms of political expression and provides evidence that department stores were selected as sites from which suffrage activities were publicised and coordinated:

> Stores everywhere volunteered their windows and their interiors for suffrage advertising. In June 1916 Chicago's Carson, Pirie Scott installed a wax figure of a suffragist in one of its windows, a herald of the coming convention of the Woman's Party in that city. At about the same time, Wanamaker's set a precedent by permitting all female employees to march in suffrage parades during working hours. In 1912 suffragists chose Macy's in New York as the headquarters for suffragette supplies, including marching gowns, bonnets, and hatpins.[24]

The shopping mall, a modern day extension of the department store, has similarly been chosen as a site for female leisure culture. The cartoon image of a woman with her charge cards hints at the way shopping has been articulated by women into a pleasurable pursuit. Buying something special for oneself is one of the few routes by which the traditional reproducer of men and children reproduces herself. Middle-class adolescent girls who have yet to take on the responsibilities of careers and families experience the leisure side of consumption more fully. For girls, the mall represents a female substitute for the streets of male adolescents. Mall corridors resemble city streets in both appearance and function. They offer the same active and anonymous sites for adolescent loitering, places to meet friends, to 'girl watch' and 'boy watch,' but within a more restricted and supervised setting. Girls at the mall experience the added attraction of shopping, an activity closely connected to their socialisation, to female bonding, and to cultural expressions of identity.

The shopping mall is the site around which female spectator correspondence with star and video texts coalesces. 'Madonna is everywhere,' writes one biographer, 'there is even a mall in California that people have nicknamed 'the Madonna mall' because so many girls who shop there try to look just like her'.[25] In response to the popularity of Madonna Style, Macy's Department Store created a department called 'Madonnaland' devoted to the cropped sweaters ($30), cropped pants ($21), and a variety of jewelry accessories such as crucifix earrings and outsize 'pearl' necklaces ($4-$59) resembling those worn by Madonna. The department became the location for the mobilisation of Madonna fans in the summer of 1985 when Macy's sponsored a Madonna look-alike contest to coincide with the star's New York concert date. To provoke attendance, Macy's ran a full page ad in the *Village Voice* with text designed to capitalise on fan familiarity with Madonna's video, *Material Girl*, and with the movie, *Desperately Seeking Susan* in which she co-starred and performed the song, *Into the Groove*.

JRS!
DESPERATELY SEEKING MADONNA LOOK-ALIKES

Join our Madonna Day contest, Thurs, June 6 in Madonnaland on 4, Macy's Herald Square. If you're a brassy material girl, get into the groove and prove it . . .

The overwhelming response was featured on both MTV and the ABC Evening News where Madonna wanna-be's revelled in their new found fame. On camera, they gushed that they too 'wanted to be famous' and 'be looked at' like their idol, Madonna. For one magical moment, in front of Peter Jennings and ABC viewers, it came to pass.

Cyndi Lauper's style has also proved to be an inspiration for the ready-to-wear market. *Seventeen* ('Funky Frills'), billing itself as Young America's Favorite Magazine, disseminated word of the Lauper-inspired fashion accessories: black rubber bracelets, twelve for $4 (Maripolitan); multicoloured rhinestone bracelets, $9 each (Medusa's Heirlooms); black leather wristband with rhinestone cluster, $26 (Michael Morrison MX); Gun-metal and rhinestone bracelets, $30 each (Maripolitan).

The appearance of music video displays in Juniors departments in stores at shopping malls across the country is a further testament to the connection between consumer girl culture and music video. While Lauper and Madonna are not the only videos featured in the displays, it is their styles that the marketplace has scrambled to emulate.

That style diffuses into fashion so readily should come as no surprise. The market reacts to popularity and new cultural forms with striking speed. But the context of consumer girl culture and its representation in music video texts, star styles, and fan response reveals the extent to which the market is also used for female symbolic expression. Consumer culture has economic consequences, but it is still resilient and responsive to consumer interaction. Girl consumer culture is not merely a reproductive incorporation, for in practice, it branches into a gendered support system for girls. Similarly, MTV videos may codify male adolescent ideology, but they also allow female authors and audiences to command their own symbolic vision.

For girls and women who have shared in the experience of fashion innovation; in style as a vehicle for self-expression, group identity and subversive pleasure; in the imaginative cultures of shopping malls and mediated texts as backdrops for fantasies and enactments of personal or social change, the female address videos of Lauper and Madonna produce a field of gendered interpretations. The fan response of the Lauper dress-alikes and Madonna wanna-be's demonstrates how the textual strategies of female performers can cohere with female spectators' cultural experience to create a powerful correspondence between text and audience.

7

Rock Video: Pleasure and Resistance
Sally Stockbridge

The dominant cultural opposition between male and female as it relates to the process of looking, (at film specifically) was described by Laura Mulvey in 1975, where the spectacle of the mainstream narrative was seen to be one in which the female figure was the object of an erotic gaze: she was an object of male desire centred within the male character within the film and the male spectator within the audience, placing them both in a position of power and based on the assumption of patriarchal heterosexual desire.[1] It is indirect address since the character does not look out at the audience. The audience is a voyeur upon the action within the film. The narrative is described as being frozen so that you (the male spectator) can gaze at her body (just as the male character within the film does). The prevalence of indirect address within mainstream cinema is the rationale for its association with voyeurism. The momentary freezing of narrative so that the male can gaze at the female is called spectacle, and relies on the masculine/feminine opposition where the female is the object of the gaze and passive and the male is the subject of the gaze, powerful and active.

The main object of this essay is to reformulate notions of spectatorship and the gaze in relation to male and female performance in and around rock clips. The analysis is, of course, concerned with textual characteristics but it could also be extended to an exploration of dance, fashion and the audience. The activity of audiences or fans has been the subject of subcultural analysis in the work of Dick Hebdige in particular and both subcultures and pleasure in articles by Lawrence Grossberg and Angela McRobbie.[2] Subculture theory emphasises the activity of the fans in reappropriating the music and is aligned with resistance and opposition. But, equally, Grossberg and McRobbie generally agree that the pleasure of the rock and roll body is tied most directly to movement and dance. I intend to explore here the pleasures of these texts for male and female rock fans in relation to three key factors:

Performance, of both rock stars and fans.

Direct Address within rock clips which produces a different kind of gaze and different performer-audience relationships than those that pertain within film.

Fantasy, which offers both pleasures and forms of resistance for fans in relation to both the rock clips themselves and in relation to dominant cultural definitions of pleasure and desire.

It is my argument that audiences or fans take from the clips elements which produce meanings for them that are not necessarily those intended or determined by the texts. Within this context is, quite crucially, a theory of how the gaze (at the clip) operates, which calls into question the dominant cultural opposition between masculine and feminine.

All rock clips may be considered to be spectacle as described in the work of Jane Feuer on Hollywood musicals.[3] She argues that address switches within these films from indirect address within narrative segments to direct address within segments which involve a performance of a dance and/or a song. Here the character/star gazes out at the audience, a situation that does not occur in realist narratives, and usually only in the modernist *avant garde*. This return gaze, characteristic of direct address, undermines voyeurism and puts the character into a position of power over the audience that did not exist with film's indirect address. It must be said, however, that rock videos are most frequently viewed on television and direct address is the dominant mode of address in that medium. In the Hollywood musical, in rock clips and on television, both male and female stars can 'look back' at the audience. The rock star can be said to be both object and subject of a gaze. Therefore, if the rock star is female, the dominant cultural construction of femininity as passive object may be undermined. This accords with the philosophy of

French feminist Hélène Cixous who also questions the masculine/ feminine opposition as it is aligned with active/passive, subject/ object, powerful/powerless assumptions.[4]

Cixous' argument concurs with another crucial factor in the analysis of clips: Constance Penley's use of fantasy in relation to the position that spectator/audiences or fans may take up toward characters in a text.[5] According to this theory, the spectator is not fixed or homogenised in relation to gender identification or desire (masculine or feminine) but is shifting and mobile, contradicting psychoanalytic positions. Music video clips tend to reinforce this and the shift by the rock star, both male and female, between indirect and direct address tends to facilitate this mobility. Rock videos operate in multiple ways in relation to the positioning of the subject and object of our gaze and in relation to the representation of masculinity and femininity or sexual difference.

Cixous reminds us that the adjectives 'masculine' and 'feminine' are qualifiers of sexual difference, difference that is not defined by anatomy. For, as she says, 'there are men who do not repress their femininity, women who more or less forcefully inscribe their masculinity'. Cixous avoids the classification of sexuality as male or female which are biological definitions. The adjectives masculine and feminine refer to a heterogeneous range of possibilities within any individual libido, and this is where fantasy also plays a part. Constance Penley also mounts an argument that the means of identifying spectators via the perspective of fantasy as the setting and articulation of desire is changing:

> An investigation of the construction of fantasy seems to provide a way of accounting for sexual difference which acknowledges difference, but which in no way seeks to dictate or predetermine the subsequent distribution of that difference (in terms of sexual identity) in any given film or for any given spectator, male or female. (This is in part at least because in fantasy) all the possible roles in the narrative are available to the subject: he (sic) can be either subject or object and can even occupy a position 'outside' the scene, looking on from the spectator's point of view . . . it is only the formal positions themselves that are fixed (there are 'masculine' and 'feminine' positions of desire); the subject can and does adapt these positions in relation to a variety of complex scenarios, and in accordance with the mobile patterns of his or her own desire. (Not least of the advantages of a theoretical perspective on film in terms of fantasy, finally, is that it) presents a more accurate description of the spectator's shifting and multiple identifications.[6]

Her argument allows for different conceptualisations of voyeurism in relation to male and female bodies, which is a fundamentally different position from that taken by E. Ann Kaplan. Kaplan takes up the issue of address and the gaze, linking it to post-modernism and television which is considered to be different from previous art movements and genres because it allows 'several different positions for the spectator to take up in relation to sexual difference'.[7] However, she doesn't discuss 'different positions' in relation to identification, or the look at the male rock star by the female (or homosexual) spectator or fan.

Kaplan begins by detailing the number of videos featuring females as central figures which, on MTV is rather limited, going on to discuss what she describes as the post-modern feminist and constructions for the male gaze.[8] What is important is that despite an opening assumption that television allows for several different positions, the only positions that are discussed here are those which accord with the Lacanian approach to subjectivity. This is presented as if it were an unproblematic finished body of theory that merely awaits application to empirical material.[8] There are several things that are not accounted for, or taken into account, not least the insights of Cixous and Penley discussed above.

Kaplan's chapter is an example of a work which takes the conception of the male gaze as given, omitting the possibility of voyeurism on the part of the female spectator or fan. There is an omission of the necessary construction of rock stars as stars to be gazed upon, irrespective of sex, by fans both male and female. The rock star is a body always coded to-be-looked-at whether male or female. This encoding comes from pop discourses about rock stardom as much as it does from filmic representation strategies. Rock stars' bodies and faces are plastered over album covers, magazines and posters before and after they get into rock clips. Female fans pin up posters of male rock stars too, their 'look' must be taken into account. When Kaplan analyses the use of the star's face in her category of 'romantic videos', she links them, again through the uncritical use of psychoanalysis, to the face of the mother and pre-oedipal pleasure. In so doing she misses the need for the face to feature in rock videos in order to indicate stardom and also because of need for this as a strategy of the record company for selling the rock star. As Goodwin argues, 'the presence of promotional strategies goes curiously unnoticed in post-modern textual analysis, as if industry and texts were unrelated.'[10] Production of multi-textual and multi-contextual sites of meaning such as posters, magazines, etc., are omitted in favour of an analysis centred on MTV and the application of the Lacanian thesis/model.

This essay is based on television across a range of Australian rock music programming but acknowledges the existence of other sites of meaning production from radio to record cover. Commencing with the Penley and Cixous positions that, while the male gaze is inscribed as the dominant or hegemonic subject position in mainstream Hollywood film, it cannot control aberrant readings even of *that*. Rock video plays with aberrant reading positions partly through the direct address of television, taking up modernist codes but using them in a fashion similar to their use in the Hollywood musical as discussed by Feuer. What is important is that the spectator is not considered to be fixed (by theory) into one position and the clips' construction cannot be described solely in terms of a hegemonic male gaze as the determining structure. This also questions the assumption that texts function by representing something or *one* thing. As Lawrence Grossberg has argued:

> 'when applied to rock and roll the assumption does not seem false, merely incomplete: particular instances of rock and roll may represent different things for different audiences and in different contexts'.[11]

Thus, it is argued that the context of viewing and use of rock clips can influence the diversity of (sex) roles available and the mode of address can cut across established conventions (of the gaze) and produce, or reproduce, a diversity in the audience that is already there (rather than imposed). Rock videos take many forms, including narrative and spectacle (and other visual imagery including computer graphics and animation). Their meaning varies depending upon the context in which they are viewed, and the context or positioning of the viewers or fans. There are thus three major factors to be explored in relation to rock clips:

Performance

Performance operates in a number of ways, affecting spectator-performer relationships differently in different contexts, making the viewing situation and use of clips variable rather than fixed. Performance in relation to rock includes: live performances to an inside audience; the televising of this to audiences elsewhere watching television, or simultaneously by the use of large video screens to the audience at a distance from the stage. Thus, the screen reproduces the simultaneous performance on stage — a performance of a performance (the audience can often watch both); the rock video of the performers on television or on a large screen to an audience in a dance club or pub; and it must also include audience interaction with performers and spectator performance on the dance floor. This can include the dress or fashions worn by the spectators as part of their performance and filmed performances. For example, Punk was considered 'access' music. There was no distance between punk rockers and their supporters. Distinctions between audience and performers are blurred at punk rock concerts. Another example would be Madonna emulators or 'wanna-be's'.[12] Emulating Madonna was also a safe way of expressing 'unsafe' sexuality for teenage girls.[13]

Direct Address

Direct address predominates in non-narrative clips and in segments of otherwise narrative clips, a situation that is relevant to their status as spectacle and display and which incorporates both female and male artists. This point is of greater importance when it is considered in relation to the notion of the usually controlling gaze of the (male) spectator within dominant discourses. The idea of looking is connected with a theory of power, relationships of activity and passivity and to heterosexuality. What is at stake is not just male and female sexuality, but male and female power.

Fantasy

Fantasy operates in relation to these clips by allowing for the possibility of multiple and not gender specific spectator positions. There are differences within masculinity and within femininity both on the screen and in relation to the desires of the spectator/fan.

These arguments incorporate a significant shift away from the dominant theoretical formulations of the gaze, or the process of looking, and how it relates to both males and females. Males, for example, are not usually recognised as potential objects of the gaze in the way that women almost always are, that is, as erotic objects. Neale and Willemen argue that looking is displaced away from the male body and located 'more generally in the overall components of a highly ritualised scene'.[14] Morse also describes a ritualised performance of males in relation to football on television.[15] She suggests that the eroticism in the gaze at the male sports star is disavowed partly through the manner in which the gaze itself is commentated. Thus, Neale and Willemen disavow the eroticism of the gaze as

Morse does. She describes it as a specular gaze which is free of uncomfortable homo-eroticism because it is narcissistic. The sports
stars are seen as ego-ideals or role models rather than objects of
desire.[16] This avoids or disavows a number of difficult questions that
need to be raised. Firstly, what happens to the look of the female
viewer at the body of the male? As in the work of Kaplan this possibility is never mentioned. Secondly, are male bodies never eroticised
for either the male or the female viewer? Finally, is the 'performance'
spectacle not one that involves both female and male characters, as I
have already argued? If we follow Mulvey and Kaplan, spectacle is a
representational strategy producing objects (female) for our (male)
contemplation, but all cinema, all visual and performing arts do
this. Some also produce subjects which return our gaze, and who are
female as well as male, which returns us to rock clips.

Sport, according to Dyer and Morse, may be the most common
contemporary source of male imagery but it is not the only one. In
sport, Dyer argues, the body quality that is promoted is muscularity
— as a sign of power which is constructed as 'natural', 'achieved' and
'phallic'.[17] In rock clips muscularity might or might not be
emphasised. There are differences between various rock clips in relation to the representation of masculinity and the way in which it is
tied to sexuality and to subject/object relations of desire. In sports
broadcasts the sportsman is the object of the male gaze but, according to references already cited, it is not sexual. This is not the case
with rock clips where rock stars are established first and foremost as
being there to be looked at — in admiration or with sexual desire.
These issues and others will be addressed in relation to the following
clips:

Kids in the Kitchen	*Something You Said*	(Aust)
Bronski Beat	*Smalltown Boy*	(UK)
Olivia Newton-John	*Let's Get Physical*	(Aust)
Weather Girls	*It's Raining Men*	(USA)
Cyndi Lauper	*She-Bop*	(USA)
Renee Geyer	*All My Love*	(Aust)
Do Re Mi	*Man Overboard*	(Aust)
Dance Like a Mother	*You Ain't So Tough*	(USA)
Marigolds	*Waiting in Line*	(Aust)

In rock videos there are different constructions of the gaze and
differences within representations of masculine and feminine sexuality, representations which utilise and which undermine dominant

constructions of masculinity in relation to muscles, sport, and machismo and which also serve to undermine dominant discourses of the supposed active/passive aspects of the gaze as they are related to sexual difference.

Commencing with the Australian group, Kids in the Kitchen, it is clear that they, like INXS, rely upon their lead male singer as the central focus of all of their rock clips. He looks directly at the camera and is usually centre frame. He is also the one whose fame and fortune is constructed and followed in fanzines like *Countdown* magazine. Scott Carne is the focus of much teenage girl adoration and speculation. These young male bands are established as the focus of female desire, the female gaze.

> She loves Kids in the Kitchen and Go West and says that posters/ pictures/interviews — anything to do with Kids in the Kitchen would be a very satisfying snack . . .[18]

In the clip, *Something You Said*, there are also Japanese girls, there to be looked at, passive and virtually immobile, but looking out at the camera. It becomes apparent that the 'you' of the song isn't necessarily the Japanese woman, it is you, the spectator. The address is direct. The Japanese affectation was a fashion of 1985, Melbourne. The 'Kids', not *men*, perform for us, but it isn't muscularity that is emphasised, it is their youth. The body of the rock star is coded as ego-ideal and as an object of desire. Again, a letters page makes this quite clear in relation to another young male rock star:

> Ralph, I totally agree with you, if they think George Michael puts a shuttlecock down his pants they would have to be mad because anyone who has seen him in his videos and on his posters will see that it is all his MEAT! He doesn't need any shuttlecock, he has enough there to feed a nation of sex crazed women.[19]

A different form of looking exists in the British group Bronski Beat's clip *Smalltown Boy*. Here is a narrative in which the sportsman clip (diver/swimmer) is represented as an object of masculine physical perfection and desirability, but not for our gaze. He is the object of the lead male singer's gaze. The address in this clip is the third person of narrative cinema but it is not patriarchal heterosexuality that is signified and reproduced. Rather, the gaze within the clip relates to homosexual desire.

Richard Dyer has written much about the eroticising of signs of masculinity in a homosexual context and this is certainly the case in the clips of Bronski Beat (and Frankie Goes to Hollywood). J. Weeks suggests that this calls into question the naturalness and inevitability of heterosexual object choice, and underscores the fact of sexual diversity.[20] But, it also problematises the dominance of the male heterosexual gaze within film theory. This issue of sexual diversity finds expression within the rock clips of female artists as well.

In *Let's Get Physical*, Olivia Newton-John transforms some fat and flabby Australian men into phantasms of masculine physical perfection. She moulds them in relation to her desire and cultural notions of the perfect male body. However, they are produced eventually not for her gaze, but for *their own*, and perhaps their male audience.

In *It's Raining Men*, the Weather Girls are actively pursuing *their* own desires for male bodies, aided and abetted by Mother Nature. Their desires are served by the muscle-bound males who are sent to satisfy them as well as the younger women in the street who need the 'earth mother's' assistance. However, this clip is interesting because it is operating in a number of ways. The muscular males do serve to reinforce a specific and dominant construction of masculinity — that the bigger the muscle the better. It also dresses them in the garb of the 'flasher' — raincoats and little else. The power within the clip is in the hands of the earth mothers, but the representations of manhood here could work to undermine this. There is also the possibility that such masculine images fit more easily within the pages of a gay male magazine. Identification and the look of desire can work in a number of ways in this clip. Whatever the position taken, they are there as beefcake, but they operate as active participants in their positioning as objects of desire, or desirable objects.

The beefcake theme is continued within Lauper's clip *She-Bop*. She reads a beefcake magazine in her car before sidling up to the motorbike boy. This constructs her as the active pursuer of her own desire. And, *this* desire does not have to include an 'other' as object. Lauper's 1985 clip eulogises auto-eroticism or masturbation, and not unlike her *Girls Just Want to Have Fun* video, it centres pleasure within oneself rather than through the good graces of someone else. But again, this is a clip which can be interpreted in more than one way.

Renee Geyer's position within her clip, *All My Love*, is very similar to that of the singer in Kids in the Kitchen. She occupies centre frame and sings directly to camera which is the dominant positioning and mode of address in clips, also utilising dance movements in time to the beat, but she does not share this space with band members as in

Kids in the Kitchen video. Instead, she is represented against a backdrop of fantasy situations expropriated intertextually from Hollywood cinema. It is an upbeat love song and, again, the 'you' of her address is you, the spectator. It is by no means clear that this spectator must be male, however; the backdrop collage does represent heterosexual love, and one could argue that this is the subject matter of the clip. It is fairly unproblematic, but does not negate the possibility of the multiple levels of fantasy described by Penley.

In Do Re Mi's clip *Man Overboard*, the subject is again probably heterosexual love, but it is by no means unproblematic. The performance of the band and the female singer is interspersed with voyeuristic segments of suburban relationships, couples in various domestic situations. The object of the song and of many of the shots is the Australian male. However, this Australian male is a very unsatisfactory and undesirable representation of masculinity. The female lead singer isn't clearly signified as the object of a desiring male gaze. She is more likely, perhaps, to be a subject of identification for female members of the audience in relation to the disastrous results of heterosexual desire, rather than its representation as desirable romantic love! The song itself is cynical and not at all romantic. As the first track to be released off their album, *Domestic Harmony*, it ironically represents domestic disharmony.

Another somewhat cynical clip is Dance Like a Mother's *You Ain't So Tough*, which is a parody of the Robert Palmer *Addicted to Love* rock clip. Palmer's rather egoistic clip is decorated with female mannequin-styled models who stand behind him pretending to play musical instruments. They are only there to be looked at and serve no other function. Here Kaplan's theoretical argument is vindicated, 'the camera freely plays with their eyes, heavily lipsticked mouths, and legs, rendering them passive objects of (male) desire'.[21] Dance Like a Mother include in their clip, male models with expressionless faces who take the place of the female models in the Robert Palmer clip. Here, the female singer and female guitarist's performance is intercut with cutaways to naked male torsos and males preening in front of mirrors. In other shots the two of them lean over a wall to sing and laugh about this masculine narcissism. The women are the powerholding owners of the gaze, but their voyeurism is subversive and ironic. The men are placed in the position of objects, a position usually reserved for women. Here, it is the men who are decorations, and they are the ones who are at a disadvantage. The same shots are used for the male models — faces and crotch shots — as were used for the female models in the Robert Palmer clip, but masculine performance is seen to be 'all an act', a masquerade.

Unlike the rock clips already discussed, the Marigolds' *Waiting in Line* returns us to convention; the convention of the gaze as it pertains to Hollywood realist cinema. It is a clip of a conventional song about a girl 'who is on his mind'. Its conventionality is reinforced by borrowed stills, intertextual appropriations from old black and white movies. Female film stars of the forties in various attitudes of 'to-be-looked-at-ness' feature here. They recline in scant clothing, staring out to the left or right of frame, or they pose provocatively looking directly at the spectator who is, by implication and dominant cultural construction, male. Their posture is passive, they are the observed, the objects of a gaze. All of the males in this rock clip, on the contrary, are active. The band is shown in performance and the inserted film segments of male actors are all action sequences.

Teresa de Lauretis and Hélène Cixous argue that the polarisation of sexual difference into masculine/feminine is a product of patriarchal culture founded on ideas of dominance. De Lauretis argues that there are differences between women, and arguably, then, also between men. Representational forms do not always reflect this level of difference. However, it is reflected to a degree across rock clips which are by no means homogeneous in their music, style, or representational strategies. Renee Geyer is not Cyndi Lauper, who is not The Weather Girls or Madonna. The Bronski Beat are very different from Heavy Metal and they are generally positioned differently in their clips. Control over representation is now quite frequently within the hands of the artist, and is frequently a result of collaboration between clipmaker and artist. Especially as an artist becomes more popular and more well known, the image is not necessarily the direct product of a multi-national record company, as it was for most girl bands of the fifties and sixties.[22] More diversity is now possible.

It becomes apparent in the clips dealing with male and female artists that, although the dominant theory is that looking is power and masculine, and being looked at is powerless and feminine, this is an oversimplification. Just as Dyer argues in relation to photographic models, the artists prepare themselves to be looked at and the artist or cinematographer constructs the image to be looked at; what we see is a collaboration between those who have created the image. Also, both male and female artists address their audiences, representational strategies are not fixed in relation to dominant theories of sexual difference or address. This situation, therefore, shifts the relations of activity/passivity in relation to power for both the male *and* the female artists. In clips, unlike film, the world to be looked at is also looking out, it is aware of its public-ness and invokes it. It is not, therefore, the same kind of voyeurism (of dominant theory). The spectator is not given the same illusion of controlling the gaze. The stars are not simply the object of the spectator's gaze, they are also, simultaneously, the subjects of their own gaze. The subject/object opposition no longer pertains.

In this essay, a number of elements have been foregrounded which are relative to the text and to the spectators/fans, suggesting a lack of uniformity that is not simply eclectic or pluralistic, but potentially rebellious and disruptive of dominant representations and ways of thinking. To suggest that rock clips operate in multiple ways, offering not *one* reading position or use, does not remove unequal social power divisions between men and women and within these categories. However, it does represent the possibility of different interpretations and appropriations including those not simply determined by the text. The concept of fantasy that I have used provides an argument that identification does not have to work along gendered or heterosexual lines. Equally, the fantasy associated with rock stardom and fashion does not necessarily serve to obliterate social awareness. Fashion can also be subversive or parodic. It is my argument, then, that rock clips and their associated accessories such as fashion and style are not simply standardised new commodities reinforcing dominant positions, nor are they completely subversive products of a rebellious, non-conformist or *avant garde* impulse. Rather, they allow for a range of interpretations and uses because of their lack of uniformity, and because of the various contexts in which they appear.

The textual qualities of spectacle and direct address shift the discourses of the gaze as male power, to one that includes the eroticism of the male rock and roll body, as well as that of the female, and if direct address can empower the male rock star it can also empower the female. Performance becomes a quality of the text and of the audience. Pleasure is not simply looking, but also participation. Rock clips are not the same as live performances but they are sometimes used that way, especially in dance clubs. The various aspects of address, performance and fantasy should be seen as opening out the meaning and function of rock clips at least in relation to male and female performance.

PART THREE

Women and Television Genres

Chapter 8. Women's space: the restroom at the 14th Precinct. *Photo:* CBS.

The private . . .

. . . and public lives of Cagney and Lacey. *Photos:* CBS.

8

Cagney & Lacey: Feminist Strategies of Detection

Danae Clark

The connection between *Cagney & Lacey* and feminism can be traced back to 1974 when Barbara Corday, one of the show's creators, made her husband, producer Barney Rosenzweig, read Molly Haskell's feminist attack on the film industry, *From Reverence to Rape: The Treatment of Women in the Movies.* According to Corday, Rosenzweig became 'enlightened' when he encountered Haskell's point that women had never been portrayed as buddies in film or television, and thereafter he was committed to producing a female buddy movie.[1] Unfortunately, executives in the entertainment industry had still not attained enlightenment. Corday developed a movie script of *Cagney & Lacey* along with Barbara Avedon in 1974, but it was not until 1981 that CBS finally produced it as a TV-movie and (based on its high ratings) subsequently developed *Cagney & Lacey* into a weekly series.

While *Cagney & Lacey* may have been inspired by feminist film criticism, its continued existence has been attributed to its predominantly female viewing audience. When the show was cancelled during its first season, executive producer Rosenzweig managed to keep it on the air. But when *Cagney & Lacey* was cancelled again after its second season (1982-83), thousands of letters sent in by viewers convinced CBS that *Cagney & Lacey* had a dedicated and sizeable audience. According to Rosenzweig, 'a lot of women, especially younger women, had been identifying almost fiercely with the show'.[2] They were not the traditional starstruck fans, he added. 'They were affluent, well-educated people . . . working women [and] college students'.[3] Overwhelmingly, women responded to *Cagney & Lacey*'s 'complex, real women characters' and 'honestly portrayed women's friendships'.[4] This held true even among women who tended not to care for 'the usual cop shows'.

Cagney & Lacey has certainly challenged the stereotypes found in earlier police dramas such as *Police Woman*, in which a highly sexualised Angie Dickinson was put into dangerous, suggestive situations only to be rescued by her male partners. But the importance of *Cagney & Lacey* to feminism lies beyond its presentation of a new or 'better' image of women. As a text that specifically addresses women and women's issues, *Cagney & Lacey* potentially challenges the boundaries of patriarchal discourse at the same time as it allows viewers to actively enter into the process of its meaning construction. Thus, as I hope to demonstrate in this essay, the 'fierce identification' experienced by the show's female viewers may derive from their participation in and empowerment by the show's discursive strategies. In particular, I will argue that *Cagney & Lacey* empowers women and encourages women-identified constructions of meaning through a combination of its narrative form, its representational codes, and its structures of looking.

Narrative Strategies/Feminist Strategies

Barney Rosenzweig summarises *Cagney & Lacey*'s narrative construction when he says '[t]his is not a show about two cops who happen to be women; it's about two women who happen to be cops'.[5] While *Cagney & Lacey* is categorised as a police drama, this aspect assumes only minor significance. The major aspect, or real drama of the show, revolves around the personal lives of Christine Cagney (Sharon Gless) and Mary Beth Lacey (Tyne Daly) both inside and outside the 14th Precinct. Although these two aspects are interwoven in any given episode, they differ significantly in their narrative structure. As in other police dramas, the protagonists of *Cagney & Lacey* are presented with a case to solve, the criminal is apprehended or outwitted, and a sense of order is restored at the end when the case is either solved or dismissed. But the drama of Cagney and Lacey's lives continues beyond a single episode. Unlike the linear, cause and effect progression of the police subplot, the main plot is open and fragmented. We don't know from any cause and effect structure what Chris will decide about marriage or how Mary Beth will cope with having breast cancer. More importantly, we eventually learn about their decisions and feelings through dialogue, not action. Because of this, the narrative structure of *Cagney & Lacey*'s major plotline seems more characteristic of the soap opera than the classical realist text.

According to Tania Modleski, one of the chief differences between these types of texts is that the soap opera appears to be participatory in a way that the realist text almost never is. In soap operas, 'action is less important than *re*action and *inter*action', and this is one reason, she says, that fans insist on the soap opera's 'realism':

> Despite the numerous murders, kidnappings, blackmail attempts, emergency operations, amnesia attacks, etc., . . . [one] knows that these events are not important in themselves; they merely serve as occasions for characters to get together and have prolonged, involved, intensely emotional discussions with each other.[6]

Cagney & Lacey differs from soap operas in relegating the more outrageous events to the police drama subplot, while the more 'realistic' events of the two women's lives provide the occasions for intense, ongoing discussion. Yet, like the soap opera, *Cagney & Lacey* contains a combined narrative structure that permits closure on a subsidiary level while remaining open on another level.

Modleski argues that the televisual flow of soap opera broadcasting creates a narrative structure that combines commercials and program content. The commercials that interrupt the soap opera diegesis, she says, present the viewer with mini-problems and their resolutions, 'so after witnessing all the agonisingly hopeless dilemmas presented on soap operas, the spectator has the satisfaction of seeing *something* cleaned up, if only a stained shirt or a dirty floor'.[7] The difference between *Cagney & Lacey* and more traditional soap operas, however, resides in the way this combined narrative structure functions within and in relation to the show's diegesis. Like the advertisements on daytime television, many of the commercials interspersed during a *Cagney & Lacey* episode depict women as domestic servants or sexual objects whose aim in life is to please others. Yet such depictions stand in contrast to the messages found within the show itself. Although Mimi White suggests that the commercials act as a 'necessary supplement' or conservative balance to the more progressive content of *Cagney & Lacey*, female viewers may experience them as incongruous rather than a complementary feature of the show's diegesis.[8] Within the episodes themselves, Cagney and Lacey are portrayed as active, intelligent agents of change outside the world of domestic labour. And it makes a difference that the women who clean up the problems encountered in the police mini-dramas are the same ones who draw us into the dramas of their personal lives.

Another major difference between the soap-like structure of *Cagney & Lacey* and soap operas themselves, is the way that viewers are invited to participate in the problem-solving process of characters' lives. According to Modleski, soap operas provide the spectator with training in 'reading' other people, in being sensitive to their needs and desires. She equates this skill in reading with the function of the woman in the home who must be attuned to the effects of the world upon her family. Since the soap opera's multiple plotlines demand multiple identification on the part of a viewer, Modleski argues that these texts activate the gaze of an 'ideal mother' who has no demands of her own.[9] Similarly, Charlotte Brunsdon suggests that soap operas 'call on traditionally feminine competencies [sensitivity, perception, intuition] associated with the responsibility for "managing" the sphere of personal life'.[10] In relation to *Cagney & Lacey*, however, a viewer's active reading is potentially influenced by two important factors: the experience of female bonding that is strengthened and explored through Cagney and Lacey's interaction, and the emphasis that their interaction places on decision-making — a skill not generally associated with traditionally feminine competencies.

Various strategies are used in emphasising the decision-making process in *Cagney & Lacey*. In some cases, viewers are not presented with the outcome or immediate effects of the characters' decisions. For example, in one episode, Chris struggles with the question of marriage and finally decides against it. But we never witness a scene in which she tells Dory, her fiancé, about her decision. The effect of such a strategy is not to deny Chris's ability to confront the consequences of her decisions, but rather underscores the fact that she was able to reach a decision that most appropriately benefited her own needs and desires. Similarly, when Mary Beth learns that she has breast cancer, textual emphasis is placed on her deliberation over the options available to her rather than the treatment she decides to receive. In a soap opera, her medical treatment would have become the object of spectacle as well as an occasion for other characters to engage in prolonged, involved discussion. The absence of this occasion in *Cagney & Lacey*, however, serves to emphasise women's active control over the decision-making process.

From time to time, other female characters are brought into the decision-making process. In the two-part episode on sexual harassment, for example, Chris decides to press charges against a superior officer who threatens to withhold a job promotion if she refuses to comply with his sexual demands. To ensure his conviction, she seeks the testimony of a woman who has been also harassed by him. But because the woman had succumbed to his threats, she is afraid that her co-operation will result in the loss of her job and the promotion she had been promised. Although Chris' statements about the need for women to speak out against sexual harassment in the workplace are met with resistance, the woman finally comes forward. But the episode concludes *before* she delivers her testimony. The outcome of her decision (winning or losing the case) thus becomes less important than the decision-making process itself. In this way textual emphasis is placed on the difficulties and risks that such decisions pose for women within patriarchy. Or, more significantly, emphasis is placed on the need to reach effective and empowering decisions on such matters.

In contrast to this textual strategy, other episodes emphasise the characters' confrontations with the decisions they have made. For example, three seasons after Chris decides not to marry Dory, she receives a marriage proposal from David. In this episode, however, Chris struggles silently with the issue, then confronts David with her decision. Perhaps the show's writers wished to avoid reiterating the decision-making process represented in the earlier episode, but the effect of this strategy is to emphasise Chris' ability and courage to stick to and follow through her decisions. Thus, long-time viewers who are familiar with the Cagney character are not only rewarded with the 'absent scene' but are encouraged to identify with her subsequent action. In other situations, the follow-up action becomes an integral part of the decision-making process. When Chris finally admits to having an alcohol problem, for example, her realisation is not in itself constituted as a solution. The process also includes her decision to attend Alcoholics Anonymous and announce publicly: 'My name is Christine, and I am an alcoholic'.

When the decision process is represented in terms of reaction and interaction, rather than action, *Cagney & Lacey* invites the participation of the spectator to complete the process of meaning construction in ways that are meaningful to her. Cagney, Lacey, and the show's other characters, provide a 'concert of voices' that inter-changeably listen to and provide feminist as well as non-feminist options to problems that affect women and women's autonomy (e.g., rape, sexual harassment, pregnancy, and breast cancer).[11] While not all women have had the same experience of these situations, the knowledge and experience they do have *as women* allow them to identify with discussions of what options are available, what decisions might put them in control, and what discursive strategies are appropriate for arriving at these decisions. When the characters' subsequent actions are represented, viewers may additionally identify with the desire and courage to follow through on such decisions.

Above all, viewers are encouraged to identify with the role that female bonding plays in decision-making. Although the relationship between Chris and Mary Beth has been strained and challenged over the six years of the show's existence, the two women depend upon each other for support and constantly reaffirm their friendship. The text thus acknowledges women's need to talk to each other (without male intervention) and also suggests to the female viewer that the positive support of women can help her in coping with the problems encountered under patriarchy. A good example of female bonding and the way it enters into the decision-making process occurs during the episode in which Chris decides not to marry Dory. Chris and Mary Beth begin discussing this decision in the rest room at the precinct house, then move to a public bar. Initially, Mary Beth makes reference to how they neatly wrapped up their case (closure of the narrative subplot), but this is followed by five minutes of uninter-rupted dialogue about the pros and cons of marriage. Mary Beth, who is happily married, takes up an argumentative line in favour of marriage, while Chris stresses why it is not right for her. Finally resolving their differences by recognising the need for personal choice (and a woman's right to make that choice), their friendship remains solid. This scene allows a female spectator to engage in the dialogue from a variety of perspectives while being encouraged to identify with the female bonding that is sustained.

When decisions involve the issue of female bonding itself, additional strategies come into play. These strategies are less com-promising in the sense that divisions among women are not easily tolerated. For example, after Chris is made sergeant, she occasionally pulls rank on Mary Beth and insists on a plan of action that her partner opposes. Mary Beth's confrontation with Chris on this issue often produces heated accusations and threats (including the dissolution of their partnership). But, ultimately, Chris recognises that her attempt to establish a hierarchical relationship is an improper and intolerable option that only serves to weaken their collective power. In other instances, patience and silence are shown to be necessary correlatives to verbal confrontation. When Chris is struggling with alcoholism, Mary Beth aggressively confronts her with the truth of her situation, but thereafter quietly stands vigil at her bedside. When the two women are shown together, clasping hands at the AA meeting, the unspoken and unquestioning support between them makes the issue of female bonding as important as the issue of alcoholism.

The viewer's relation to *Cagney & Lacey* thus contrasts markedly with the viewer-text relation Modleski suggests for the soap opera. Although both texts provide women with multiple points of view, the *Cagney & Lacey* viewer is not addressed as an 'ideal mother' with no demands of her own. On the contrary, *Cagney & Lacey* calls upon women to examine what their demands might be and how they might articulate them. This relation between textual strategies and reading practices most closely resembles the framework and goals of feminist consciousness-raising groups in the sense that women are encouraged to join in the discussion of women's issues and find answers that will empower them. The aspect of female bonding, which privileges trust among women and assumes a crucial, supportive role in the process of women's decision-making, has prompted one critic to suggest that *Cagney & Lacey* offers 'a nascent feminist ideology within the context of mass art'.[12]

Codes of Detection

At the risk of contradicting the points made in the previous section, I would now like to suggest that no discernible separation exists between the police drama subplot of *Cagney & Lacey* and the drama of the main characters' lives, and that the show can also be read in relation to certain textual strategies found in the detective genre.

It is commonly thought, for example, that the detective undertakes two simultaneous investigations — one involving the world of crime, and the other the sphere of sexuality. In the process of detecting the truth, the former precipitates the latter and, ultimately, the question of sexuality assumes primary importance. The typical male hero of such texts is forced to encounter his own sexual anxieties in relation to another (usually female) character. Annette Kuhn explains it thus:

It is often the woman . . . who constitutes the motivator of the narrative, the 'trouble' that sets the plot in motion, [and] the film's resolution depends on [his] resolution of the particular 'woman question'.[13]

Cagney & Lacey works against the generic boundaries of traditional detective fiction by usurping the male's privileged role as representative of the (patriarchal) Law. Yet, significantly, the text continues to centre on the 'woman question'. This focus challenges and often reverses the relations of power that structure traditional (male-defined) detective genres such as *film noir*. Within *film noir*, for example, the woman question is generally resolved by determining the guilt or innocence of women, and guilty women (by virtue of their independence or expression of sexual desire) are killed, punished, or otherwise eradicated from the text. But within *Cagney & Lacey*, women (i.e. Chris and Mary Beth) assume the voice(s) of judgement concerning female sexuality while attempting to resolve the trouble that patriarchal structures create for women. Resolution of the woman question thus becomes a resolution of the issues that affect women's autonomy and expression.

The power and credibility of Cagney and Lacey as heroines derive from the text's refusal to separate the public and private aspects of their lives. In other words, Cagney and Lacey are not defined solely by a private (sexual and familial) identity, but also in relation to a public (professional) role. According to Jane Tompkins, '[The] public-private dichotomy, which is to say the public-private *hierarchy*, is a founding condition of female oppression'.[14] This dichotomy, in other words, results in women's objectification and confinement, privatising their functions within the home while privileging the role of men as decision-makers in the public sphere. The dissolution of this distinction in *Cagney & Lacey* can thus be read as an attempt to represent women in more empowering social relations. As women engaged in a demanding profession, work forms an integral part of Cagney's and Lacey's experiences and provides a context outside the home in which decisions are discussed and acted upon.

The lack of separation between public and private in *Cagney & Lacey* can also be read in less progressive terms. According to Mimi White, consideration of the private, domestic sphere allows 'feminism [to be] explored in the context of the traditional, middle-class nuclear family' and prevents any real challenge to the institution of the family itself.[15] The nuclear family, from this perspective, becomes the standard against which all social relations are judged. Thus, the welfare mothers that Cagney and Lacey encounter in their police work can appear pathetically incomplete without the emotional and economic support of a 'good' husband. In addition, the programme resists any radical interpretations of the family such as happily-committed gay or lesbian couples, with or without children. The only homosexual represented in *Cagney & Lacey* is Chris' next door neighbour, Tony, who is single (and seemingly celibate). Although Chris herself has no husband or children, White argues that 'her familial situation is explored in relation to her father and brother'.[16] [Significantly, the homosexual next door is male; any interaction between Chris and a lesbian neighbour would place into question the decidedly heterosexual orientation of one of the show's stars.] The Laceys, meanwhile, suggest a prototype of the American nuclear family.

The representation of the institution of the family may, on the other hand, serve as a vehicle for the expression of frustration and non-fulfilment of desire. According to Sylvia Harvey, 'one of the defining characteristics of *film noir* is to be found in its treatment of the family and family relations'.[17] While the presence of the family may appear to legitimate and naturalise the dominant social values embodied in the patriarchal nuclear family, it may also serve to expose the 'intolerable contradictions' and suppression of desires that this institution sustains. If, as I am suggesting, *Cagney & Lacey* can be read according to certain textual strategies found in the detective genre (which finds its most exaggerated interpretation in *film noir*), then the show's representation of 'broken, perverted, peripheral' family relations may actually be founded upon the *absence* of the family.[18]

During the 1986-87 season, the Laceys move from their small apartment to a suburban house in Queens. The purchase and renovation of the house represent the fulfilment of their dreams (and, by extension, the fulfilment of the American dream) as a family. During this period, the bonds between Chris and Mary Beth weaken, and Mrs. Lacey seems more cheerfully domestic than ever before. But domestic bliss is interrupted when it encounters the conservatism, racial prejudice and violence of white, middle-class suburbia. In one episode, Lacey is summoned to a nearby house where a woman has been physically battered by her husband. The frightened wife denies the occurrence, and the husband maintains his innocence by holding to the myth that spouse abuse never occurs in 'nice' neighbourhoods. Lacey eventually succeeds in getting the man convicted, but her pleasure and security in her new surroundings are undermined. In this episode and others, the nuclear family is portrayed as a site of violence and instability. In relation to this depiction, the Laceys appear *not* as an ideal family, but as a family group struggling to survive where no ideal exists.

The institution of the family also provides a context in which other issues, such as racial and economic differences, can be explored. Differences between Cagney and Lacey, for example, are defined as much by class standing as by marital status. While Cagney claims the working-class background of her father, she more obviously embraces the upper-class interests of her (deceased) mother. Chris regards Mary Beth's 'low culture' tastes with some disdain, and Mary Beth often feels impelled to defend her latch-key childhood and working-class husband against Chris' more economically-privileged existence. While these conflicts are never resolved, neither are they erased. The exploration of class differences within the context of the family rather serves to create greater awareness of the family's social and economic effects on women.

This awareness is heightened through Cagney and Lacey's contacts with other women. Welfare mothers, for example, are not represented simply as women without husbands, but as economically-disadvantaged women who are victimised by a variety of patriarchal, capitalist institutions. During one investigation, Cagney and Lacey encounter a woman who is sleeping with her slum tenement landlord. When Cagney tells her that she does not have to exchange sexual favours for a place to live, the woman replies, 'You mean *you* don't'. This exchange foregrounds the experience of a woman (or class of woman) who is ordinarily absent from televisual representation; at the same time it foregrounds differences between women. Thus, far from being a commentary on family life, such an exchange points to the larger issues of women's oppression and offers a 're-visioning' of women's social relations. Within this context, the traditional family loses its force. *Cagney & Lacey* challenges a unified concept of the family by exposing its internal strife, by exploring the economic and political conflicts that exist *between* families, and by insisting on establishing a connection among women across family lines in spite of — or, rather, because of — their differences. As Teresa de Lauretis notes, textual representations of feminism succeed to the extent that they can generate an understanding of how women are 'constructed and defined in gender across multiple representations of class, race, language and social relations'.[19]

As these examples suggest, the lack of separation between public and private in *Cagney & Lacey* works as a narrative strategy to highlight social issues while reinforcing the idea that the personal is political. The investigative structure can translate personal conflict into public concerns and anchor viewer identification to a specific political stance, especially when the police subplot and the drama of characters' lives are integrally connected in an episode. For example, at a time when Mary Beth is trying to cope with her son's decision to enlist in the military, her police work brings her into contact with a WW II veteran who proudly shows off his war decorations. The man becomes a target for Mary Beth's displaced frustrations (since she feels she cannot interfere with Harv Jr.'s decision). But the fact that this man turns out to be a murderer in civilian life substantiates her outrage towards the stupidity and false pride of war. Harvey, Mary Beth's husband, occupies an important position in relation to this issue. He not only shares his wife's views about the military, but explicitly critiques Reagan's Central American policies. In this particular case, then, the personal and the political coincide to reinforce viewer sympathy with a pacifist stance and to discourage identification with militarism.

Aside from Harvey's supportive role as husband in *Cagney & Lacey*, his character is often used to signify opinions or positions that the show's stars do not articulate. Other minor characters who take up controversial stances are also featured in episodes — especially when the social issue in question is not explicitly feminist. In addition to Harvey's liberal (sometimes bordering on socialist) working-class position, for example, Detective Marcus Petrie repeatedly takes a stand against racism, insisting on the recognition of his racial difference as a way of confronting the racist attitudes of others. Thus, in contrast to White's suggestion that 'minority positions or deviations from the mainstream are introduced but are framed and held in place by more familiar, conventional representations', minority positions often serve to *replace* or critique conservative points of view.[20] The positions assumed by minor characters may be seen by some as a diversion tactic or safe method of keeping a more conservative representation of Cagney and Lacey intact. On the other hand, it could be argued that these additional voices work in concert with the women's own political agendas to suggest a broad-based feminist approach to social problems.

The investigative structure of *Cagney & Lacey* can be summarised as a 'struggle between different voices for control over telling the story'. Working in conjunction with its soap opera strategies to provide multiple points of view and identification, *Cagney & Lacey* uses codes of detection to uncover the 'truth' of women's social relations. While the show departs from the traditional detective genre in significant ways, and its investigative structure might work just as well if Cagney and Lacey were members of a different profession (e.g., medicine), the authority invested in these women as representatives of the Law makes its comparison with the detective genre both profitable and unavoidable. According to *Cagney & Lacey*'s newly-emerging law governing crime and sexuality, women are presumed innocent, the voices of many different women are examined, and women's struggle to assert control over their own lives is legitimised.

Reclaiming the Look

One final way in which *Cagney & Lacey* challenges patriarchal discourse and encourages women-identified constructions of meaning is through its economy of vision. In fact, it is this aspect, more than any other, that most clearly distinguishes *Cagney & Lacey* from other texts. Dominant theories of spectatorship maintain that traditional (male-governed) texts are founded on a subject/object dichotomy that places a male subject in control of the 'gaze' and positions the woman as object of his look. Since the woman becomes the passive raw material for the active gaze and visual pleasure of the male, the female viewer's possibilities for identification become extremely limited; she must choose between adopting the voyeuristic (sadistic) position of the male subject or the masochistic position of the female object.[22] But this model of spectatorship does not describe the viewer's relation to *Cagney & Lacey*. As I have pointed out in the previous sections, female viewers are more likely to feel empowered by their identifications with Cagney and Lacey. Thus they experience a pleasure in viewing that cannot be explained in masochistic terms.

Cagney & Lacey provides an alternative viewer-text relation that breaks up traditional structures of looking in several different ways. First of all, the show's female characters are in possession of the look. By virtue of their authority to control the process of detection and narrative action, Cagney and Lacey define the text's point of view and vision of social relations. Thus, they not only act as subjects of narration, but rarely become the objects of a male gaze. It could be argued that it is precisely because Cagney and Lacey are not the fetishised objects of male desire that they are able to assert control (a condition that would conversely explain Angie Dickinson's powerlessness in *Police Woman*). However, this control is not necessarily a control *over* men. Instead of reversing the traditional relations of looking and objectifying men as the fetishised objects of female desire and power, *Cagney & Lacey* attempts to break the pattern of dominance and submission altogether. Even though the text privileges the woman's point of view, reverse discrimination is not seen as the answer to women's empowerment.

Cagney & Lacey actively works to frustrate the traditional relations of voyeurism and fetishism by avoiding scenes which would ordinarily result in an objectification of women. For example, in episodes on spouse abuse and child abuse, viewers are not privy to scenes in which women or female children are physically assaulted, thus discouraging a sadistic and voyeuristic identification with violence against women. Likewise, in the 1988 episode on acquaintance rape, where Chris is attacked by her date, we do not witness the actual rape. This strategy allows the program to focus on the social and political implications of rape without objectifying a woman in the process.[23] Sharon Gless's character *is* marked as sexual; like other television stars (male and female) she is portrayed as desiring and desirable. But the episode draws a line between desirability and objectification to make the point that no woman − even (or especially) a sexually active woman − deserves to be victimised by the crime of rape.

The relations of looking established between women in *Cagney & Lacey* also challenge traditional economies of vision. Since women are not isolated from each other as objects for male consumption, women have more freedom to initiate and act upon relations with each other. The de-eroticised images of women, in other words, permit women to interact as *subjects*. This sort of re-visioning requires women to look beyond the surface level of a woman's image and to place into question male-defined images of women. Thus, women are perceived by other women not as sexual objects, but as the victimised subjects of patriarchal desire. *Cagney & Lacey* does not foreclose the possibility of erotic identification − a point that lesbian viewers can substantiate − but the female viewer's *objectification* of female characters is discouraged. Since *Cagney & Lacey* looks behind the image to examine women's oppression and encourages identification with the various struggles that women encounter, viewers are less likely to identify these women as fetish objects. In this way, *Cagney & Lacey* offers a vision of female bonding that simultaneously threatens patriarchal definitions of sexual relations and offers female viewers a point of identification that is neither sadistic nor masochistic. This results in more empowering (rather than power-filled) social relations for and among women.

Another way that *Cagney & Lacey* avoids the objectification of women is by shifting the viewer's attention from sight to sound. In other words, greater emphasis is placed on the voice (what women say) than on the image (how women look). As Mary Ann Doane notes, '[the] voice displays what is inaccessible to the image, what exceeds the visible: the "inner life" of the character'.[24] Thus the voice can be seen as 'a potentially viable means whereby the woman can make herself heard'.[25] *Cagney & Lacey* provides 'an isolated haven' for the voice of women within patriarchy, through the creation of woman's space. Within the enclosed space of the police car or the rest room at the 14th Precinct House (spaces which are both public and private), Cagney and Lacey speak to each other without male intervention and are free to explore and affirm the dimensions of female partnership. The importance of this woman's space (and the female bonding that occurs within it) is underscored by the fact that the show includes at least one such scene in every episode.

Other textual strategies in *Cagney & Lacey* rely on the voice (e.g., the reaction and interaction evident in the process of women's decision-making). But when examined in relation to the gaze, strategies involving the voice take on added significance. The voice is sometimes placed in counterpoint to the gaze — a strategy that allows *Cagney & Lacey* to play with the conventions of voyeurism. For instance, when Cagney and Lacey are in the precinct house rest room, the camera often focuses on their reflections as they primp themselves in front of the mirror. But within this woman's space, the role of the image becomes undermined. Either the woman's concern with her image is shown to be a diversionary tactic (a way to avoid discussing the real issues at hand), or the image itself turns out to be a false or incomplete source of information (it is, after all, only a reflection). Viewers are thus discouraged from investing any identification or voyeuristic pleasure in the image. To gain access to the characters' inner feelings we must actively look beyond the image and listen to rather than look at the characters.

In other instances, the voice and the image combine in ways that explicitly usurp male privilege. In the episode on spouse abuse, for example, Chris' ACLU boyfriend, David, is the trial lawyer who gets the accused husband convicted. But instead of showing the actual courtroom scene, the site of David's authority and expertise, the event is recounted verbally in the women's rest room. Mary Beth performs for Chris the details of the trial by playing David's role and speaking in his place. In this way, the woman's voice is privileged and Mary Beth, instead of David, receives recognition for all the hard work she put in on the case. Although Mary Beth makes a 'spectacle' of herself during this scene, the woman's space provides a safe environment for her performance while it, once again, allows a woman to speak and to be heard.

Finally, *Cagney & Lacey* tampers with the conventions of voyeurism through the use of masquerade. As Mary Ann Doane notes, '[t]here is always a certain excessiveness, a difficulty associated with women who appropriate the gaze, who insist on looking'.[26] In order to maintain control — over the narrative, the look, and her own body — a woman must destabilise the image and confound the masculine structure of the look. One option is to give (male) viewers more than they bargain for. Thus, instead of refusing the familiar trappings of femininity, a woman might *flaunt* her femininity, play the game of femininity, by using her own body as a disguise. This masquerade allows a woman to distance herself from the image (to refuse complicity with objectification) while she demonstrates and controls the representation of her body.

In *Cagney & Lacey*, the detectives often adopt disguises in the service of their undercover work. While these disguises generally connote a power of action that extends beyond a woman's sexualised form, the occasions of feminine masquerade provide a direct commentary on the issue of female representation. In a 1987 episode, for example, Cagney and Lacey go undercover as hookers to catch a mugger. In their role as women dressed up as women, they display an excess of femininity — mounds of makeup and hair (wigs of unnatural color), revealing dresses, feathers, jewellery — that creates a ridiculous image of the female form. The masquerade allows Cagney and Lacey to expose the sadism of male desire, i.e., 'those "ogling" eyes that turn women into pieces of meat', as Cagney remarks. Moreover, when the detectives change into their street clothes and assume a different identity, they deconstruct this fetishised image of woman and expose male-defined femininity as a mask that can be worn or simply removed. At the end of the episode (after they have successfully closed the case), Cagney and Lacey return to the privacy of the woman's rest room and conduct a ceremonial ritual in which they burn their costumes. Once free of the burden of their feminised images, Cagney remarks, 'We are better cops now, Mary Beth'. 'And smarter', replies her partner.

The characters' understanding of this issue has been represented as an ongoing process of development. In an earlier episode, for example, Cagney and Lacey are assigned to work with a Hollywood 'bimbo' (Cagney's term), who seeks a taste of real police work in connection with her starring role in a television cop series. (The episode seems to be an obvious and quite conscious comparison between *Cagney & Lacey* and *Police Woman* that permits the show to comment on its own construction of women's images.) Cagney feels that the woman's highly-sexualised appearance (excessive femininity) undermines the seriousness of police work and makes life difficult for other women (i.e. Cagney and Lacey) who have struggled against sexual stereotyping. When she expresses this disgust to Mary Beth in the rest room, the actress emerges from a rest room stall and confronts Chris's attitudes. She explains that as a single mother she has taken the role for financial reasons and that she too abhors the image she represents/flaunts. This feminist twist on 'a man's gotta do what a man's gotta do' allows *Cagney & Lacey* to question women's complicity in the game of objectification while it encourages its viewers (and characters) to see female representation as masquerade.

Other uses of masquerade are more celebratory than pedagogical. When Cagney and Lacey dress up as fruits for a game show, and when they perform a Rockettes number for a police awards banquet, their disguises invite laughter rather than critical reflection. In circumstances such as these, masquerade provides an occasion for play and the detectives do not comment directly on the conventions of female representation. Nonetheless, their disguises act as a visual statement on the fluid, potentially subversive quality of the female image and women's ability to change and control the parameters of its representation. And this is finally what *Cagney & Lacey* is all about: the empowerment and pleasure that women gain from representing themselves (to themselves). If the makers of *Cagney & Lacey* occasionally celebrate and flaunt this pleasure, many female viewers, including myself, feel that they have earned the right to do so.

Visual playfulness and other disruptions of conventional representation do not automatically mark *Cagney & Lacey* as a radical text however.[27] As Julie D'Acci has noted, the show's representations are often rooted in liberal notions of feminist politics which perceive 'social change and difference for women (as) simply a matter of equal rules, equal jobs and equal representation'.[28] Its liberal politics thus tend to promote individual accomplishment (i.e., representations of women who have 'made it') and pluralism (i.e., many different types of successful women) as a means to correct the social imbalance of a white male dominated culture.[29] Yet, *Cagney & Lacey*'s pluralism of representation should not be confused or equated with the show's discursive strategies of detection. In spite of its apparent liberalism, the text opens up the possibility of a reading practice that goes beyond a mere identification with certain stereotypes or roles and engages its female viewers in a process of locating and (re)articulating women's positioning within social practices. This becomes possible because *Cagney & Lacey* actively works to create viewing positions which empower the text's female viewers as political subjects.

9

Women and Quiz Shows: Consumerism, Patriarchy and Resisting Pleasures

John Fiske

US television has broadcast over 330 different quiz and game shows, most of them in day time, most of them aimed at women. In Australia and the UK, a day's television without a quiz show of some sort is rare, and frequently at least one example of the genre rates in the top ten program. The role of game shows in women's culture is problematic, and in this chapter I wish to explore the questions of how far they bear the forces that subordinate women, and to what extent they enable these forces to be opposed, evaded or negotiated.

Quiz shows, along with soap opera, are often considered as one of the lowest forms of television. The fact that low critical standing coincides with their appeal to women should alert us to the possibility that the reasons for denigrating them should be sought not in the shows themselves, nor in their role in women's culture, but rather in the disciplinary power of patriarchy to devalue anything that resists, threatens, or evades its power. It is the function of this book to interrogate patriarchy, so let us take quiz shows seriously; let us posit that they can play active, pleasurable roles in women's culture and investigate what those roles and pleasures might be.

The approach I wish to take is to follow some of the main lines of argument attacking quiz shows, and suggest that their error lies not in their analysis of the semiotic features of quiz shows, but in their evaluation of the roles such meanings play in women's culture. I wish to concentrate on three of these semiotic features or discourses common throughout the genre and discuss each with reference to one particular show. These discourses are those of consumerism, the family, and romance.

Woman as Consumer

Quiz shows are a cultural product of consumer capitalism. They foreground commodities, they blur the distinctions between themselves and the commercials embedded in them and the rewards that they offer are those of the commodity system. In short, they relentlessly address and position the woman as housewife and consumer. But in the consumerist, capitalist society in which we live, the *only* cultural resources are those provided by the system and those social forces that govern it. This is as true of language and systems of representation as it is of commodities. A whole range of recent cultural theories, particularly ideological and feminist, have argued with great sophistication and persuasiveness how the interests of the dominant are served by the systems they control. But these theories need to be mitigated, if not contradicted, by studies focusing on *how* the subordinate make use of these systems. The art of everyday life, according to Michel de Certeau, is the art of making do: people make do with what they have, and if all they have are centrally provided resources, the point at issue becomes what people might do with them, rather than what they might do to people.[1]

Without such an emphasis, it becomes difficult, if not impossible to conceive of subordinated groups, such as various groups of women, having any culture of their own: they would become merged into the mass so feared by the Frankfurt school. There is no 'authentic' folk culture for the subordinate to draw upon: 'high' culture is available and of interest to a minority only (within which women have difficulty in establishing a place for themselves) and no alternatives exist. Women's oral culture, or gossip, however, makes use of a language deeply inscribed with patriarchal values, but uses it in a feminine way. Similarly I would argue that women can use commodities (and quiz shows as cultural commodities) in ways that negate or evade the economic and gender power of the system that produces and distributes them.[2]

The New Price is Right is the consumerist quiz show par excellence. The contestants are nearly all women, and the knowledge required is what our society treats as 'women's' knowledge: that of the prices and comparative values of commodities. The show consists of a variety of games and competitions in which the winner is the one who best judges commodity prices and values; who is, in other words, the best shopper. But if all the show does is to reproduce and repeat women's role in domestic labour, why, we must ask ourselves, should they find it popular and pleasurable? If women are the shoppers for the family in real life, why should they choose to fill their leisure with more of the same?

While recognising that the show clearly addresses women as consumers, we must also recognise the differences between the conditions of consumption on the show, and those of consumption in domestic labour, for it is in the differences that the pleasures lie for women.

The most obvious of these is the difference between the public and the private. Consumption in everyday life is essentially a private affair. Its skills go largely unrecognised and unapplauded. This lack of social acclaim for women's knowledge and labour is part of the strategy to silence them under patriarchy. *The New Price is Right* is characterised by noise, cheering and applause; the studio audience's enthusiasm verges on hysteria, the successes of the consumer contestants are wildly applauded. There is a strong element of the carnivalesque here, and for Bakhtin, the carnival was the occasion when the repressions of everyday life could be lifted, when the voices of the oppressed could be heard at full volume, when society admitted to pleasures which it ordinarily repressed and denied.[3] The essence of carnival was the inversion of the rules of everyday life, necessitated by the need to maintain the oppression of a populace that would otherwise refuse to submit to this social discipline. So the forces of carnival are opposed to those which work to repress and control the everyday life of the subordinate.

Two main forms of liberation are expressed in the game-show audience's enthusiasm: the first is to give public, noisy acclaim to skills that are ordinarily silenced; the second is simply to be 'noisy' in public; to escape from demure respectability, from the confines of good sense that patriarchy has constructed as necessary qualities for 'the feminine'.

Women, particularly those from the lower socio-economic groups who form the core of the show's audience, are subordinated economically as well as socio-politically. This economic subordination takes two forms: the limited amount of money available to women and the ownership of that money. For women fulfilling the traditional feminine role of unwaged domestic labour, the money is the husband's. Earning and providing for the family is socially linked to masculinity, while spending and managing that money therefore becomes the feminine. In *The New Price is Right*, money is replaced by knowledge: masculine money by feminine knowledge. The show symbolically liberates women from their economic constraints and in so doing liberates them from their husbands' economic power (one of the many ways patriarchy has constructed and subordinated the feminine).

There is one other difference that needs addressing and this is the one between work and leisure. Shopping as part of domestic labour has a quite different meaning to shopping as part of leisure. Shopping for the family confines a woman to her role as housewife and mother; shopping for fun, however, is a liberation from that role. Rachel Bowlby points out that the department store was the first place to which a woman could go in public, unaccompanied, and be both safe and respectable. Shopping malls today meet similar needs (Fiske, forthcoming).[4] So, in women's culture, shopping for oneself has quite a different meaning to shopping for the home: the one is leisure, liberating and recreational, the other is labour, confining and subordinating. Shopping, in all quiz shows, is leisure and fun, not labour. Women (or men) shopping for fun enter quite different social relations with the commodity system to when they shop from necessity. These relations are much less subordinating; in fact they contain significant elements of empowerment.

The New Price is Right treats the skills of consumption in a way that removes them from the sphere of subjugated, silenced domestic labour and repositions them in the sphere of liberated, acclaimed public leisure and fun. This inversion is carnivalesque in that it relies upon the pleasures for the subordinate in resisting or evading the forces that subordinate them in a moment of carnival. This inversion and evasion draws attention to the apparatuses of economic and gender subordination, for moments of liberation, however brief, by definition derive their pleasure from their opposition to the forces of oppression. Carnival necessarily contains subversive elements which expose the social norms for what they are: arbitrary and therefore ultimately changeable; rather than as they normally appear: natural, universal laws.

The excessive quality of carnival performs a similar function. By exceeding the norms of society it exposes both their arbitrariness and their function as social discipline. 'Excess' is behaviour, pleasure or meaning that is out of control; 'the norm' is the conceptual police-man, an agent of social discipline working in the socio-political interests of those with the power to define and establish it. It is significant how much of women's culture is characterised (by patriarchy) as 'excessive'.

Women as Family Managers

Closely allied to the discourse of consumption is that of the family. The woman as consumer and the woman as family nurturer are overlapping roles. As its name suggests, *Family Feud* situates the woman firmly within the family. The game is played between two families of four and consists of guessing which were the most common answers given to a question by a random sample of a hundred people. The winner is the person (or family) who best understands or empathises with what other people are thinking. It is a democratic form of knowledge in that it depends upon majority belief rather than factual truth; it is inclusive rather than exclusive, for it does not distinguish clearly between those who possess it and those who do not; and its distribution throughout society lies outside the control of those with social power.[5] This is a bottom-up knowledge, not a top-down one. It is also an 'interior', domestic form of knowledge and is thus a particularly feminine one. If the knowledge used in *The New Price is Right* is that developed by women to manage the economic resources of the family, the knowledge used in *Family Feud* has been developed to manage the family's emotional resources. It is knowledge of people, and how they are thinking and feeling that enables women to manage and smooth relationships within the family.

Though the families are of both sexes, females predominate, and the role of leader or spokesperson is almost invariably a woman. Adult men are comparatively uncommon contestants, though boys and younger men appear fairly frequently within the families. Women's leadership roles, normally confined to the domestic sphere, here become public: they speak for their families in a way that has traditionally been the role of the male. *Family Feud* may appear to offer fewer and more muted resistive pleasures than *The New Price is Right*, fewer opportunities to escape the repressive discipline of patriarchy, but the contradictions are still there within it.

Women and Romance

Perfect Match, however, is a different matter entirely. It has arguably the most progressive gender politics of all quiz or game shows, and deserves its success as the ratings hit of the mid 1980s on Australian television.

The game consists of a 'wooer' of either sex choosing a date from three members of the opposite sex. Each has to answer the same three questions asked by the wooer, who can hear, but not see, the dates. The studio audience and, of course, the viewer, can both see and hear. The date chosen by such 'human knowledge' is then compared to the wooer's 'perfect match' who is selected 'scientifically' by a computer. If the human knowledge and scientific knowledge coincide, that is if the wooer chooses his or her scientifically 'perfect' match, the couple win extra prizes. But their main prize is always a date, usually on a short luxurious holiday. The central segment of the show consists of a previously matched couple returning to tell of their experiences on their date, both 'live' together in the studio, and separately on tape as they were each interviewed immediately afterwards.

The progressiveness of this show lies in a number of features which tend to minimise the differences between male and female sexuality. These differences have been established during the development of patriarchal capitalism and the nuclear family which it produced in order to naturalise patriarchal power (see below).

The structure of each show equalises the genders, for each show has two games, in one of which a woman chooses from three men and in the other, the sexes are reversed. The responsibility for initiating the relationship, the open control of the process of romantic choice and the more passive role of being selected are explicitly shared equally between the genders.

More importantly, perhaps, feminine sexuality is freed from the responsibility and respectability of marriage. Women, like men, are expected to find pleasure in their sexuality and no longer have to justify this pleasure as cementing a marital relationship, or at least a relationship in which marriage is the object. Women can 'rage' and find pleasure on their dates and in their social life in a way that has been traditionally defined as exclusively part of masculine sexuality. Women are free to enjoy it in a way that is almost never shown unjudgmentally elsewhere on television. (In TV dramas, women enjoying their own sexuality for the pleasure and control it can offer them are generally punished in the narrative.)

Of course, this 'liberation' from the discipline of patriarchal definitions of sexual differences is never complete, and, indeed, the show would not be popular if it were so. The traditional forms of patriarchal control are there to remind us what is being evaded: the title sequence has all the trimmings of traditional romance — soft focus, hearts, pinks and blues, romantic music — but they are so exaggerated as to parody traditional romantic values. Parody is a subversive form, for it exposes and mocks the essential features of its object. Here its object is the patriarchal conventions of the romance narrative. The growth of the romance genre throughout the nineteenth century paralleled the growth of the nuclear patriarchal family and the redefinition of feminine sexuality to fit within it, so the parody of that which is to be escaped from is a powerful part of the progressive gender politics of the show.

This release from patriarchal discipline can also be seen in the central segment when a returned couple tell of their experiences on their date. Much of the appeal of this segment lies in those couples whose dates were 'failures', whose matches were far from perfect. The characteristics of each that annoyed or alienated the other are openly discussed and laughed at, and in particular, the women tend to comment freely and enjoyably about the men's shortcomings. What is important in this is that the women show no guilt at the 'failure' of the date. They are freed from the feminine responsibility to manage the emotional life of the couple (or family). Such guilt, of course, is the internalisation of patriarchal discipline, and therefore is not considered an appropriate masculine feeling at the 'breakdown' of a relationship.

Women's Culture Within Patriarchy

I have concentrated in this chapter on the meanings that quiz shows might have for their women fans, and attempted to account to some extent for their popularity with women by means other than the 'cultural dope' theory.[6] Women are not cultural dopes. They are not complicit in, nor do they find pleasure in, their subordination under patriarchy. Of course, women's responses to this subordination may range from the oppositional to the (fairly) comfortably accommodating. In this chapter I have made oppositional readings of quiz shows which can be made by any among the subordinate against the thrust of dominant ideology and social power. It is important to stress that these are the tactics of those among the subordinate who choose not to oppose the repressive system head on but make guerilla raids upon it and seek out its weak points, the places where it can be turned against itself. Subordinated groups have to make do with what they have, and what they have is what the dominant system provides. The art of everyday culture is the art of making do, an art at which women excel through many generations of oppression, and from whom other subordinated groups have much to learn.

The study of the popular culture of subordinated groups (and *all* popular culture is the culture of the subordinate, even if it may use the cultural commodities of the dominant as its raw material) should direct itself to the tactics of 'making do'. Of course quiz shows are not radical texts. They do not attack or subvert patriarchal commodity capitalism with revolutionary zeal. Indeed, like all cultural commodities, they bear the ideology of the system that promotes and distributes them. But mass culture is not popular culture: popular culture is made at the interface between the cultural commodity system of mass culture and the practices of everyday life.

The generic conventions of quiz shows intextuate the values of patriarchal capitalism: quiz shows and the dominant definition of femininity (and hence of masculinity) are all the products of the same society. The urbanisation and industrialisation required by capitalism set up new social relations that developed steadily throughout the nineteenth century. Urbanisation fractured traditional communities and produced the need for the nuclear family; industrialisation set up new forms of difference between work and leisure (the concepts are quite differently related in rural economies) and between the domestic and the public; capitalism set up new relationships between production and consumption, earning and spending. And all differences were mapped onto equally new constructions of gender difference. So the masculine was associated with the public, work, production, and earning; the feminine acquired an opposite association with the domestic or private, leisure, consumption and spending. Domestic work was not recognised as labour because it was lost among these newly-acquired associations with femininity.

The role of women within this evolving social system became more and more that of housewife and mother within the nuclear family. The romance developed as a genre to train women for marriage, to propagate the idea that women's fulfilment was to be found in the slot prepared for them by patriarchal capitalism. So femininity was cast as romantic, sensitive, weak, and finally complete only when immersed in the needs of others, particularly those of husband and children; that is, the family. This feminine, domesticated sensitivity, centred around others, created for women the role of the family's emotional manager to parallel her role as manager of its material resources. So it is not surprising that patriarchal capitalism should address women through quiz shows as romantic, as consumers and as family managers, for that is precisely the way it has constructed femininity over the two centuries of its existence. But it is equally predictable that women have developed ways of responding to this persistent address which do not acknowledge its truth.

If quiz shows are popular with women (and they are), they are so only because they bear not only the ideological voices of the dominant, but also the opportunity to resist, evade or negotiate with these voices. Indeed, they would not be popular if they did not contain both opposing forces. Reading relations reproduce social relations. As women's lives under a patriarchal social order involve a constant variety of tactics with which to cope with the constant forces of subordination, so women's textual culture must contain the same patriarchal forces against which women's readings and textual pleasures are created. Women's texts that ignore patriarchy or that show feminine values in total control over the masculine, or existing on their own apart from the masculine, cannot be popular in a patriarchal society because they lack the lines of relevance to most women's material and social positions.

My account of quiz shows has not centred on their hegemonic thrust, for that does not account for their role in women's culture: it accounts only for their ability to serve men and the capitalist economy. Of course the shows carry the implicit definitions of femininity that oppress women: such definitions must be there in order to be evaded or resisted. In the standard host and hostess pair, for example, the traditional gender stereotypes are rigorously enforced. The male is in control of the show; he asks the questions and controls the flow of knowledge. The female is the domestic, interpersonal manager who introduces the contestants, displays fashion and portrays total happiness with her subordination. But she also fits the 'showgirl' image, albeit a girl-next-door inflection of it. She portrays the traditional 'woman on stage for display', and as such is in contrast with the everyday women contestants who compete, perform and frequently win. In *Sale of the Century*, the contrast between the women contestants competing successfully on equal terms with men, and the vapid, glamorous hostess, is the contrast between the real and the plastic, between the everyday woman and an image that embodies the only femininity that men can control. It is this conflict between two meanings of femininity that generates the pleasure and that opens up gaps in patriarchal hegemony for resistant feminine readings. So, too, in *Perfect Match* there is a contrast between the way it restricts the sort of women who appear on the show to those that fit the dominant stereotype (white, young, employed, conventionally attractive, heterosexual) and their behaviour on the show which breaks free from the oppression within that stereotype. *The New Price is Right* expresses the contradictions between consumption as a sign of women's subordination and as a means of women's creativity and power.

The quiz genre as a whole works with two different types of knowledge that are mapped into gender differences.[7] There is a 'factual' knowledge, which can be gauged as right or wrong against external, public criteria. This is essentially masculine, public knowledge. *Mastermind* (with its masculine title) and *Sale of the Century* employ this type of knowledge.

The other type is an experiential, 'intuitive' knowledge, a knowledge of people, of how they are feeling and thinking. This is the knowledge of *Family Feud* and *Perfect Match*. It is a feminine knowledge. In *Perfect Match* the 'masculine' knowledge of the computer is often in direct contradiction with the 'feminine' knowledge of the contestant and viewer, yet it is not accorded any privilege or power; the contradictions are open. The genre as a whole shows women coping equally well with both types of knowledge, able to move successfully across this arbitrary boundary between the masculine and the feminine.

The popular appeal of quiz shows for women lies in the starkness of the contradictions they embody. On the one hand they embody most nakedly the discourses that subordinate women — those of consumerism, of romance, of the family — but on the other they offer great opportunities for these discourses to be subverted, inverted and turned back on themselves. The act of making do is the act of making the discourses of subordination into ones of empowerment for the subordinate.

10

Male-Gazing: Australian Rules Football, Gender and Television

Beverley Poynton and John Hartley

Professional Australian Rules football is a man's game. Men play, coach, promote, officiate, ministrate, commentate and follow the footy. It seems only natural, therefore, that the transformation of football into television would produce an audience for the game that is similarly gendered.

Although I* am not going to qualify this statement statistically, the fact is that some women — and not just the mums, wives and girlfriends — do attend matches and do watch football on television, and I am one of them. So what interests me is the systematic exclusion of this fact from the discourse of football.

The television coverage of football has been called a male soap-opera, but compared with soapies themselves it sells a different kind of froth. This is a full-bodied brew, with lashings of sweat, the odd trickle of blood and perhaps a dash of defeated tears. It is the kind of viewing that a man could work up a thirst with, and what could be a more compatible programming accompaniment than the beer advertisements that cheer the time between a goal scored and the recommencement of the game at the centre ball-up? The mannish image is a cliché, but it is a marketable cliché, one that serves to

---

* The first person pronoun in this paper should be taken to refer to Beverley Poynton.

illustrate the alliance between sport, media, capital and a specifically Australian representation of masculinity.

This alliance began in earnest with the inception of televised Australian Rules, just one year after the media coverage of the 1956 Melbourne Olympiad had demonstrated the spectacular potential of televised sports. The electronic appropriation of the game produced changes that were initially cosmetic: certain passages of play were modified to accentuate motion and to deliver a more frenetically-paced set of images for the small screen. But since those early days the Australian media industry, within the overall context of economic production, has precipitated the restructuring, refinement and commoditisation of the game itself.

Some twenty years after the first experimental telecast of Australian Rules, the conservative Victorian Football League (VFL) — the governing body of the professional game — has yielded to the pressure of an intense campaign to create a national league. This has made sponsorship a far more rewarding proposition, and one upshot has been the unprecedented move to a fully-sponsored competition of summer-season night games, broadcast live. For the purists there is something irreverent, almost sacrilegious, about footy in summer. But although it is not the sort of weather in which to play a hard game, sponsors have endorsed the belief that summer provides the ideal beer-drinking conditions for the evening armchair spectator.

Unlike football, television is not played out within fixed boundaries. Since footy hit the big time to become a professional spectator sport, that quaint motif of regional rivalry which once characterised the game and endeared it to a hard core of suburban barrackers has subsided into nostalgia. The significance of the game as a localised event has been superseded by footy as television entertainment because the scope of a television audience can be defined as national, which is clearly more than any match, however grand, however final, can claim. As an industry largely motivated by profit and audience maximisation, television offers conditions tailor-made for the promotion and popularisation of the game and for an expanding revenue from associated advertising. In this whole new ball-game, regional attendance just does not rate.

Equally non-rating is the individual player's allegiance to the club to which he was assigned as a boy and youth. It is a competitive business, becoming a League player, but it does pay off. The professionalism demanded by League football means that a player must be determined, committed, upwardly mobile and aim high to score the money and prestige; but the ultimate measure of success for the professional player is to become a national media personality, or even an international media star, if Mark 'Jacko' Jackson's brief foray into American network television can be taken as a precedent.[1]

In the business of football, star players make great assets. Not only are they valuable for their contribution to the team, they also represent an investment to be cleared and acquired by clubs when the time is opportune and the price is right. Player trading was a long-standing practice in footy history, but now it is part of the glossy revolution in the packaging and marketing of the game.

The expansion of the *Victorian* Football League to fourteen clubs, including specially selected State teams from New South Wales, Queensland and Western Australia, has facilitated the identification of Australian Rules as *the* national football code, despite the strong support for Rugby (Union and League) and soccer in various parts of the country. With the idea of an indigenous, nationally-celebrated brand of football comes the potential for international promotion and export.

The nationalisation of the VFL (in this instance, an initiative of the private sector to maximise available resources) has coincided with one of the most energetic periods of nation-formation in Australia since Federation, leading up to the officially-promoted 1988 Bicentennial celebrations. The cultivation of an idea of 'nation', of a 'national identity', of myths and symbols that are supposed, for Australian people, to be comforting, cohesive and readily identifiable, has become an ideological imperative for both government and corporate enterprise, who associate themselves with selected, evocative Australian images in the media, especially in television commercials and continuity.

This merger of corporate culture with national imagery has paid dividends to all concerned. The relationship between government, corporations and the Australian nation is rendered ideologically as immutable and inviolate, but the strategy conceals the necessity for government to refine and promote a national identity which will not only win acceptance within the expanding arena of international capitalism, but also secure popular approval at home. Political and economic intentions, and inequalities in the social order, are discreetly elided so that the representational credibility of a caring state and a corporate conscience can be sustained.

Sport holds a privileged status in Australian culture and Australians are reputed to take pride in being a nation of good sports.

But it is only the youthful sporting elite who make it to the television screen, so the Australian obsession with sports includes the rather less strenuous exercise of sitting back and watching. The domestic armchair becomes the most important sporting venue when the game is changed from doing to looking. But the transformation from body-contact to eye-contact also changes the rules. The game is brought to the spectator, and the television set is the turnstile. The masses of fans who pour through that electronic gate are, however, participating in more than sport. Capital investment turns sporting culture into a market, and thus sport into a commodity. The armchair enthusiasts who turn on the television are giving the nod to the intervention of capital, which transforms the whole game, literally calling the shots.

The Australian media's representation of sport is a dynamic constituent in the construction of the Australian nation, inter-relating capitalist production, politics and ideology through techniques of visual display and commentary. Sport expounds values that are conventionally prescibed in the rhetoric of war, industry, nationalism and ultimately masculinity — values such as competitiveness, discipline, strength, aggression, valour, implacable optimism, mateship, disrespect for constraining authority and an uncompromising determination to win (though not necessarily at all costs).

The apogee of the televised sporting event is the Olympiad. A fullblown spectacle telecast live, worldwide, the Olympic Games provides a showcase for space-age technology and the ideological aggrandisement of sport. Television coverage of the Games valorises the notion of sport as a universalising force, that can dissolve national boundaries and secular and religious ideologies with the reverential ignition of the Olympic flame and a transcendental flick of the television switch.

The Australian equivalent of this spectacle would be the VFL Grand Final. The Grand Final marks the annual climax of the League competition and the culmination of yet another season of footy. But it also represents a celebration of Australian cultural identity, staged as a ritual event in grandiose style. The VFL Grand Final as a televised sporting event is sent by satellite, live around the world, but its significance is scaled to appeal to a national rather than an international audience.

So what is the specifically Australian appeal of Australian Rules football, and in what manner is the Grand Final embellished to make it not simply a game of footy but a spectacularly Australian entertainment event?

It is two hundred years since Captain Arthur Phillip planted the British flag into the virgin earth of this ocean-locked continent and ceremoniously announced its secondment into imperial service as a site for penal settlement. The celebratory carnival which has been programmed to commemorate the Bicentennial year, and the other 199 years of white Australian history (at least in New South Wales), provides a timely stage for the consideration of Australia's cultural origins and contemporary representations of identity.

The nature of the land, of sacred significance to Aboriginal cultural experience, found no register within the European consciousness. The colonial attitude to the land was one of confrontation and hostility. You claim ownership but you have to work to cultivate, civilise and remake the land before it may become economically productive, and only then may it be rendered meaningful. From the meanings generated by this exploitation of the land there emerged two opposing themes which implanted in an ideological as well as an economic way the sapling colonial society into its new environment. These were the themes of the city and the outback, of urban existence *versus* 'going bush'.

Vestiges of these divisions still remain in the contemporary Australian consciousness, albeit divested of the particularised and partisan social identifications which they once encouraged. The urban centres and the outback made the first deep impressions on the *tabula rasa* of Australian social history (a *tabula* coloured white of course), but it was the characters in this setting, and the roles they played in the begetting of a nation, which generated the myths deemed necessary for national unity.

From colonisation to the constitution of the Commonwealth at the turn of the century and beyond, white Australian society could claim one outstanding feature — the disproportionate number of men in the population (Western Australia, for example, did not achieve gender balance until 1947). White Australian society was, at this seminal time in its history, an overwhelmingly male affair. The characters who charged the imagination of a nation arose from the crowd, but the crowd was mostly men. From that brutal beginning there emerged the myths of a manliness which became the focus of public adoration and worship. The myths idealised a masculinity which was aroused from general social intercourse and individual intimacy between males.[2]

Masculine relations were essentialised into a code of ethics which found its exemplar in the phenomenon of mateship — a reverence for fraternity rather than paternity and the reification of the concept of the singular male friend. Particular attributes of manliness found their ideal and their embodiment in the Aussie hero whose imposing figure, set against an indifferent landscape, looked good, attracting the admiring gaze of the crowd as an object of specular pleasure.

And so it happened that sentiments of national identity and motifs of masculinity were readily available for expression in the Australian game of football. The game sets up a relationship between the male body as an object of visual pleasure, and a masculine viewing subject (extending from individual to crowd to nation), but it also works to conceal the homo-erotic implications of this relation by coding the spectacle into ways of looking which both sanction and disavow any homo-erotic content.

This specular dynamic positions women very firmly on the outer, but then a distanced point of view is often the best way to observe the action. So how do interested women regard football?

Theoretical pursuits aside, my involvement with Australian Rules was established in the conventional manner. If you are born into a family of footy followers and you live in the same area for any length of time, the odds are that you will barrack for a team and you will go to watch them play and then you will watch the television coverage. In its parochial form, before it became a national spectacle, a footy team could inspire a sense of community (and of its continuity). There was a kind of pedagogical function associated with football. Australian children learnt to identify with their immediate social and geographic environment, their territory, through their footy team. You wanted your team to win the premiership and your gender seemed inconsequential, although it never occurred to me that I might actually want to play the game. The fact that my gender made me ineligible to play was never questioned.

Now, as a parent, I go to watch my sons play in the junior division and my support for the local junior club involves canteen duties (which generate the bread and butter finances for junior football) and participation in the committee. This is a mere repetition of the traditional division between women's work and boys' play.

But in between the footy experiences of childhood and parenthood I discovered the plenitude of football's representational counterpart — television football. When you look at it closely, television footy does not resemble the real game at all. The television

game is played with an assortment of images which are convention-
alised and thus predictable. These ingredients of television footy
could be itemised as follows:

> program title sequence
> men in action
> talking heads (all men)
> statistical readouts
> miscellaneous shots (the crowd, individuals)
> embellishments (cheer-squads, costumed mascots, pre-game and half-
> time displays)

All this imagery is overlaid with a commanding commentary, the
diegetic roar of the crowd and a robust passage of music to signal,
like a siren, the program's outer limits.

For the moment let us leave aside the recipe that turns footy into
the intriguing fictions that could qualify it as soap opera for men to
imbibe and an interesting text for women to digest. What attracted
my interest were the images of male bodies. Here were barely clad,
eyeable Aussie male bodies in top anatomical nick. The cameras
follow their rough and tumble disport with a relentless precision, in
wide-angle, close-up and slow-motion replay. With the commentary
turned down and with some music the imagery may be released from
its imposed fixity of meaning and the performance enjoyed as
choreographed spectacle: lyrical, flagrantly masculine, and erotic.

The visual effect was fascinating, but I suspected there was something slightly perverse about this way of watching. Football is a
man's show, right? Audience-land is populated with six-pack-toting,
militantly heterosexual men, who'd deck you for implying they were
perving when they gazed on other men's bodies.

I don't think television footy is designed for the gratification of
voyeuristic women. Neither do I suspect any covert conspiracy to
titillate homo-erotic desires. On the contrary it seems to me that the
carnal connotations of the *men in action* imagery are vigorously and
persistently effaced by the processes of the text. Man may be reluctant to gaze at his exhibitionist like, but all the same in television
footy male bodies are objectified in the display of their physical
prowess. The relation of looking and being looked at — a relation in
which conventionally the feminine body is rendered as the object of
specularity — is tenuously reversed, although men still retain their
subjective dominance as spectators or audience.

The specular exchange from objectified male bodies to masculine
viewing subject excludes women in a way that is a reminder of the

original Grecian Olympics, where women were forbidden as spectators because the male athletes competed in the nude. In patriarchal
societies, carnivals of masculine exhibitionism bypass the reluctance
of the male gaze by denying feminine spectatorship, although the
reluctance may be that of history — the ancient Greeks made a civic
virtue out of pederasty, but that is all the more reason to exclude
women from public displays, presumably. The Greeks were the
classic pragmatists, elevating the relation of masculine body/mascu-
line gaze to an ideal — a homage to purity of form. By supplanting
difference with an aesthetics of purity, they showed no reluctance in
their homo-erotic gaze.

Aussie footy cannot assume the same gendered exclusivity. In
contemporary Australian society, women are permitted to watch.
Feminine infiltration into relations of looking, however, places
demands upon the text. The visual element has the potential to be
read erotically. For a male audience voyeuristic contemplation implies homo-eroticism. The suggestion that the pursuit of pleasure in
footy is associated with a subliminal stimulation of homo-erotic
desires is outrageously unacceptable in a society long conditioned to
acknowledge heterosexuality as the standard. Any wayward tendencies on the part of the visual element therefore require a certain
vigilance from other components of the text. It is sound and, specifically, commentary that undertakes the regulation of visual excess.
The commentary produces a verbal articulation of the visual flow. It
incorporates description of form, narration of the action and personal comment, all of which anchors the text to the genre and to the
discourse of sport.

Pity the footballer whose public image strays from his position
and function in the team and on the field, to be singled out by the
media as a showpiece of sex-object speculation. Sydney Swans'
talented full forward Warwick Capper, of the short, tight shorts,
flowing blond locks and pout is a prime example of the media's un-
ease in dealing with masculine sex-objectification. Capper had the
dubious privilege of being the object of media promotion by his
club's advertising agency, not for his obvious, match-winning skills,
but for his good looks, his sex appeal.

The Sydney-based agency underestimated the football public's
pious regard for their sport. Sydneysiders are new to the game. Their
attention-seeking attempts to compensate for a lack of tradition
have been vilified by the moralistic conservatism of the aptly-named
Victorians. For Capper, the outcome is metaphorical emasculation,

particularly by the press who relish the opportunity to poke fun at his publicity-prone physical assets. Sex and sport just do not mix, except in jest. The good commentator practices abstinence from the subject when calling the action.

State of the art in calling the action is ABC Channel 2's *The Winners*; a slick, pacy production, professionally presented and institutionalised within national television broadcasting. The six o'clock scheduling every Sunday evening between March and September is a ritual as reliable as the 2 pm centre bounce-down the previous afternoon, and followers of *The Winners* attend to the program as conscientiously as supporters attend the Saturday match — but in far greater numbers. While the matches are regional, *The Winners* is a national event with a national audience, winning for the ABC a good performance in the ratings game.[3]

Given the premise that actuality is transformed by the intervention of television, *The Winners* is thus not about footy but about its representation. The actuality that is recorded by the cameras is organised by a process of selection (the edited replay of two matches, then a further selection of highlights) and then integrated into a mode of studio presentation, and the combination produces the format of the program. The sequential elements of this format are as follows:

Titles, visual and aural (musical) denotation of the program;
talking head of anchorman (Drew Morphet);
first replay with voice-over commentary;
table of progressive scoring in the match (V/O Morphet);
talking head of anchorman;
second replay with V/O commentary;
table of progressive scoring in match (V/O Morphet);
talking head of anchorman;
interview — vox pop in talking head mode;
talking head of anchorman;
table of the league ladder (V/O Morphet);
table of leading goal-kickers (V/O Morphet);
highlights from the two featured matches and others;
talking head of anchorman;
best 'mark of the day' with slow motion replay;
best 'play of the day';
talking head of anchorman;
table of next week's fixtures (V/O Morphet);
talking head of anchorman;
best 'goal of the day' with slow-motion replay;

slow motion segment ending in a freeze-frame overlaid with closing titles (credits) and theme music.

The game of football is subject to an institutionalised code. Umpires are authorised to conduct the play, but they also have the power to book transgressing players, who must then face a VFL tribunal and possibly suspension. Similarly, the formation of the crowd is subject to codes. Displays of particular colour combinations signify club supporters who view the match from the privileged position of the members' stand or from the outer, but always from outside the boundary. This basic demarcation is policed for transgressions.

The action of the game itself, though coded, is continuous and unpredictable. But in *The Winners*, football is transformed into discrete and formalised, that is predictable, representation. Televisual codes conventionalise the program, legitimising it as a genre of television (sport). However, this is not to say that the viewer is incapable of resisting the dominant 'legitimate' reading. The program hovers game-like on the boundary between the conventional codes of television sport (display, analysis, personal comment and professional impartiality) and other representations (othernesses?) which are produced by specular relations between viewers and football as spectacle.

The conventional codes utilised in the representation of sport are fundamentally verbal. The working history of these codes includes the word-media of press and radio. However, the visual and aural sequence which marks the introduction of *The Winners* is literally speechless. This is a characteristic of nearly all introductions to television programs regardless of content or genre. In its juxtaposition of titles, theme-music and a montage of images, *The Winners* establishes a signifying cue which is recognisable to the viewer, thus particularising the flow of televisual broadcasting and fulfilling the medium's prerequisite for program identity.

What identity for the program is encapsulated in the opening title sequence?

It is introduced with a musical fanfare. The cultural tradition of the fanfare, still popularly acknowledged, is that of signifier for the imminent public appearance of an exalted figure or event. In this television text, the fanfare heralds the construction of a relation between the viewer and 'what we are about to receive' — the spectacle. The image which accompanies the fanfare is a revolving aerial shot of the MCG (Melbourne Cricket Ground), a circular island of green surrounded by grandstands packed with spectators (the capacity crowd suggests that this is the Grand Final). The titles provide the linguistic component of the proclamation:

'*The ABC presents — The Winners*'

This springs up from the centre of the field, anticipating the centre-bounce which signals the commencement of the game. The camera's circular motion complements the aerial image of the arena, producing a visual articulation which suggests the motif of the ball (repeated in the footy shaped logo behind the anchorman). The aerial point of view privileges the position of the television spectator as against those represented below, but the intrusion of the title on the screen also connotes the omniscience of television's institutional position and point of view — all-seeing, all-knowing and impartial — decidedly above the popular weakness for one-eyed views and one-sided positions.

The introduction continues with a series of Quantel images over a single shot which moves upwards from ground level, along the tiers of spectators, to follow a multitude of ascending balloons (semiotically registering both the motif of the ball and the rising excitement) and ending with the balloons floating against an azure field of sky.

The spatial articulation of the sequence from spectators to the release of balloons, to balloons abstracted, elides the specificity of the images to construct a transcendental mythic meaning — VFL Grand Final footy, with its mass display of devotion, as a spiritual experience, inspiring higher idealistic notions in which skill, change, struggles, goals and the altruistic victory of the game are universalised, and footy becomes a metaphor for life.

The Quantel shots produce a screen-within-a-screen effect, superimposing on the mythic representation of the long take underneath a representation of football that is structured by discrete, grounded images, organised as narrative:

A team running onto the field;
a mark;
an airborne football;
the ball gliding through the goalposts;
players leaping;
another mark;
a confrontation;
the winner's cup held aloft.

The temporal succession of shots is synchronised to the beat of the theme music — a bold, brassy tune in traditional marching rhythm. The militaristic echoes of the music accentuate the narrative theme of battle and victory, but the conditions for subjective pleasure are reproduced in the music's foot-stamping rhythm which orchestrates the masculine action into a repetitively performed choreographic routine. Even differences in musical pitch have a corresponding visual signification — marks are scored in the higher pitch.

In the introduction to *The Winners* there are no spoken words to anchor the meaning. The viewer enters into a special relation with privileged images (they have been selected, combined and scored), and this relation produces a complex of representations — footy as spectacle, as myth, as epic narrative (dramatically condensed) and as physical performance.

Connotations of an objectified and aestheticised masculinity (as myth, narrative and bodily display) are also evident in the closing credits. But there are differences. There is no narrative structure in the closing credits, although the images are cued in Morphet's closing remarks — he says, typically, 'And in the concluding segment watch out for . . .'. Also the use of slow-motion, close-up and freeze-frame intensifies the representation of masculinity as bodily display. When the display features male bodies in close contact, as it often does in the conclusion, the homo-erotic productivity and pleasure of the image is foregrounded.

The titles and credits function as program boundaries, and their marginal status permits this covert representation — and covert pleasure. It is from within these boundaries that the legitimising codes which structure television football as the representation of sport are played out.

Australian Rules footy is represented as the national sport and the locus of essentialised Australian masculinity. One ideological motivation for advancing the concept of the all-Australian nation has been the recognition of Australia's multi-cultural origins and of the contribution made by ethnic communities, not least to footy. The current ethnic mix of players and fans of Aussie Rules includes no Asian players, but a relatively strong contingent with southern European origins (Italian, Greek, Slav), despite the lure of soccer, and — most significantly — a consistently strong representation of Aborigines. Some of the mightiest players the game has produced have been Aboriginal: Graham 'Polly' Farmer, Sid Jackson, Ted 'Square' Kilmurray, Barry Cable, Maurice Rioli, the Krakouer brothers, Stephen Michael and so on.

Racial origins are underplayed in the represention of the game, but as a sporting and social activity, footy has proved remarkably accessible to blacks throughout the country and particularly in those areas, like the north-west of WA, with large Aboriginal populations. The WAFL (West Australian Football League) has maintained a system of recruitment whereby the clubs are allocated specific regions in which they can scout for talent. For young Aboriginal men the opportunity to play League football promises not only distinction and renown among their own people but also an otherwise rarely attainable status in white society.

The strength of play and support and the desire to maintain an Aboriginal cultural identity is gradually gaining ground. If the remote Aboriginal communities can forge competitive footy teams, urban followers may see the incursion of all-Aboriginal footy into the mainstream of the game. Maurice Rioli, former VFL player (Richmond), WAFL champion (South Fremantle) and runner-up Brownlow-medallist, is keen to pursue the potential benefits from this kind of promotion for fellow-Aborigines. Rioli is a rover no longer, but in his new position as the Department of Sport and Recreation's first sports consultant for Aborigines, he has demonstrated his abilities in another direction by hosting a Tiwi and Bardi Aboriginal football tour. The Tiwi and Bardi teams played their first exhibition match as a preliminary to a League fixture.[4]

Barefoot or booted, Aboriginal players command physical presence in television culture which they can use to promote their culture and history. Aborigines can lay claim to a truly indigenous status and their show of strength in Australian Rules is a powerful emblem of the game's indigenous character and of the significance of Aboriginal involvement with footy in the development of a popular Australian mythos.

White players tend not to be as altruistic. Football guarantees their all-Australian masculinity, but you've got to be an individual man to extend your footy-affiliated body into activities of promotion and profit unrelated to the game. Capper's individuality is packaged *à la* pop star to register adolescent sexual appeal. Because he is not identified as a man's man, Capper's masculinity is trivialised, neutered by the self-conscious wit of those committed to the masculine sensibilities of an imagined male audience. (That he might be seen as a *woman's* man is ignored by the footy commentators; such possibilities are left in the defter and less squeamish hands of the popular women's magazines.)

Mark 'Jacko' Jackson's masculine individuality, on the other hand, gets good press. The locus of attention in Jacko's imposingly big and ugly form is his mouth. It is a vulgar, toothless cavity but it displays high energy mobility when engaged in vocal antics, or a grimace for the cameras or the crowd. Jacko is a most effective mouthpiece for aggressive product promotion. His boisterous larrikin individuality is commoditised in the compelling monosyllabic utterance that has made him famous in America: 'Oi!' Not even a word, let alone a catch-phrase, 'Oi!' has infiltrated American popular culture successfully enough to make Jacko a millionaire, and Energizer a leading brand of battery.

Jacko's 'Oi!', Capper's bum, Aboriginal feet; the simulacra of masculinity in electronic culture. But they are not just different members of the same male body. They represent different, incommensurable maledoms; a contesting play of identifications on the field of masculinity. Just as there is a power struggle on the footy field between competing teams, one of which always *wins*, so there are contending masculinities, not reducible to a single essentialised 'maleness', and here too it is not a matter of free choice but of winners and losers. Capper's masculinity is leered and laughed at — feminised by the television mediators. All-Aboriginal footy does not appear to be a matter of masculinity to observers on the outer so much as a matter of race — more to do with the politics of Aboriginal advancement than with the gender of the players.

For the paying customers of popular culture, Jacko's endearingly shouted 'Oi!' marks him as champion. While certainly not the 'fairest and best', Jacko's noisy, energetic masculinity is proving to be a real crowd-pleaser. His uncompromising ugliness is unambiguously male, but for the paying customers it is offered as a generic label, not as one brand name among a shelf-full of different and competing identifications.

11

Class, Gender and the Female Viewer: Women's Responses to *Dynasty*

Andrea L. Press

Theoretical Context: Hegemonic Theory in Cultural Context

Throughout its history, television programming in the US has presented us with a view of our society which sometimes tones down, but more often ignores outright, the very real class differences which separate us. Television has in many respects misrepresented women's changing historical relationship to work and family overall. In this chapter, I discuss how women of different social classes respond to, talk about and use television images, particularly the images of specific television characters in the prime-time soap opera *Dynasty*.

Critical media analysts have often used what they call the theory of hegemony to explain the content and influence of the mass media in complex societies. According to hegemonic theory, the mass media play an ideological role in society, reinforcing and encouraging general world-views and specific beliefs which help secure the position of those groups already in power. Some powerful analyses have illustrated the hegemonic content of media products, including television's news and entertainment programming.

Studies of media reception, however, particularly those which illustrate the possible operation of hegemonic processes in reception, have been slower to develop. Two competing traditions have characterised the developing study of audience reception. One, little affected by broader cultural considerations, employs an essentially experimental model, favouring the study of audience response to discrete instances of media exposure. My study is situated in the second tradition, which advocates a more culturally contextual method for the study of media reception. This tradition has been heavily influenced by the cultural theory in both sociology and cultural studies. The school of cultural sociology and the interdisciplinary tradition of cultural studies assert that the ideological facets of media influence can be best understood when studied within the context of the broader set of beliefs and traditions which characterise the particular audience studied.

I set out to study American working-class and middle-class women's interpretations of television entertainment. Because my study was motivated by the sorts of critical questions which sociologists and feminist researchers have asked before, I expected to find differences between the social classes of women in the American context, adding up to a different relationship to television reality and television characters for working-class and middle-class women — evidence, in effect, that the hegemonic process takes different forms in different social groups. In the American context it was not clear that these differences would indicate more critical consciousness and sentiment among working-class women. I expected the opposite, in particular because of the muted history of resistance among the American working-class vis-a-vis cultural matters in particular. My suspicion was that in the American situation the mass media were in fact powerful instruments of accommodation and domestication, perhaps particularly for members of the working classes.

Methodology

Deciding upon a working definition of social class in order to guide my choice of informants was more problematic. The class issue, particularly when applied to women's class membership, is not a simple one. Even when sex is not considered, class divisions in our country are far from clear. Over the past two decades, there has been a tremendous amount of debate in the sociological literature over what are the operant class divisions in the United States at present. From a strictly Marxist point of view, classes are defined in terms of the positions of different occupational groups vis-a-vis the mode of production. If a group produces surplus value, it is defined as working-class; if it does not, it is not working-class. A Weberian approach to class analysis focuses more on other realms of life, apart from the economic. Classes consist of groups which share a common set of circumstances and expectations in life, which is determined by measurement of the distribution of goods, rather than their relationship to production.[1]

Typical sociological models of class differences determine class boundaries with reference to one's position within the division of labour.[2] As Tom Bottomore notes, Marxists have had problems in relating the social stratification of capitalist society to the basic social classes as defined in their model.[3] However, both Marxist and more traditional sociological models of class have in common their stress on structural position in determining class membership, as opposed to the belief and values of the individual which the Weberians have traditionally stressed.[4]

Nicos Poulantzas offers perhaps the most systematic attempt to formulate a Marxist theory of class applicable to modern capitalism.[5] When we search for workers who produce surplus value in contemporary capitalist society, we are struck by the large number of workers who cannot be said to do so; where to put white-collar workers, service-sector workers, etc? E.O. Wright argues that, when applied to the United States, these criteria yield a small number of workers indeed.[6] He offers a theory of contradictory locations within class positions, arguing that the new middle class under monopoly capitalism contains features of both the traditional Marxist proletariat and the bourgeoisie.

The assessment of women's class position adds a new wrinkle to an already complicated picture. Most male theorists of class have assumed that women's class position is to be determined from their association with men, usually their husbands or their fathers. Frank Parkin states well the accepted position:

> Now female status certainly carries many disadvantages compared with that of males in various areas of social life including employment opportunities, property ownership, income, and so on. However, these inequalities associated with sex differences are not usefully thought of as components of stratification. This is because for the great majority of women the allocation of social and economic rewards is determined primarily by the position of their families — and, in particular, that of the male head. Although women today share certain status attributes in common, simply by virtue of their sex, their claims over resources are not primarily determined by their own occupation but, more commonly, by that of their fathers or husbands. And if the wives and daughters of unskilled labourers have some things in common with the wives and daughters of wealthy landowners, there can be no doubt that the *differences* in

their overall situation are far more striking and significant. Only if the disabilities attaching to female status were felt to be so great as to override differences of a class kind would it be realistic to regard sex as an important dimension of stratification. But in modern society the 'vertical' placement of women in the class hierarchy, through membership of a kin group, appears to be much more salient to female self-perception and identity than the status of womanhood *per se*. It is perhaps for this reason that feminist political movements appear to have had relatively little appeal for the majority of women.[7]

The popular opinion holds that women have more in common with men in their class than with women outside it. Anthony Giddens agrees with Parkin, arguing that in fact women's own work is peripheral to the class system.[8] Marcus Felson and David Knoke offer evidence that indeed, women themselves evaluate their own class membership in terms of their husband's income and class position.[9]

Feminists have, over the last two decades, disagreed with this position. Joan Acker argues that we should look at the mother's status as a criterion for class membership of women, and that a woman's mobility should be considered in the light of her mother's status (presumably, those elements of the mother's status which are independent of the father's status). Blau offers evidence to support this theory in noting that, for working-class girls, maternal aspiration is a critical determinant of their eventual possibilities for class mobility. Cynthia Epstein supports Acker's theory by asserting that individual girls, at least in the middle class, need role models showing them that marriage and careers can be combined.

Mary Ryan attacks the male view of women's class membership on historical grounds. She argues that in nineteenth-century America the structural similarities between working class and middle-class women outweighed incidental differences between them, and leaves open the question of the legacy inherited by us in the twentieth century. Ann Oakley notes that the roles of working-class women became more differentiated from those of middle-class women as the nineteenth century wore on.[10] With the establishment of a doctrine of female domesticity as an ideal — although the doctrine did permeate downwards from the middle to the working class — economic reality prevented most working-class women from living up to it, as they were forced to work outside the home in the vast majority of cases even into the early twentieth century. It may be true, therefore, that significant differences between the position of women in different classes may be a comparatively recent phenomenon.

More radical feminists have been arguing for several decades that women constitute a separate class or even culture in our society. Helen Hacker argued early that women actually constitute a separate subculture, with their own language and idioms, distinct from men, although she did not specify to which *class* of women she was referring.[11] Later, theorists of patriarchy argued that the primary division in our society was between men and women, rather than between more strictly defined economic classes. Kate Millett claimed that 'our society is still a patriarchy', in that all the power continues to rest in male hands.[12] Hartmann and Bridges and Chris Middleton claimed that patriarchy operates independently of women's class position.[13]

More recently, feminists have begun to question these blanket positions, paying more attention to women of the working class and possible differences, as well as similarities, between these women and women of the middle and upper classes.[14] My project falls within this tradition. What I have done is to select women who would be defined as working-class according to traditional, sociological measures. For the most part, this means that either their fathers or their husbands are engaged in blue-collar work — butchers, printers, factory workers, dancing instructors, hairdressers. In the case of women brought up solely by their divorced or widowed mothers, I have taken the mother's occupation into account. In the case of independent women, I have looked at their own occupation in making my judgement. In some cases, when someone's husband, father or single mother worked in a job which appeared to be borderline (unskilled clerical work, for example), I have considered education (lack of high school diploma, or high school diploma alone) in addition to occupation as an indicator of working-class status.

My middle-class informants were professionals, most of whom had attended college and receive an A.A., B.A., or an advanced degree. I determined the women's class status in their group in the same way in which working-class women's status was assessed.

I used snowball sampling as a means of finding my informants.[15] In snowball sampling, one starts with one member of the desired group, and asks that person for a friend, neighbour or relative in order to continue interviewing within the same class group. In order to avoid the bias sometimes inherent in this sampling method, in which sometimes the fact that all of the individuals in the 'snowball' are somehow connected with one another, I used several snowballs to start off each group. Like Lillian Rubin, I interviewed women at the start of each snowball who came to me in a variety of ways: through waitresses I met, friends who taught working-class students, a working-class church, hairdressers.[16] Like Rubin, also, I conducted my interviews in different communities surrounding the San Francisco Bay area, but excluded Berkeley since its population is so unrepresentative of the country at large.

My interviews lasted for at least two hours, sometimes more, and often included follow-up interviews and visits. While I used an interview schedule[17] as a general guide, rather than sitting my informants down to ask them questions, I wanted them to talk to me about television and about their lives in a freer manner. I therefore left my questions open-ended, and let the interviews travel in directions which seemed most consonant with the women's particular interests and views on the subject. Many interviews I did yielded little information of value for the study, unfortunately, in part because of this open-ended format. However, I am convinced that I would not have gathered the valuable information I did had I created a more closed, structured interview situation. In the end, my total sample consisted of 41 informants, including 20 working-class and 21 middle-class women. Interviews were taped and later transcribed. In addition, I wrote notes directly following each interview regarding the general tenor of the interview, my impressions of my informant, and other miscellaneous details. It is from this data that the following information was culled.

Dynasty: The Real World of the Fabulously Wealthy

Dynasty is a prime-time soap opera which revolves around the lives of two extremely wealthy Denver families, the Carringtons and the Colbys. Blake Carrington (John Forsythe) and Alexis Colby (Joan Collins), once married and now divorced, are the respective patriarch/matriarch of each clan. Blake is now remarried to Krystle (Linda Evans). The show revolves around both the businesses but primarily around the personal adventures, trials and tribulations of Blake, Alexis, Krystle and their respective children and other assorted relatives and acquaintances.[18]

The way in which *Dynasty* is structured provides several issues which make it a particularly fruitful focus for a discussion of the way in which television is mistaken for reality. *Dynasty* is first and foremost an American fable. The show offers to us a vision of what it would be like were our wildest fantasies of material success fulfilled. *Dynasty*'s vision gratifies our most extremely avaricious desires at the same time that it teaches us the generic soap-opera moral that family, above wealth, guarantees happiness, and the rich are often more unhappy than the poor.

Female images on *Dynasty* are particularly interesting as well. The two main female principals — Alexis Carrington Colby and Krystle Jennings Carrington — embody our society's dichotomous good-and-evil view of the female character. Krystle is almost entirely good, a prime candidate for the label of 'perfect woman'. She is identified primarily as a wife and mother, although on and off she has worked at various jobs. Overall, Krystle provides emotional support for virtually everyone on the show with the exception of Alexis and assorted other enemies of the Carrington family. Her one flaw seems to be that she once had an extramarital affair; but that is long past and her marriage is now as strong as ever.

Alexis, an aggressive, power-hungry and enormously successful career woman, can be seen as evil personified. She is everything our culture tells us that good women are not: powerful and lusting after even more power, extremely sexual and not above using her sexual allure for personal gain. Her only redeeming feature is her apparently genuine concern and love for her children. These two women embody the often cited 'good-bad' woman dichotomy which has pervaded representations of women in the Hollywood film and has now, apparently, entered the realm of television images as well.[19]

Working-class in my sample reacted to *Dynasty*, and to the glamorous world it represents, in one of two ways. Some liked the show, and watched it regularly. Some did not. But the interesting difference between working-class women who both liked and watched *Dynasty* and middle-class women who liked and watched *Dynasty* is that the working-class women who liked the show felt that it was realistic, several indeed seeming to like it *because* it was realistic. With this observation, my study adds a class dimension to Ang's less specific findings correlating viewer appreciation of *Dallas*, another very popular prime-time soap opera, with the perception of this show as being realistic or true-to-life.[20]

In my sample, working-class women overall were much more apt than were middle-class women to state a preference for television generally which they perceived to be realistic, as indicated in statements like the following:

> I don't like something that I don't think can really happen. I guess I like real life stuff.

I like more realistic shows on TV, I guess because they make more sense to me.

It's more realistic stuff, you know? It's not a lot of garbage and it's like that show is what can happen — really happen, whereas a lot of these shows, they make everything seem like peaches and cream, you know? I like realistic stuff.

It's a very good story. I thought it was cute. It was real life.

Now I like things that . . . I mean, things that are plausible is what I really like. Things that can happen. They show all kinds of things now. That's the kind of thing I like. The thing that they show you that is going on that is true. Why? Well, because it's happening around me. That I find very interesting. I like to be informed, I like informative shows. I think we should all face reality. If we're living in this world, we better know what's going on around us, and what might be in store for us whether we like it or not.

Middle-class women, on the contrary, liked *Dynasty* while consciously believing, or at least stating, the show to be quite fantastic rather than realistic, as I will illustrate in the following discussion. In fact, some middle-class women were quite capable of identifying closely with characters and situations on the show, relating them to situations, feelings, and problems they have had or have experienced in their own lives, while at the same time quite firmly discounting the realism of the show in sweeping, general terms.

Overall, middle-class women were more likely than women of the working-class to display the attitude that television generally is not a very realistic medium. They seemed to have expectations from their experience of television watching other than that they would be confronted with realistic images, as, for example, in the following statements:

I take it with a grain of salt, I really do.

I don't think I really took television all that seriously.

Several seemed to desire more realism in their viewing experience. They either denigrated television for being something other than realistic, 'TV is a joke, a big advertisement'; or stated a preference for film over television for the reason that in film, characters are more finely and realistically drawn than they can be on television series, given the limitations of prime-time conventions, as evidenced by the following quotation:[21]

I know it's because they have such short scenes [on television]. And I find that very insulting. Because life is not one person walks in the door, talks for two seconds and then the person walks out. The scenes are all about twenty seconds long. And it's a big joke to think that this person enters and exits within twenty seconds. I guess that's my gripe about the show [*Dynasty*], is because it doesn't really show — like movies do. The reason that I think I like movies is because characters are more developed. You see them communicating for longer periods of time. You get — you feel like you know them better because you have more to judge than just short little one or two word scenes.

Another woman, who felt she had learned a great deal about her children and their generation from the movies to which they brought her, said:

Then I began to see those movies because I realised that I had better relate to what my children were into or surrounded by. Just that simple. [re *The Graduate*]: And I never thought it was possible, but obviously a thing like that can happen. And that's what I'd think; I had better face reality. If that's what's going on, you better find out about it.

In the case of the show *Dynasty*, middle-class women, while maintaining their scepticism of the show's realistic nature, seemed able simultaneously to identify with particular characters and situations in the show to a much greater extent than did the working-class women with whom I spoke, as I attempt to demonstrate in the discussion which follows. Herein lies the central paradox of my findings: how is it that middle-class women seem both to doubt television more entirely, yet to identify with it more closely, than do their working-class counterparts? With this observation perhaps I add a new dimension to Horkheimer and Adorno's observation, which concludes their now paradigmatic essay, 'The Culture Industry: Enlightenment as Mass Deception':

The triumph of advertising in the culture industry is that consumers feel compelled to buy and use its products even though they see through them.[22]

I rephrase this comment to now ask why this is true in the case of the middle-class consumption of television, and less true in the case of the working-class, who do not see through the industry's products as readily, but resist their messages more forcefully when they do.

In some women, particularly women of the working class, mistaking television for reality takes quite a literal form. In the case of *Dynasty*, these women imagine that, fantastic as the show's characters may appear, these images must be representative of reality in some respects. These women display almost a blind faith in the sociologically representative nature of television images. One working-class woman, for example, comments on the character of Alexis (Joan Collins):

> She's supposedly a career woman, but she was not a career woman like I associate career women to be.

This woman goes on to compare Alexis to other career women that she knows in her life. It is particularly interesting to note how easily she discounts her own experience, which is that she has never met nor known of a woman like Alexis, for the view that 'there must be women like Alexis', which she believes because this image appears on prime time television:

> Well, the career women that I know socially and see about, I mean, they are women who are very average women. You can't figure *her* out; she's really far above the average in many ways — in her love approach, in her money spending, her clothes, her dress, I mean, that's a very different standard from the average person. But there must be women like Alexis in *Dynasty*.

Or another woman:

> INTERVIEWER: Do you think there are women like Alexis?
> Yes, I'm sure there are.

Contrast the views, that 'there must be women like Alexis', with these statements by middle-class women:

> No one could be like an Alexis.

And another woman:

> I think Alexis' story is absolutely far-fetched and ridiculous. Nobody can be that rotten. That's my honest opinion. That is absolutely unreal. Absolutely unreal.

Quite a contrast in the interpretation of images! The far-fetched Joan Collins character, Alexis Carrington Colby, is a character who would stretch anyone's imagination. She is brilliantly and consistently successful in business, and her sexual allure is so powerful that no man can resist her. Yet while middle-class women — even *Dynasty* fans — perceive the exaggeration in this portrayal, some working-class women seem to accept it, and its reality, at face value.

One middle-class woman goes on to critique *Dynasty*'s lack of realism more generally:

I don't think the things on *Dynasty* are plausible. They make you feel that because people are rich they have nothing but problems. And then always jumping into bed with someone else, and I really don't believe that. I don't believe that at all. Just because a person is rich, doesn't put them in a different category and make them different from other people.

While this woman may be similar to the working-class woman quoted above in her lack of experience with rich people, she is more apt to criticise the televised images with which she is presented.

It is interesting, however, that both the middle-class and working-class women quoted above criticise *Dynasty*'s lack of realism or accept its images as realistic on the basis of the belief that, essentially, rich and poor people are the same. Both overlook differences between the two, but they do so in different ways. The middle-class woman quoted has noticed, and subverted, *Dynasty*'s ploy: to make us think that rich people have many more, and more serious, personal problems than do those who are poorer. Rich people, she claims, are emotionally the same as poor; they're not fundamentally different, nor do they act so. They simply have more money. In contrast, the working-class woman quoted simply doesn't notice that the fundamental differences between people she has met and those pictured on the television screen is the economic class in which each travels. There must be, she claims, women like Alexis Carrington Colby out there somewhere. Perhaps accidentally, she simply has not met them. The level of material wealth which *Dynasty* portrays is perhaps so threatening to some women that they cannot think rationally or consciously about the material discrepancies between their way of life and what is shown on the screen.

In addition to the denial of their own experience of reality in favour of the televised version, one can sense in the statements of both working-class and middle-class women their groping for the proper words with which to conceptualise class differences, armed as we all are with concepts and a vocabulary which steadfastly ignore the importance of class in our social system. By promoting a level of identification which in effect urges viewers that 'we are all the same', a show like *Dynasty*, whose principals sport lifestyles which in fact differ radically from those of the vast majority if not all of its viewers, contributes heavily to the class-blind quality of our society's language, and our vision of ourselves. Most perniciously, this blinding seems particularly effective in the case of working-class women. Middle-class women seem able to maintain more distance from this particular 'we are all the same' message. They see sameness on an emotional level rather than on a material level ('no one could be as rotten as Alexis').

Materially, it is quite another story for working-class women. One middle-class woman describes the level of material prosperity portrayed on *Dynasty* as a goal:

> If you view it as a goal and become frustrated because you're not like that and you don't have furs and you don't have chauffeurs and you don't go on jets — on your private Lear jet here and there . . . I think it's okay — I don't look at what they have as much as the way they react to other people.

Working-class women do not seem to view the *Dynasty* way of life as a goal, or in any similar vein. Working-class women rarely comment at all on the level of material difference between the *Dynasty* lifestyle and their own. Perhaps it is simply too threatening for them to examine this issue in much detail, their prospects for upward mobility being much more limited than, at least, the way middle-class women perceive their own to be.

Let us examine further the nature of middle-class women's identification with, and involvement in, the show. Consider this middle-class woman, an avid *Dynasty* fan, who qualified her description of the pleasure she takes in the show as follows:

> Well, I have to tell you, I watch it really with a grain of salt. I mean, John says I don't want to watch that! That's filthy! But I laugh at it. I really do. I laugh at it. I know that nothing like that could ever really happen.

And this woman:

> I watch TV shows like *Dynasty* and *Dallas* for the fun of it. I know I don't believe in any of that stuff really.

These statements qualifying their identification with the show, contrast strongly with both women's description of their strong relationship to and heavy involvement with the show.

The first woman describes her involvement: '*Dynasty* is what I call my *vice*!'. She goes on to phrase her addiction to the show in terms which closely parallel the way in which middle-class women described and justified their addiction to romance novels in a recent popular study.[23] Janice Radway found that the primary function of romance reading for the middle-class women she studied was that the act of reading itself gave them time away from their duties to husbands and children, time for themselves alone. This respondent describes the act of watching *Dynasty* in terms which are very similar:

> That is something I do really for me, that it feels very selfish. Because sometimes John wants to watch something on Wednesday nights but he can't because I have to watch *Dynasty*. I won't even let him record it because I have to watch it when it's on.

The women Radway studied felt it was selfish to claim time for themselves alone. This woman feels it is selfish to claim television time for something she alone wants to watch.[24]

What is most interesting for our purposes here is the way in which this middle-class woman denigrates any supposed realism of the show *Dynasty* at the same time that she tells us how much she enjoys it and that she is virtually addicted to it. The second woman quoted above goes on to confirm this pattern; her transcript consists of pages and pages of detailed discussion of the *Dynasty* characters and of various plotlines which have appeared on the show.

Middle-class women consciously believe that much of the content of the television they watch is unrealistic. In addition, as we saw in the case above, they are often somewhat embarrassed about how much television they watch. It is interesting that the woman quoted above frames the activity of watching *Dynasty* as a 'vice.' Television watching is a somewhat illicit activity, with a negative connotation (vice), particularly when one watches alone, perhaps especially for a woman alone. Of course, women of both classes tended to denigrate the activity of watching television. Many women began their interview with the disclaimer 'But I don't watch television', often proceeding to offer detailed accounts of the television shows and characters which they do in fact watch, often quite regularly. This initial tendency to underestimate the extent of one's television watching is perhaps in part a response to the professional sociologist, in front of whom people want to seem educated and intelligent. But it is also probably a result of our more general cultural denigration of the activity of television watching. Yet if women of both classes are slightly embarrassed about their television watching habits, the firm disclaimer of television's realism belongs primarily to the middle-class alone.

The sense of literal and material reality with which working-class women in my sample receive *Dynasty* is illustrated further by the literal way in which they talk about the show. Consider, for example, the following comments made by working-class women about characters and incidents on *Dynasty*:

INTERVIEWER: Who do you like on *Dynasty?*
RESPONDENT: Krystle. I like Krystle.

INTERVIEWER: What do you think of Alexis?
RESPONDENT: She's arrogant and she's real snobby and she'd do anything to better herself. Walk on anyone and she doesn't care if she disgraces them. Definitely not like me.

INTERVIEWER: But you identify more with Krystle?
RESPONDENT: Yeah. And I think Fallon is changing more to be a nicer person too. She's changing into a much nicer, sweeter person.

Another woman talks of *Dynasty* in this way,

> Who do I like? Oh . . . Krystle's just wonderful! And Alexis is just . . . just horrid! She's just a mean lady. She's . . . I don't know. I feel that she carries that through even, you know, when she's not that character. It's just her. She's . . . She's just isn't the least bit . . . nice. What can I say? Krystle just is so warm and loving and Alexis just always seems to be cold and calculating and looking out for what's best for Alexis, even though many times, you know, it almost costs her children.

She continues:

> I don't think Krystle is like that. Krystle is always looking out for the good of everybody else. Everybody comes to her to discuss problems. You know? Deep emotional sort of things. Where Alexis, nobody trusts. If you did fill her in on something she'd use it against you eventually.

Both of these women take the meanings offered by the show itself literally, at their face value. There is no irony or critique in their talk. When asked whether Krystle functions as a role model, both unhesitatingly reply that she does. The first woman responds:

> Krystle is very sweet and caring. You know, just a pretty, really nice person.
> INTERVIEWER: Perfect, a perfect woman?
> RESPONDENT: Yeah, maybe, you know.
> INTERVIEWER: Is that kind of your ideal of what you'd like to be?
> RESPONDENT: Oh yeah, I would, sure, like to be like that, but nobody's perfect.

The second woman:

> INTERVIEWER: Do you feel Krystle is a good role model for women? Would you like to be like her?
> RESPONDENT: Oh, *sure!* I mean, to look beautiful all the time! I mean, it's an unrealistic existence, but it . . . It's neat. You know, I'm kind of

like up there with a goal, an unrealistic gaol. What she does in her life is good.

Another working-class woman offers the following:

I don't care for . . . what's her name? . . . Alexis. Can't stand her. Can't stand her sister's books either. There's something that goes against me. I don't know why truthfully. Now which is his wife? The blond? I like her.

All offer little or no critique of the good/bad split in images of women which are present in any surface reading of the show's text.

Contrast these responses with the following replies culled from middle-class transcripts:

INTERVIEWER: Which of the women [on *Dynasty*] do you like?
RESPONDENT: Alexis. Because she's fun, you know, she's amusing. She's like . . . they make her out to be this real evil woman. But she's, you know, she's real independent. She goes after what she wants and she's a bitch.

This woman goes on to describe her reaction to the character of Krystle:

I really can't stand what's-her-name . . . Linda Evans. Krystle . . . ugh! She is such a bad actress and just really . . . Well, they all are but . . . She's real one-dimensional, just like, 'Oh, Blake!'.

Another middle-class woman mirrors these views:

I hate . . . I don't like Krystle. Well, I don't hate her. But I don't like her. Because too many scenes I've seen her on her knees or in a similar manner [sneers] talking to Blake like he is *the* person of the world and she has to show all respect for him. I don't like her. She doesn't speak back to him, she doesn't really give him any . . .

When asked about Alexis, this woman replies that it is the unreality of her character which bothers her:

Alexis . . . Well . . . No one could be like an Alexis. Or maybe there are women like Alexis, but they couldn't have things go right for them all the time like she does, I don't think. I guess . . . I kind of feel like if you do things like that, you're really going to get it some day.

Contrast this view of Alexis with the working-class women's repeated comments that there must, in fact, be women like Alexis in reality.

Both of the women quoted above seem to have deeply emotional responses to the show. They give relatively long, involved answers when asked for their responses to particular characters, and go on to describe particular scenes and plotlines and their reactions to them. Yet, unlike the working-class women cited earlier, both deny that they identify with any of the characters. The first woman quoted simply says 'no' when asked whether she identifies with any of the *Dynasty* characters. She goes on to describe an episode of the show with a great deal of comic distance:

> Someone just took Fallon's baby. They're trying to figure out who. And the ex-wife Alexis is gonna try and marry that guy she almost killed having sex with [laughter] . . . Colby. Oh, it was great! They tried to convince you that they're having such strenuous sex that this guy had a heart attack. So they had like fifteen minutes of cavorting with all this music and stuff. Then all of a sudden he goes GASP! GASP! [laughter] . . . I can't freaking . . . and Alexis gets really pissed and she starts slapping him across the face and going, 'You can't die, you can't die, you asshole! We have to get even with Blake! We want revenge!'. And she's slapping him. And you think he's dead, but then it turns out he's in this oxygen tent. So she's gonna marry him and somehow they're gonna get revenge on Blake. And then, they just found out that Blake has this long-lost son that was kidnapped when he was a little baby and this guy's gonna come in from Montana and claim to be the Carrington son because the other one just left the series. And what else? Oh, and Claudia's gone bonkers. They thought she had the baby last week but it turned out she just had a doll.

Notice that as she is describing a scene which was obviously meant to have a great deal of dramatic impact, i.e. Colby having a heart attack, this woman is quite detached from the surface level of the show's meaning. Rather, she is quite in touch with what she perceives to be a comic undercurrent of the show. She finds it hilarious that an elderly man was shown having a heart attack while having sex with Alexis. What identification processes, if any, are occurring for this woman are unclear. Whether on some level the comic pleasure she takes in Alexis's character, which she exhibits in the first set of quotes above, derives from an identification with her, is difficult to determine. If this identification does take place, it is not on a conscious level. This woman is an ambitious professional woman and does share certain qualities with the character of Alexis, so an unconscious identification between the two is certainly a possible source of at least some of her pleasure.

The second middle-class woman quoted also denies that she watches *Dynasty* because she identifies with characters or situations. In fact, she offers a quite unrelated reason for her addiction to the show:

INTERVIEWER: Do you know why you like watching the show?
RESPONDENT: Well, maybe this won't help you, but I think I watch it because I like to see what clothes they wear, I like to see how their hair is done.

But when asked whether she likes to see these things in order to copy them, she denies this emphatically, saying that to her *Dynasty* fashions are an interesting 'joke':

INTERVIEWER: Do you want to try and look like them?
RESPONDENT: No.

INTERVIEWER: They have *Dynasty* clothes now. They have this whole line of designer suits and things.
RESPONDENT: I think it's the biggest joke in the world! Those dolls . . . I think it's a joke!

INTERVIEWER: You would never go out and buy a *Dynasty* dress?
RESPONDENT: Never ever! I think that's the stupidest thing in the world!

INTERVIEWER: Do you think they're pretty . . . the dresses and stuff they wear?
RESPONDENT: Some are. Some are. But some are not. Some I don't like at all. I'm not a real clothes person.

This, at least, is the reason for watching *Dynasty* of which this woman is most consciously aware.

She goes on, however, to display an involvement with the show which belies this detached account of her interest in it. It seems she is particularly interested in the marital relationship between Blake and Krystle. It became clear in the course of the interview that this relationship, and the problems the two have faced, remind her of her own relationship with her husband, and of certain problems they have faced together. She specifically comments on the quality of the communication between the two, an issue she has found to be particularly central and often problematic in her marriage. She is very critical of the way in which characters on *Dynasty* communicate, or fail to communicate, with each other. She herself has found that open communication has been necessary to preserve the quality of her marriage.

For instance, one set of *Dynasty* episodes involved a plotline wherein both Blake and Krystle each received pictures showing the other in compromising positions with a member of the opposite sex. Blake immediately confronted Krystle with the pictures he had received, showing her apparently kissing the man she worked with. For several episodes he argued and tormented her, demanding to know the meaning of these pictures. Meanwhile, Krystle herself had received similar pictures of Blake which showed him in apparently compromising positions with a female friend. All through Blake's cross-examination of her, however, Krystle refused to reveal that she had received similar pictures.

The middle-class woman quoted above had these comments to make on this situation:

> Krystle doesn't really give him any . . . I mean, with those pictures. Why didn't she tell him that she had gotten similar pictures? But no, she had to wait. I woud have yelled at him so many times! She's just . . . I don't like her at all. She's a wimp!

And, further, regarding Blake and Krystle's marriage:

> I think she ought to talk more to him. She hasn't even talked to him. I mean, they haven't yelled about it. They haven't gotten it all out. So I hate to see the marriage fall apart without trying to talk about it first because . . . I guess they're both innocent, from what we've seen on TV, it looks like they're both innocent. They don't realise that it's only hurting their marriage for them not to talk. They're both holding things back that would ease the whole situation if they only talked about them.

And more generally:

> Well see, I have this general gripe. My general gripe is none of them really speak their mind. They're always sort of being asked to speak their mind and a lot of times they don't. And you don't admire that. Because they don't realise that it's only hurting themselves.

The argument she makes regarding Blake and Krystle's marriage, and regarding the desirable level of communication in relationships more generally, is paralleled by this woman's later discussion of the important function of communication in her own marriage. As she sees it, her own function, like Krystle's, is to bring out into the open issues that her husband, left to his own devices, would never discuss.

> Okay. My husband's somewhat like that. He'll say . . . rather than bring it up, I'm going to protect you by not bringing something up. I'm going to hold it in and I'm going to try and cope with it. And I object to that because I feel that . . . especially in a relationship, especially in a marriage . . . you want to air out all these things because what's gonna happen is you bring up these resentments. They're gonna sometime have to be aired out anyway. So I try to get him to tell me every little thing that bothers him . . . that I know bothers him. Because I know it's going to come back to me at some time later on anyway. And so he doesn't need to

feel the need to protect me because it's going to be harmful in the long run.

Her critique of Krystle's inability or unwillingness to bring up difficult issues with Blake, particularly concerning the adulterous picture incident, is based on this theory regarding her own role in communication in her own marriage. What is interesting is that elsewhere in her interview, this woman had mentioned some communication problems that she and her husband were presently experiencing, noting that she and her husband 'haven't done a whole lot of talking' recently, since she had been inordinately busy in school of late.

Another middle-class woman, a teacher, had lately decided to stay at home full-time with her small child. Having worked full-time as a teacher, and at other jobs, this decision was a new one for her, and she seemed to be experiencing some conflict over it, as evidenced by the fact that she had attempted part-time work, but had given up because she felt that her child was seriously disturbed by her absence. Her conflicts are perhaps heightened by the fact that she herself was brought up by a maid while her mother went to law school and then worked full-time as an attorney. She was attempting, she told me, to do a more effective job of child-rearing than did her mother, although her decision to stay at home flies in the face of the feminist assumptions prevalent in our culture and in the media generally.

This woman focused her discussion of *Dynasty* around the specific conflicts between work and family which Krystle had been experiencing just prior to the time of her interview. Krystle, having recently given birth to her first child, Kristina, had just gone back to work on a horse farm, having felt that simply remaining home to care for her child was insufficiently stimulating and fulfilling. My informant had this to say about Krystle's situation, which clearly resonated with her own:

Lately, she [Krystle] hasn't been too good. I mean, that horse is really starting to . . . (laughs) I don't know about it. I don't think it's right. I really don't I guess that — with her baby, I feel that she's taking time away from her child that she shouldn't to go spend with her horse.
INTERVIEWER: So you agree with Blake when he said, 'Your place is here, with Kristina!'?
RESPONDENT: Yes. Yes, I do. And I believe that she's entitled to have outside interests, but from what you see on the television, it seems the horse is taking a primary role that I don't think is right. If she spent as much time with Kristina as she did with the horse, you know, and she

spent as much time with the horse as she spent with Kristina I would say it's fine. But I don't think that the time allotted to each is appropriate.

INTERVIEWER: Even though she can afford all the help she needs?
RESPONDENT: Exactly. I think nobody can take the place of the mother in the home.

She goes on to further discredit Krystle's decision to go back to work by linking it to adulterous desires for her partner, Reese:

INTERVIEWER: Why do you think Krystle has gone back to work?
RESPONDENT: Why I don't know. I guess I've never given it much thought. I guess that maybe she's attracted because, well, isn't what's his name, Reese there? I guess that there's a bond there that existed before her and Blake were ever involved and maybe she feels young and beautiful being around him, vs. *being an old mother with kids at home.* (Author's italics.)

Nevertheless, the way in which Krystle's dilemma reminds this woman of her own conflicts and choices is even more clear as she continues:

An identity crisis, really! Even the beautiful Linda Evans feels it sometimes. You know, I think everybody once in a while would like to shun their mother garments and go out and be a swinging single for a night. But I think it would take one night and you'd be so happy to be home. At least I would.

The conflicting images in these statements interpreting Krystle's actions — from being an 'old mother with a kid at home' who is 'shunning her mother garments', versus the feeling of in the end being 'so happy to be home' — indicate that, for this woman, *Dynasty* does indeed resonate with conflicts and choices she has faced in her own life. In fact, discussion and interpretation of the show seem to be means by which this woman plays out or tests her ideas, particularly those fraught with some uncertainty or conflict.

Here, then, we have another example of the way in which a middle-class woman uses aspects of her identification with a *Dynasty* character, and the plotlines within which this character is embedded. As seen in the example quoted above, she is critical of the quality of Krystle's relationships. But in particular, Krystle's choice between work and family echoes conflicts she herself has lived. Criticising Krystle's choices, and finding support for her criticisms in her interpretation of fictive events on *Dynasty*, is a way for her to justify and to bolster her own decisions.

Conclusion

This study raises the possibility that the categories of class and gender are crucially important for the study of media audiences.[25] In the case of *Dynasty*, we find working-class women identifying very generally with some of the female characters on the show. Overtly, their reading of the show is non-critical. What is particularly noticeable about their responses to this show is that working-class women speak very little to differences between the *Dynasty* characters and themselves. Instead, they focus on what similarities there are between their own personalities and those of the *Dynasty* characters. Differences in lifestyle between themselves and that of the *Dynasty* characters are obviously noticed but are not very often the subject of working-class women's comments. The fact that differences between these lifestyles are not forefronted in working-class discussions of *Dynasty* leads to the suspicion that *Dynasty* operates hegemonically for these women, either in some way helping them live vicariously through the show and thereby ignore dissatisfactions with their own lifestyle, or simply to blur perceptions of their own lives through the television image.

Middle-class women, on the other hand, speak quite differently of *Dynasty*. Unlike the working-class focus on sameness, middle-class women focus on differences between themselves and the *Dynasty* characters they discuss. In the process, they are often quite critical of these television characters in ways that working-class women were not. In several cases, middle-class women use their identifications with *Dynasty*'s characters in order to help them conceptualise conflicts they experience in their own lives, particularly those involving the form and quality of different relationships in which they participate.

At the same time, on a very general level middle-class women consciously refuse to be taken in by the conventions of realism which characterise this, like virtually all, prime-time television shows. They repeatedly maintain that *Dynasty* depicts a very unreal picture of life among the fabulously wealthy. Yet their active identification with the show's characters and situations presents an interesting contrast to their denial that it is 'real' for them; this gives us a clue that on some level middle-class women are responding to *Dynasty as though* they considered its image to be real, or at least real enough to elicit responses in terms of sameness or difference to the *Dynasty* characters.

Jane Feuer notes that prime-time soaps give viewers a chance to feel morally superior to the fabulously wealthy, who are most often shown embroiled in melodramatic family issues which let viewers in on their less-than-admirable personal qualities.[26] Middle-class women do in fact respond to themes in *Dynasty* which offer them an opportunity to feel superior to the characters involved. In fact, such plotlines seem to appeal to them precisely because they touch on areas of moral or relational conflict within women's lives which they themselves may be attempting, not entirely successfully, to solve. The soap may show characters who are failing even more dismally at solving similar problems. Such depictions may simply be comforting to watch, or at the very least allow women a 'mental worksheet' with which to solve their own, related dilemmas.

One possible interpretation of my results is that working-class and middle-class women are responsive to different aspects of the hegemonic images that *Dynasty* presents to them. Middle-class women, in identifying more with the characters and their family situations as depicted on *Dynasty*, can almost be said to be responding to a gender-specific hegemony as it is presented on this television show. I use the term 'gender-specific' because it is specifically to female characters, and even more specifically to their roles within the family, that my middle-class informants responded in their discussions of this show.

The form this gender-specific hegemony takes is complex, however. Even in the two examples I have shown, we see in discussions of *Dynasty* situations and characters contradictory uses of our society's gender ideologies. In one example, we see a woman invoking an extremely conservative, anti-feminist ideology to criticise Krystle's excursion into the work-world after giving birth to her child. In another, we have a woman criticising Krystle for not being more assertive in her marriage, a criticism decidedly non-traditional in its origin (although in some respects this woman draws on traditional ideas about femininity in asking Krystle to be more communicative and, thereby, in effect, to take greater responsibility for holding her marriage together). While I am reluctant to draw firm conclusions from this limited number of examples, even this small subset of data illustrates the complexity with which women respond to ideologies of femininity and of the family as they appear on television. For our purposes here, it is most important to emphasise the difference between middle-class women, who invoke these ideologies in order to criticise the show's characters in their discussions, and working-class women, who invoke them only to affirm the depictions which they view.

Working-class women may be said to respond less to this gender-specific hegemony and much more to what I term the class-specific aspects of *Dynasty*'s hegemonic images. Rather than identifying with specific female characters and their roles within the family, working-class women responded to those aspects of *Dynasty* which they felt depicted a lifestyle they found interesting — and pleasurable — to witness. Overall, their responses to the show's characters, their personalities, and the situations in which they found themselves were less critical than were those of middle-class viewers. In light of these responses, it is possible that the type of hegemonic power which *Dynasty* represents for working-class women may be more related to its overall depiction of life among the fabulously wealthy rather than to its representation of specific characters and their problems — in my terms, more class-specific (focused on material aspects of life) than gender-specific (focused on personal, inter-personal and familial relationships).

We can only conjecture as to the consequences of each sort of reception for women's interpretations of their own experience in the world, both materiallly and relationally. In this chapter, I have emphasised differences between the way women of different social classes discuss one particular television show, *Dynasty*. Whether these findings can be generalised to apply to the reception of other shows, and other television genres, and their bearing on television reception by other social groups, remains to be demonstrated in future studies.

Chapter 10. Warwick Capper of the Sydney Swans.
Photo: The West Australian.

Chapter 12. London billboard. *Photo:* M.E. Brown.

Chapter 10. Australian Rules Football — the Sydney Swans.
Photo: The West Australian.

12

Motley Moments: Soap Operas, Carnival, Gossip and the Power of the Utterance

Mary Ellen Brown

This chapter stitches together a patchwork of material drawing from the narrative practices of television soap operas, conversations with soap opera fans, Mikhail Bakhtin's analysis of carnival and laughter, and reflections on the nature of women's talk, especially gossip, and its status as 'feminine discourse'. All these elements in our discussion can themselves be related to the concept of patchwork. The non-hierarchical juxtaposition of various stories in a soap opera, or of various subjects in women's gossip, can be described as a set of 'motley moments', and the particoloured motley dress of the jester is emblematic of the capacity of contradictions to provoke a carnivalesque laughter. It has also been argued that the process of bricolage, of piecing together ready-made but heterogeneous elements into a new creation, is characteristic of many of women's cultural practices, ranging from traditional craft skills to storytelling techniques.[1]

The dictionary definition of gossip illustrates the way that women's talk and friendship may be viewed quite differently in masculine and feminine culture.

> *Gossip*, n. (*arch*) a sponsor at baptism . . . : a woman friend who comes at a birth: a familiar friend . . .: one who goes about telling and hearing

news, or idle, malicious, and scandalous tales. . . . (O.E. *godsibb*, god-father, one who is *sib in God*, spiritually related).

The woman friend or relative who, in the first definition, comes to give comfort and spiritual support at times of crisis or transition, establishing an ongoing network of mutual support and obligation between women is seen in the latter definition from outside the women's network as a threat, as the agent of a subversive and malicious information service. In contrast to the overwhelmingly negative characterisation of the talking and intimacy that are part of women's oral culture, there are many positive terms for men who speak publicly: bard, preacher, orator, or soothsayer. If we are to regard television as a medium that draws more strongly on oral than literate modes of thought and formal construction, as has been suggested by, for example, Fiske and Hartley, then it is clear that the soap opera fulfills many of the same functions, and attracts much the same sort of criticism, as the figure of the gossip in women's oral cultures.[2] What is it then that is so threatening about women's gossip or about soap opera?

Part of the answer may be found in the recurrent labelling of women's cultural production as vain, idle, trivial, or trashy. More than the content of such gossip, it is its aimless style that is apparently most objectionable. The Biblical admonition by St. Paul to ignore 'fables and endless genealogies, which minister questions rather than godly edifying' (Timothy 1.4), suggests that it is the open-endedness of such talk, its refusal to direct itself to higher purposes, that is at stake. Unmotivated talk that raises questions, explores possibilities, and continues for its own sake, for the joy of talk, implicitly denies that language is capable of embodying the one true word that is at the basis of official Christian dogma. The presentation of fables and endless genealogies in contemporary television soap operas meets with the same disgust from many television critics, who conversely applaud serious and informative night-time television. Soap operas are concerned with the stuff of traditional women's culture not only in the subject matter (i.e. domestic matters, kinship, sexuality) but also in their style. In particular, the importance of talk in soap opera plots indicates the basis of orality that persists in television in general, and affirms the power of talk in creating and maintaining relationships. Can we maintain that soap operas and what may be described as women's oral culture are part of a materially existing 'feminine discourse'? Are they connected by more than the negative ways in which they are both described in dominant discourse? The modes of operation of conventional history and ethnography have made it difficult to confirm such a connection because so little of women's domestic culture has found its way into writing.

The dimensions of women's oral cultural networks in the past have been obscured by the emphasis in ethnographic studies on how oral traditions as texts relate to place, which is defined in terms of family and village structures. Such models of oral transmission have obscured women's connections and relationships to other women because the centring of the analysis in male-controlled property individualises women's connections to the male-defined patriarchal family. Women's place in such a model is always indirect, defined by their relationship to the household head. The networks of women who generate and maintain women's oral culture always operate within and between households and in the gaps in traditional ethnographic analysis. In ways that vary among different cultures and historical periods, women have always been materially isolated, usually in a domestic setting.

Social separation along gender lines is common in one form or another, to most, if not all, European-based cultures. For example, in nineteenth century Italy, it was commonplace for sisters, daughters-in-law, aunts, mothers, grandmothers, nieces, godmothers and friends to come together to perform such women's work as sewing or weaving; and usually women from a number of neighbouring communities would be represented in such a gathering. The performance of songs, the telling of tales, the arrangement of marriages, discussion of health problems, kinship gossip and work-related hints might all form part of women's talk on such an occasion. Yet in terms of the hierarchical model of the family as a component of the village, and ultimately of the state, this confluence of women was hardly recognised. Thus, folklorists studying the variation of European ballads had recourse to the figure of the male travelling singer as the main source of innovation and change in the tradition.[3] The peripherality of the concerns expressed in women's talk to the 'important' public issues of power, war and commerce led to the characterisation of women's culture as trivial and idle, if not actually evil in its distraction of thought from higher things.

I have maintained in earlier work that American daytime soap opera is closely related to women's oral culture.[4] Like folk culture, women's oral culture is practised informally outside established institutions and is recognised, though differently characterised, by both insiders (women themselves) and outsiders (men, dominant institutions). Other strands of oral culture drawn on by soaps include, in Britain, working class culture, and in Australia, teenage oral culture. This earlier work linked soaps to orality, arguing that soaps are not so much based on dominant literate cultural traditions, as on oral speech and thought patterns, which often employ codes and conventions that do not 'make sense' in literate cultural traditions.[5]

One of the most striking features of soap operas in this regard is the openness of their narrative form. In other television narratives, even when characters and some plot elements are carried on from one episode to another, the episode tends to be defined by the presentation of one major story. Whereas traditional literary narratives have a beginning, middle and end, soap operas consist of an ever-expanding middle.[6] The lack of a conventional introduction is compensated for by greater narrative redundancy in soap operas, i.e. the presentation of the same or similar situations in numbers of different scenes and the characters' frequent retelling of their own and others' histories.

The novice viewer of soap opera will experience an episode of a soap opera very differently from the fan, whose long-term knowledge of the soap opera, its characters, their histories and its narrative conventions brings a depth of significance to the action that is not available to the novice, who needs the interpretations and explanations of the knowledgeable viewer in order to make sense of what is going on in the narrative. The same is often true of orally-transmitted narratives. For example, interpretation of the narrative significance of one particular version of a song will be quite different when it is informed by the knowledge of previously heard versions of the same or similar stories in the culture. Traditional literary narratives, which of course also include their own set of cultural preconceptions, attempt to make the narrative self-explanatory within the limits of the piece. They also rely much more on psychological motivations to 'explain' the narrative development — the characters' actions stem from the sort of person they are. Part of the construction of a realistic character is consistency of behaviour in different situations. By contrast, soap opera characters often behave quite inconsistently, depending on their past and present relationships with other characters, and also on the actor who plays the character. Part of the talk about soap operas by knowledgeable viewers turns on comparison or awareness of such contrasts. Whereas inconsistent characterisation is usually considered to be a fault because it may detract from the pleasure of the reader in literary narratives, inconsistency in soap operas is understood to be an inescapable consequence of their process of production, and does not appear to affect the viewers' pleasure. Similarly, in traditional oral narratives, there is little or no attempt to explain character's actions in psychological terms; these actions are generally functions of the plot which behaves in accordance with generally accepted, if problematic, cultural precepts.

Many of the characteristics commonly found in both soap operas and oral traditional narratives can be related to their process of production, which in each case takes place in real time. Both narratives require that the audience's attention be held from moment to moment, in contrast to written narratives which can be put down and taken up again, and in which the reader can backloop if necessary to retrieve forgotten or skipped information. As Robert Allen, writing about the early radio soap operas, has pointed out:

> In radio . . . the *listener*, not the narrative, was the commodity being sold; thus, closure became an obstacle to be overcome in the attempt to establish regular, habitual listenership (author's emphasis).[7]

The same observation applies to contemporary television soap operas, in which the aims of the producers and advertisers to reach the widest possible audience of consumers exist in a complex, mutually dependent relationship with the pleasure of the viewers. Just as in live performance the performer adapts the song or tale depending on the audience's receptiveness and responses, so soap operas have been and continue to be comparatively responsive to the interests of viewers. For example, Robert LaGuardia reports that in the 1970s 'if a show had slipped half a point in the ratings shares, the poor writer would be given orders to make someone pregnant to get the numbers back up'.[8] Annie Gilbert reports that networks keep track of fan mail in order to monitor the popularity of particular stories (which is judged most successful if the fan mail is split 50/50, but possibly changed if the reaction is mostly one way), and of particular actors, whose part in the show might be expanded if their popularity was increasing.[9] Conversely, viewers might exploit this responsiveness of the producers by organising campaigns to 'rescue' popular characters perceived in danger of being killed off.[10] It must be pointed out that this phenomenon is most widely documented in American soaps. In Australia, where there is a much greater delay in screening, and where most daytime soap operas are of overseas origin, viewers do not generally perceive themselves as powerful in this way.

The process of producing soap opera scripts is much more dependent on viewers' reactions than in many other television narratives. In addition the managing of multiple story lines over long periods of time is another factor which affects narrative construction. Manuela Soares reports that writers favour ambiguity in their story lines because it leaves more options for future development of the story.[11] Irna Phillips, who wrote and produced many of the early radio and television soaps in America, maintained an ideal of live performance in many of her production practices. For example, she dictated all her scripts:

> (Which) allows me to play the parts of all my characters and give them dialogue that sounds like real, colloquial speech. And I avoid tape recorders. I dictate to another person to get that essential human contact, that other person's reaction to my dialogue that tells me a word or phrase doesn't sound right. . . .[12]

Phillips also preferred live broadcasting of her television soap operas long after the technology was available for delayed broadcast, because she believed that taping 'took the excitement out of the production'.[13] From the early days of radio soap operas, the scripts were produced by teams of writers. The producers or advertisers had some input into content and general principles of suitable material, the head writer would make decisions about which stories lines would be developed and how, and the actual dialogue would be written by teams of dialogue writers. Of course, story-lines would also be potentially affected by contingent factors such as actors' illnesses or departures, viewers' responses as outlined above, and even by the stage of development of similar plots in other soap operas. The version of the script that finally goes to air is therefore constrained in quite different ways from an authored literary narrative. In the lack of an individual author and in the responsiveness to a particular set of external conditions governing the final shape of the narrative, then, the conditions of production of a soap opera have much in common with the formulaic processes of oral composition, in which the broad outlines of a story passed down in oral tradition are realised in performance in different ways depending on the performance context.

So far, I have addressed the ways in which soap opera narrative is related to oral traditional forms in general; in this connection, I have argued that many of the similarities are engendered by similar processes of production that differ in significant ways from the norms of construction of written narratives. The perpetuation of many of these literary norms, such as narrative closure and psychological character formation in much television drama, has been the result of the historical evolution of these forms from literary novelistic and dramatic forms and the prevalence of a literary aesthetic in the producers and audiences. Soap operas, on the other hand, evolved in a more ad hoc fashion from radio programming that was deliberately designed to appeal to women's domestic culture. Chatty shows with a grandmotherly presenter alternating handy hints with product endorsements were an early form taken by radio programming aimed at women. Early radio soap operas incorporated advertising into the story line, and it was only comparatively late that advertising and narrative were segmented in the form now familiar to us in television soaps. In these unofficial narratives, unashamedly aimed at drawing and holding an audience for their sponsor's products, producers were less likely to consider that what they were producing was 'art', and were therefore relatively free from the constraints of literary definitions of narrative form. Furthermore, many popular entertainers had been drawn from the orally-based tradition of popular theatre. For example, the vaudeville stars Amos and Andy moved from film to radio with the slump in film production caused by the Great Depression.[14] Thus radio programming drew on non-official orally-based narrative forms in a number of different ways. It was precisely because soaps were considered unimportant and commercially-based that these orally-based narrative forms developed and evolved in radio, and, until comparatively recently it was only in daytime television programming that the characteristic narrative conventions of soap operas were evident. Prime time was reserved for literary-based narratives such as adaptations of novels, films, action dramas, or situation comedies. But the popularity of soap operas, which in fact make most of the daytime advertising revenue for the television networks,[15] has fostered, in the last ten years, a burgeoning of prime-time shows using soap opera narrative conventions in one form or another, ranging from *Dynasty* and *Dallas* to *Hill Street Blues*, *LA Law*, and *thirtysomething*. In Britain and Australia soaps like *Crossroads*, *Coronation Street*, *EastEnders*, and *Brookside*; or *Home and Away* and *Neighbours* have always been programmed in the early evening. The Australian soap, *Neighbours*, when imported into Britain, became the most popular television program in that country in 1988. Soap operas, then, are one of a number of modern texts on American, British, and Australian television that differ from dominant narrative and discursive assumptions; however, the dominant attitudes with which soap operas are often most concerned are those dealing with the position of women within patriarchy, so that the soaps differ in a way that often directly involves feminine discourse.

Feminine discourse is a way of talking and acting among feminine subjects (usually women) in which they acknowledge their position of subordination within patriarchal society. All non-mainstream groups in society can speak to each other in contexts which acknowledge their subordinate position within society and the problems of having that position defined in ways that do not necessarily represent their own perception of their world. For example, in the case of women's roles, dominant discourse often represents the position of housewife or mother in our culture as unproblematic, whereas housewives or mothers speaking to each other may not. These groups may see power relationships within these social roles as a balancing act between their own lived experiences and what the public or naturalised version of these roles or experiences represents. The knowledge of this subordination carries with it a set of assumptions about how the world is: that is, how one gets by in relation to the rules of patriarchal society. Often feminine discourse, as we define it, is parodic: that is, it makes fun of dominant practices and discursive notions. By playing in this way with the conventions of the dominant discourse, feminine discourse constitutes itself as 'other' to it, and displays a potential resistance.

I have chosen to include Bakhtin's analysis of carnival in my discussion because I am interested in exploring the potential for resistance or subversion inherent in feminine discourse, and Bakhtin's argument about the resistive potential of the discourse of mediaeval carnival is a direct parallel. Whereas I am concerned with the position of women *vis a vis* institutionalised patriarchy, Bakhtin's subject was the position of the common people *vis a vis* the institutionalised power of the Church and feudal nobility. He argued that the playful reversal of the dominant order in the carnival celebrations immediately preceding Lent empowered the common people because it involved a sense of play that could only be understood from the position of the subordinated group, whose subjecthood was thereby affirmed. If this is so, then the consciousness of subordination inherent in feminine discourse may also be potentially empowering.

In talking about carnivalesque aspects of soap operas, I will concentrate here on the power of talk in and about soaps as utterance and the manner in which this constitutes a kind of play for the audience. By play, I mean the performing of 'acts not part of the immediate business of life but in mimicry or rehearsal or in display', acts performed for recreation and for amusement.[16] Play in this sense is not to be confused with official games with official rules. In his introduction to *Rabelais and His World*, Bakhtin characterised the carnivalesque as 'a boundless world of humorous forms and manifestations opposed to the official and serious tone of medieval ecclesiastical and feudal culture'.[17]

Carnivalesque forms, ranging from ritual spectacles to various types of verbal expression, have a number of common attributes, two of which are particularly pertinent here: first, they existed outside dominant cultural practices, and second, they were based in laughter. According to Bakhtin's thesis:

> The basis of laughter which gives form to carnival rituals frees them completely from all religious and ecclesiastic dogmatism, from all mysticism and piety . . . All these forms are systematically placed outside of the church and religiosity. They belong to an entirely different sphere.
>
> Because of their obvious sensuous character and their strong elements of play, carnival images closely resemble certain artistic forms, namely the spectacle.[18]

However, carnival is not a spectacle that the people merely observe:

> . . . They live in it, and everyone participates because its very idea embraces all people . . . During carnival time life is subject only to its laws, that is, the laws of its own freedom . . . Such is the essence of carnival, vividly felt by all its participants.[19]

Bakhtin's description of carnival in relation to the Church is analogous to the position of soap operas in relation to dominant cultural forms such as so-called serious books, the news on nighttime television or sports which follow rules. Bakhtin's description is particularly clearly relevant in relation to the soaps' use of women's talk, which potentially mocks the language of dominant discourse.

Talk itself, as utterance, becomes a denial of language because it is using the abstract symbolic power of language for the particular purposes of the speaker.[20] It thereby constitutes the speaker as dominant over the language system, or at least able to control that aspect of language that s/he has spoken. The act of utterance may itself be interpreted as a claim to the discursive superiority of the speaker over the language. In this way, utterance represents a perversion or corruption of language because it demonstrates the speaker's incomplete submission to language's abstract symbolic power. On the other hand, the ideal of the silent woman constructed by dominant discourses is obedient to language's power.[21] In a sense, her silence is held up as the ultimate goal for all speakers, since the most highly prized use of language in our culture is the written. Utterance, then, unlike language, is potentially out of control, and can be a source of playful pleasure in performance. The enjoyment that many soap fans get from their favourite soap operas often demonstrates an appreciation of this dimension of the characters' speech. It is not only what is said, but how it is said that is appreciated by fans. An example appears in the following conversation with a group of Australian teenage fans of the Australian soap, *Sons and Daughters*:

ME: I'm trying to remember which one Ginny is.
L: She is the one who wears the really odd clothes she puts together with the long . . . sort of hair.
ME: She's the one that's just had that thing fall on her?
L: Yeah.
ME: So she's the one that you like?
W: She's all right. She doesn't like blend in with the rest of the *Sons and Daughters* characters, but she uses her language differently. Her odd clothes make it more interesting to her and everything, but that's about it.
L: Her character's really outstanding.
ME: What do you mean, she uses language?
L: Like soft spoken and everything, she doesn't care what she says, she's outgoing and . . .
W: Loud.

(M.E. Brown, recorded interview, October, 1986)

The group members display an extremely complex understanding of how, for example, Ginny's code of dress affects how we code her speech ('she uses her language differently. Her odd clothes make it more interesting to listen to her and everything . . .'). The interrelationship of visual and oral codes is clear to these readers. In addition, they appreciate the power of Ginny's speech in its capacity as utterance (the way 'she uses her language'). They read the style of speech used by the character Ginny as in opposition to what 'nice' girls might be allowed to say. This is a concern identified by Taylor as one of the major conflicts in ideology for teenage girls: that in this traditional age for rebellion, girls are expected to be 'nice' and silent, which the character of Ginny clearly is not ('She doesn't care what

she says, she's outgoing and . . .', 'Loud').[22] Another example of the
way that sensitivity to dialogue plays a part in the pleasure fans get
from soaps is found in the following quotation from a British fan
commenting on British soaps:

E: That's definitely part of the pleasure of it and the language. *EastEnders*, which is the new very successful British one, is set in the East End of London and the humour is cockney and it's very sharp — in a different way. It's very different, but it's the sharpness of the language that is used there. And also the black characters, their language which is different too; so it's all that and the way people talk to each other that is crucial. That's definitely some of the pleasure in watching it. It's the way things are said.

ME: Particularly the put-down I take it.

E: The put-downs, the rudeness, all very stylised really.

ME: Well, the power of the women seems to have to do with their . . .

E: Their mouths. (Laughs.)

(M.E. Brown, recorded interview, September, 1986)

Soap fans then may signal their allegiance to a particular soap not
just by talking about it, but also by playfully adopting the speech
style and persona of a particular character. As with both gossip and
folklore, knowledge about a specific soap can serve to define one's
solidarity with others within a group.[23] When such commonality is
established, the formalities of conversation among group members
are dropped, and like the carnivalesque marketplace conversations
that Bakhtin characterises as 'liberating from norms of etiquette and
decency imposed at other times', conversations within the group
become codified in a different way.[24] The same fan (quoted above) in
speaking about the British soap opera, *Coronation Street*, describes
how she and her friends put on the appropriate accent and adopt the
attitude of a particular character. One person begins a re-enactment
with a familiar line from one of the characters, and her friend will
answer back with another appropriate line of dialogue from the program. Here is an example from the interview:

E: . . . You'd be talking about things in general and you'd suddenly throw in a line from Mavis.

ME: A real line that she had said? Or one that . . .

E: You'd say something in a Mavis voice. I mean there's great lines from Bet Lynch that you . . . things like put-downs mainly, mainly prob- ably put-downs to men which is why she is popular in her role as a barmaid, how she puts people down. Because I don't know whether you've seen it, but there was this barman Fred Gee, a great big fat obnoxious bloke, who really fancies himself — you know what fancies himself means? I don't know whether it means the same thing in America.

ME: He was full of himself.

E: Really fancies himself, thinks he's a real hit with the women, but isn't actually and is extremely unpleasant and obnoxious generally. Most women find him that, and he would always get into situations when he would dress up and put on aftershave and perhaps a cravat and look absolutely ridiculous and then he would try and get off with someone.

ME: And then Bet would come in?

E: And he'd be preening himself in front of the mirror very pleased with himself and he'd say, 'How do I look then, Lynch?' and she'd say, 'Oh, you look like a well-scrubbed pig.' So you'd use that line — or you'd just really appreciate that line.

ME: So, it becomes almost like a code, that only the readers could . . .

E: If somebody was in the bar, Bet Lynch would say something to someone and they would be shocked and they'd have their mouth open, and she'd say something like, 'Shut your mouth before I drive a bus into it'.

                   (M.E. Brown, recorded interview, September, 1986)

Such utterance becomes a performance on the part of the soaps fan, acted out in the spirit of play and in the course of other conversations, and the ability to pick up on the performance also defines a fan's membership in a group, her position as part of a network of fans who recognise and speak the language and imitate its irreverent and defiant aspects. In another example, an Australian teenage fan of the American daytime soap, *Days of Our Lives*, carries a photograph of Bo and Hope, a *Days of Our Lives* couple, and shows the picture to her friends as if the picture were of real relatives or friends — a mini-performance based on a fantasy connection with these characters. This is also an act of resistance when played against parental disapproval of soaps.

    In soaps, conversations are always in process, just as the soaps themselves never end. According to Bakhtin, the experience of carnival was opposed to everything ready-made and completed. The symbols of the carnival idiom are filled with a kind of 'pathos' of change and renewal — a sense of the 'gay relativity of prevailing truths and authorities'.[25] This consciousness produces what Bakhtin calls a 'second life', a sort of parody of extra-carnival life, 'a world inside out'. He stresses that this parodic mode is far distant from the negative and formal parody of modern times because 'folk humor denies, but it revives and renews at the same time. Bare negation is

completely alien to folk culture'.[26] Such world-inside-out logic can
be seen in the play between the audience's knowledge of the fictional
world of the soap and their knowledge of the world outside the
soaps, a world in which soaps are constrained by production
budgets, the actors' desire for more money or better parts, and
failures of the writers to live up to audience expectations of various
kinds. Entering into the 'second world' of soap viewing thus involves
the knowledge of the constraints imposed on soap operas in the 'first
world' of dominant culture. Here is an example from a conversation
between American fans of *Days of Our Lives*:

S: There's a new bad person on the scene.
L: What if he's Stefano? (Laughter.)
S: Stefano's dead!
O: We don't know Stefano's dead. We just think he is.
C: No one ever found his body.
K: Some people think that Roman is still alive.
ME: Why do you think that Roman is still alive?
S: Because they didn't find his body, and, I'd swear, on one soap opera
they said Stefano's dead but they put his body on ice.
O: Roman left the program. He wasn't pleased with something — his
money or his part. Before he was killed, there was an article in *TV
Guide* or one of the books that he was going to leave, that he wasn't
pleased. I don't know whether it was . . . I think it was over his part,
the way it was developed.

(M.E. Brown, recorded interview, July, 1985)

The above conversation illustrates a carnivalesque sense of play in
the crossing of the boundary between fiction and reality. Soaps'
audiences often play with conversations about characters as if they
existed in real life. 'Real life' is, of course, contained and articulated
by dominant discursive practices, and the audience's talking about
the characters as though they were real defies that dominant conception of what constitutes reality. The extent of the viewers' willingness to entertain the fiction can be seen in the elaborate published
genealogies of soaps' characters, which assign them actual dates of
birth. There is an insistence on the value of such fantasy to certain
subcultural groups in this intertextual practice. Far more is involved
than the audience's being simply sucked in by the fictional world of
the soap opera.

Likewise, the importance of genealogies in the soaps and in
women's culture in general denies the status of the official 'histories'
promulgated in dominant discourse. Whereas history emphasises

orderly and unified cause-and-effect relationships, genealogies, according to Foucault, have an inherently uncontrollable disorder through the randomness of their development.[27] Foucault goes on to develop a broader definition of 'genealogy' which is not confined to kinship relations. It is easy to see that the genealogies (in the more restricted sense) are very disorderly indeed in soap operas, and knowledge of the former relationships and parentage of characters is an important element in gossip and discussions between fans and in their understanding of narrative developments. The difficulties faced by novice viewers in making sense of soap opera genealogies may be illustrated by the following conversation with a *Days of Our Lives* fan whose husband had begun to watch with her:

T: George got into it fairly quickly — he's got his pet hate on the program.

R: I didn't think he'd be able to follow what's going on. I reckon all the women are the same.

T: Oh, it was so annoying. It was so annoying when he first started watching. Every five minutes he'd ask 'Who's that? Who's that? What's she doing?' — and you couldn't possibly explain who she is. Like Hope and Julie. First you just say no, it's her stepmother, and then something comes up about Addie — and you say, well, in fact, her father was married — Julie's mother was her husband's wife as well. Right? And it's all ridiculous. Because all the women look alike, it took George a long time. Every time a woman came on, he'd say 'That's the one that . . .' and I'd say 'No, no, that's Gwen Davies', and this is such and such.

(R. Quin, recorded interview, June, 1987)

To the new viewer who stands outside the soaps' reading conventions, it is hard to make sense of genealogies in soaps. It is, however, through the cheerful suspension of 'first world' reading practices that soaps fans play with the construction of 'second world' meanings. In addition, kinship systems entail elaborate rules of social behaviour, and women are often entrusted with the important role of knowing who is kin to whom and at what level. The fact that kinship on the soaps is different from the dominant kinship situations operating in our culture constitutes a kind of in-joke on the subject of kinship. By contrast, more conventional narratives more rarely question or problematise kinship systems in this way.

A striking element in such reading practices is laughter. Often it is laughter at the absurdity of plot construction or characters. Bakhtin characterises carnival laughter as ambivalent:

It is, first of all, a festive laughter. Therefore it is not an individual re-action to some isolated 'comic' event. Carnival laughter is the laughter of all of the people. Second, it is universal in scope; it is directed at all and everyone including the carnival's participants. The entire world is seen in its droll aspect, in its gay relativity. Third, this laughter is ambivalent: it is gay, triumphant and at the same time mocking, dividing. It asserts and denies, it buries and revives. Such is the laughter of carnival.[28]

The laughter involved in soaps fanship groups has similar charac-teristics, particularly its ambivalence. Soaps, after all, are a form of entertainment almost universally belittled despite their popularity. The ability to see things both ways, as both humorous and serious, characterises both carnival participants and soaps fans. Take the following conversation about *Days of Our Lives*, for example:

S: Oh, Alex and Marie. They weren't married. Marie was a nun. Before she was a nun, she lived in New York. Even before that there was Tom Horton, Jr., who had amnesia and who somehow or another had plastic surgery and somehow or another he wandered back to Salem with plastic surgery and nobody knew him and he didn't know anybody.

ME: You mean Tom has a son?

S: Yeh. He fell in love with his sister, Marie. And they did their thing and they were going to get married and all of a sudden Tom Horton, Jr. remembered. So Marie got sick and she fled and nobody knew where she was for a while and then later on she went in a convent and became a nun. But meanwhile, when nobody knew where she was, she went to New York and had an affair with Alex and had a baby.

ME: Who's Alex?

S: Alex is the really bad one.

K: The consummate evil one.

S: He did Stefano's dirty work.

ME: So he and Marie had a daughter?

S: I'd forgotten about her. She got married. Who did she get married to?

K: She married Joshua. She was engaged to Jake, the Salem Strangler.

O: Oh yeh.

(M.E. Brown, recorded interview, July, 1985)

In the group discussion noted above, everyone laughed when it was mentioned that Jessica, Marie's daughter, was once engaged to the Salem Strangler. The humour takes in not only the absurdity of the specific situation but also the character's history. If one has followed Marie's story over the years, one knows that she has been subjected to the most absurdly terrible (and, because of the excess, humorous) series of tragedies that one can imagine, which may be quite different in kind and degree from those which might beset another character. Yet any other character's litany of problems would also elicit laughter. It is the cumulative effect that comes out when one is talking about them that makes them funny. However, the same viewers who, at the moment of viewing, enter wholeheartedly into the pathos of a particular situation, at the level of metadiscourse are quite capable of laughing at the same event.

In the soaps, bodies are not 'revealed' as in many other forms of representation, as individualised bodies or as objectified female bodies, the usual objects of the male gaze. Instead, the body is present in another way, quite different from the bourgeois ego or the individual biological body. According to Bakhtin, the carnivalesque image of the body is part of the heritage of folk humour that he terms 'grotesque realism', in which: 'the cosmic, social, and bodily elements are given . . . as an indivisible whole. And this whole is gay and gracious . . . the bodily element is deeply positive'.[29] In the soaps, close-ups of people at the peak of emotional conflict expose this agonistic body to scrutiny in much the same way that a grotesque image reveals too much, defying dominant rules of propriety about how much emotion it is acceptable to show. In dominant literary traditions, it is these emotional constraints and the resolved emotional conflicts that tell us everything is all right; that it is possible to live happily ever after, as the climax or closure of the realistic narrative tradition of literature would lead us to believe.

But the soaps tell us otherwise. They codify life in some humourous and grotesque ways, ways in which utterance takes precedence over the language. They help us to laugh at ourselves and the absurdities of subordinate cultural positioning. As consumers of soap operas and the products they advertise, women do participate in the process of consumption, but the extent to which women can be said to be the passive objects or 'victims' of dominant discursive practices by watching and enjoying soap operas is limited by the women's use of these same cultural forms to affirm their own positions of subjectivity in a women's discursive tradition. This breaking of the rules is a source of pleasure, and the act of taking that pleasure entails defiance of dominant reading practices which attempt to shape the construction of meaning in our culture. Because the hierarchy of dominant values is either ignored or parodied in some of the reading practices around soaps, these practices may open up new possibilities for ways of thinking about culture from the subordinate's point of view.

CONCLUSION

13

Conclusion: Consumption and Resistance — The Problem of Pleasure

Mary Ellen Brown

Women have often been thought of as a problem, as a mysterious 'other' whom we, the audience, cannot hope to understand. Classical Hollywood narrative film frequently investigates the woman, presumably for the pleasure of the male viewer. Paradoxically when the tables are turned, when women derive pleasure from popular narrative forms, the process is viewed as a problem. This contradiction is a problem for feminists and one which I would like to address in this conclusion.

Among feminist television critics, there are two distinct notions of what constitutes good television in terms of women. One notion is that television should represent women in a positive light, for example, that the number of women on television should relate to the number in the population or that women should be represented in such a way that positive role models are presented for female children. Another approach taken by some television critics is to attempt to understand how representations of women on television are used by women in response to their social positioning. In other words, the attempt is to understand television reading practices among women in relation to existing television programs or texts. But beyond the analysis of reading practices, what can be the political significance of the fact that women derive pleasure from commercial television programs, like soap operas, which are designed both to play upon their emotions and to make them consume? This chapter attempts to theorise the possibility of the political use of pleasure by women, using as an example discursive networks centred around soap opera viewing.

In terms of the first view, television's representation of women is thought to be negative. It is thought to perpetuate both the status quo and generally regressive values in the female population. The argument is that women (or any other subordinated group) will only become radical when their position in life is so unpleasurable that there is no possible choice but revolution. The second group of critics put forward the idea that there are levels of political involvement that often hinge on less obvious notions of success which make it possible for subordinated groups to resist hegemonic positioning in various ways. This second view on women and television is more concerned with what women do with what is at hand than with setting out agendas for changing the representation of women on television.

For women, politics is often close to home and can take place in the context of everyday life, and leisure time within our homes often means television. Because women are seen by commercial interests as being the purchasing agents for a number of people within the home, usually the woman's family, the cultivation of women as consumers for the family is looked upon as a primary activity of television advertising. Television advertising, however, is not just the commercials, but is also the process of moulding audiences into appropriate consumers. As Virginia Nightingale has pointed out in this volume (Chapter 2), this does not mean that television caters to women's conscious needs or desires. Feminist activists who have tried to secure more diverse images of women on television or who have tried to see that more women are employed in decision-making positions in the television establishment, can attest to the fact that although women are primary purchasers, television is not always constructed with women in mind.[1] Neither is the dynamics of the nuclear family such that women are always in control of their television sets. Sets have to be purchased, and once the television set is installed in the home, television viewing is usually managed and negotiated among members of a household. According to some recent studies women do not always come out ahead in such negotiations.[2] Control of the television set seems to be a major indicator of power structures within families; and women's power within the home can be minimal.

Television programmers assume that women have control of the set during the day and that men have control in the evenings.[3] Consequently they attempt to maximise the way that women, men and children of both sexes are able to relate to the flow of television as it is integrated into their lives. The proportion of time devoted to sport, news, talk shows, soap operas of various kinds, action dramas, quiz shows, mini-series or movies, is an attempt to marshall audiences of various configurations into buying positions for advertisers on the commercial broadcasting stations. Audiences are then 'sold' to advertisers, that is, the cost per minute for advertising time is determined by audience demographics and size.

Women's Television Genres

In the configuration of television programming choices, women are recognised by several genres of programming (most quiz shows, some talk shows, cooking shows). It is, however, the melodramatic serial, or the soap opera, which — at least in the United States — is usually considered to be almost exclusively a women's genre, although many men and boys actually watch this form as well.

The social function of soap opera, in the first view of television's relationship to women mentioned above, is to colonise women in the home as consumers and, not only that, to do it in a most insidious manner by preying on women's loneliness and desperation at being left out of the public productive relationships of the economy and denied recognition for the work they do in the home. As Ann Oakley points out, the unspoken syllogism is men/women, work/nonwork.[4] Soap opera in this view, then becomes a vital part of the ideological construct which naturalises 'women's place' in the home.

Since women's place in society in this view is both disguised and trivialised, the ambiguous and paradoxical relationship of soap opera to that position is of particular interest. As Michele Mattelart puts it:

> What is disturbing, however, is the fact that these stories still provide *pleasure* for women viewers who are critically aware of how alienating they are and who have located the mechanisms through which their work is carried on. We cannot simply ignore the appeal and the pleasure (however bitter-sweet it may be when it goes hand in hand with social and political awareness) produced by these fictional products of the cultural industry. There *is* a problem here, and one hitherto scarcely tackled.[5]

There are, then, contradictions built into the enjoyment of television soaps by women since, for the politically aware audience, the soaps can be seen as a tool of capitalism. In addition the trivialisation of soaps watching and of soaps' audiences themselves in the popular press and in general talk among people, mark the soap opera fan's cultural capital as very low. Hence the discourse of pleasure for women is overlaid with a discourse which deems soaps to be rubbish. This puts feminine viewers in a very uncomfortable position — one which belittles their pleasures. The irony here is that such pleasures are denigrated both by feminists, such as Michele Mattelart, *and* by cultural institutions like the popular press. As several studies on women and ideology point out, the contradictions inherent in women's social position leave them with the feeling that they cannot win since dominant discourse gives them one message while their life experiences give them another.[6] There are obviously tensions created by women's discursive position in relation to soap operas, and these are some of the same tensions that all women feel in relation to many patriarchal social constructs.

Feminine Discourse and Viewing Practices/Pleasures

In Chapter 12 I defined feminine discourse.

> Feminine discourse is a way of talking and acting among feminine subjects (usually women) in which they acknowledge their position of subordination within patriarchal society. All non-mainstream groups in society can speak to each other in contexts which acknowledge their subordinate position within society and the problems of having that position defined in ways that do not necessarily represent their own perception of their world. For example, in the case of women's roles, dominant discourse often represents the position of housewife or mother in our culture as unproblematic, whereas housewives or mothers speaking to each other may not. These groups may see power relationships within these social roles as a balancing act between their own lived experiences and what the public or naturalised version of these roles or experiences represents. The knowledge of this subordination carries with it a set of assumptions about how the world is: that is, how one gets by in relation to the rules of patriarchal society. Often feminine discourse, as we define it, is parodic: that is, it makes fun of dominant practices and discursive notions. By playing in this way with the conventions of the dominant discourse, feminine discourse constitutes itself as 'other' to it, and displays a potential resistance.*

---

* Page 190 of this volume.

Other authors have used some version of this term to describe what happens when a moment in popular television speaks to women viewers from the position of a particular kind of knowledge, or when a particular type of discourse is accessible only in certain conversations. Some authors have referred to this type of discourse as illegitimate knowledge or private knowledge.[7] Others have also labelled it feminine discourse.[8] Feminine discourse, in this sense, holds the prospect of empowerment for its feminine subjects. I would like to theorise on how this type of discourse can be viewed as empowering and hence to explain why it is important, in a political sense, to acknowledge the way in which women sometimes use television, despite its problems for women. My contention is that soap operas, like women's talk or gossip and women's ballads, are part of a women's culture that exists alongside dominant culture, and that insofar as the women who use these cultural forms are conscious of the form's otherness, they are practising feminine discourse.[9]

Foucault points out that history is a set of linguistic practices governed by rules invisible to the speakers involved.[10] Such a system forms a kind of 'cultural unconscious' which is not universal or archetypal, but is shaped by forces of constraint which determine what serves as truth and what is unacceptable. Media, literary, and research conventions work in similar ways — acceptable values of production or methodology serve as unwritten rules. However, because of the system of mass media consumption, it is necessary to please an audience, and it is this hegemonic interaction, the need to win and rewin audiences to dominant values, that gives popular media its power.[11] It is able to serve both capital and the people in class-structured industrial societies, even though those interests are contradictory, in short, able to make 'their/our culture mean differently'.[12] Foucault related the power to make meaning within discourse to a 'will to power' which combines with a will to knowledge. In addition, he sees all power relationships as containing within their structure the possibility of resistance:

> Every power relationship implies, at least in potential, a strategy of struggle, in which the two forces are not superimposed, do not lose their specific nature, do not finally become confused. Each constitutes for the other a kind of permanent limit, a point of possible reversal.[13]

Foucault calls this the 'rule of the tactical polyvalence of discourses'.[14]

What I am calling feminine discourse involves both empowerment as well as the requirement that its speakers and listeners understand feminine subordination. Yet they continue to speak. Feminine subjects, speaking feminine discourse, do not assume that the status quo in terms of gender roles is a natural, preordained condition. Hence they sometimes look for spaces in the system where they can speak from their own subject positions, admittedly still somewhat limited by the options available in any given time and place.

Feminine discourse involves speaking practices among women or other non-dominant groups where they can talk directly, where their opinions are valued, and where listeners share the same or similar perceptions of the world. Women's gossip is often compelling because it has this feature. Women can acknowledge their tenuous position in relation to dominant social and cultural practices and yet gain strength from the knowledge that others understand that position. As Deborah Jones says about gossip, it 'perpetuates the restrictions of the female role, but also gives the comfort of validation'.[15] The validation has to do with the mutual recognition of those restrictions by the participants in the group.

Grossberg constructs a similar position for rock and roll fans. He contends that pleasure for rock and roll fans exists outside the hegemony of ruling culture and 'cathects' a boundary for rock and roll fans marked by its otherness.[16] Cathecting is when psychic energy is attached to an idea, a part of the body, or an object. Thus when rock and roll fans form a network of empowerment by setting up boundaries having to do with their relationship to the music, they form what Grossberg calls 'affective alliances' or alliances based on feelings. It is the feelings, the emotional register, combined with the empowerment that comes from participating in the group of fans that constitutes pleasure. Pleasure for some feminine television fans can work in a similar way. By way of illustration let us look at a study by Ann Gray.

In her study of how women use home video tape recorders, Gray discusses the way that the use of such technology confirms women's traditional lack of power within the leisure activity of the home. Gray uses a system whereby women colour code those pieces of technology in the home which according to the 'commonsense' of traditional family life are considered feminine or masculine — pinks for those machines used exclusively by women, blue for those used by men and various shades of lilac for those used by both genders. According to her research:

> The 'record', 'rewind' and 'play' modes are usually lilac, but the timer switch is nearly always blue, with women having to depend on their male

partners or their children to set the timer for them. The blueness of the timer is exceeded only by the deep indigo of the remote control switch which in all cases is held by the man.[17]

Not only is control of the technology masculine in Gray's study, but her respondents also attached a value system to the programs and films watched and hired:

> It is the most powerful member of the household who defines this hierarchy of 'serious' and 'silly', 'important' and 'trivial'. This leaves women and their pleasures in films downgraded, objects and subjects of fun and derision, having to consume them almost in secret.[18]

The discourse within the home which in Gray's study devalues these narrative genres pleasurable to women, is not only picked up by the male and female children but also by the women Gray interviewed. However, when these same women connect with each other and form a support system around feminine pleasures, we have a different story. The women in her study often get together during the day to hire films they like, and they are devoted soaps fans, operating a failsafe network in which they record soaps for each other and refrain from the discussion of each soap opera episode until everyone in the group has seen it. According to Gray:

> These popular texts form an important part of their friendship and association in their everyday lives and give a focus to an almost separate female culture which they can share together within the constraints of their positions as wives and mothers.[19]

The women in the above study recognise the contradiction between their own pleasures and the pleasure rewarded by their husbands which are the same pleasures rewarded by dominant discourse which is naturalised as neutral and, therefore, assumed to be correct. It is the boundaries that these women establish in their friendship networks, constructed in relation to their fanship networks, which establish or, to use Grossberg's term, 'cathect', an alliance between these women based on relationships of pleasure. Important to these relationships is the fact that within the boundaries of these alliances the pleasure in soaps is pleasure without guilt, since within the group it is acceptable behaviour to watch soaps. The boundaries establish for them a locus of empowerment for their own brand of pleasure. The source of pleasure here is not only textual but is also contextual.

Contextual Pleasure and Genres of Discourse

Such contextual pleasure can also be looked at in terms of genres of discourse, that is places where women's material reality can be acknowledged. Genres of discourse are the possibilities of ways of speaking within specific speaking situations, an idea originally suggested by Bakhtin/Volosinov and further elaborated by John Frow.[20] Frazer comments on the fact that hegemonic discourses are supported in some situations where girls' conceptions of reality tell them a different story.[21] She cites as an example a study by Angela McRobbie where the young women speaking seemed to say that women do not go out to paid work. Instead they do childcare and domestic work in their homes. The statement was made even though most of the members of the group had mothers who did go out to work.[22] Along the same line Pendergast and Prout interviewed fifteen year old girls about motherhood and marriage. When they were talking informally with the girls, a body of 'knowledge' concerning the tedium, exhaustion, loneliness and depression experienced by mothers of young children was evident.[23] Such knowledge was usually first-hand, gathered from sisters with young children and the girls' own experiences babysitting and/or with primary childcare of younger sisters and brothers. Yet when these young women were asked in the formal interview to agree or disagree with the statement: 'It is a good life for a mother at home with a young child' they almost all *agreed* in accordance with the hegemonic notion of motherhood.[24] When returned, then, to the public discourse on motherhood by the formality of the questionnaire, the girls in general accepted the socially-rewarded idea that motherhood is unproblematic.

Pendergast and Prout distinguish between these two distinct but contradictory bodies of knowledge as 'illegitimate' and 'legitimate'. In their analysis: 'Illegitimate knowledge is not generalisable while legitimate knowledge is: the sentimental stereotype is so powerful that when one's own experience comes into conflict with it, it is taken that the experience is invalid'. The young women in Pendergast and Prout's study were interviewed alone and some indicated that illegitimate knowledge was also private knowledge, i.e. they kept it to themselves. However in Frazer's study, in which girls were analysing a story from *Jackie*, a British magazine marketed to teenage girls, the girls talked quite frankly or illegitimately in groups. According to Frazer, 'Such knowledge was shared among them, as it is among sociologists of the family, women in women's studies classes, consciousness-raising groups and the like'.[25] Her conclusion is that 'ways of talking, or 'knowledges', or 'discourse registers' will be dropped in contexts where they are not supported'. Frazer's definition of discourse register is 'an institutionalised, situationally specific, culturally familiar, public, way of talking', which seems to coincide with the definition of genres of discourse put forth by Frow. There are, in other words, speaking situations in which certain discourses, in this case feminine discourse, are legitimated.

There are also situations where such discourse registers, at first glance, seem so extreme that the dominant reading would seem to be the only one possible. Fanship networks established around daytime soaps appear, particularly to non-fans, to be this type of case since soaps so forcefully present what appear to be stereotypes of both women and men. However the parodic or ironic *use* of the medium to critique the very values it appears to represent may afford a particular type of pleasure to fans.[26] Grossberg, for example, refers to types of rock and roll specifically coded as masculine and to the possibility of a doubled pleasure when that specific type of rock and roll is reappropriated as feminine.[27] Rock and roll is often criticised for the reproduction of hegemonic notions of gender and sexuality, both in its lyrics and its patterns of consumption. Grossberg uses the example of rockabilly which is marketed as masculine and produced and consumed by males. According to Grossberg's sources, however, women bought it, sang it, danced it and participated in its styles. He gives the example of Georgia Gibbs singing *Great Balls of Fire* which gives it new meaning but, 'only because something else — its affective investment — has been changed by the insertion of the female voice into that particular apparatus'. Such an insertion — because of its difference from the expected hegemonic voice — can evoke pleasure, not to mention the 'ironic' interpretation that such a reversal suggests. Empowerment here involves the ability to see things differently. Gibbs' song becomes an ironic joke on rockabilly's sensitivity, or lack of it.

Pleasure and Politics

However, many feminine pleasures, like those of girl rock and roll fans, are underground and therefore socially invisible. Like the work of the housewife ignored in official statistics, girl rockabilly singers also recorded rockabilly 'although their recordings were rarely released'.[28] Thus the reappropriation of which Grossberg speaks may be a rare event for most women since the recordings or spaces from which the feminine is spoken often do not exist. It is in the sense of struggle for a place for women to speak and in the possibility of resistance to hegemonic gender role conditioning that becomes apparent when women *do* speak that the relationship of television to women's culture can be seen as potentially political. Critics who attempt to look at the way that television audiences use available television texts, document how women *can* use television rather than how they *should*. Often issues that are a 'problem' within dominant constructions of reality are not a 'problem' in feminine discourse as it is conceptualised here.

The example of Georgia Gibbs singing *Great Balls of Fire* is a case of feminine appropriation of a supposedly masculine genre. It is not so different from the example in Gray's study where women in the home appropriate a space for themselves by claiming the right to a so-called women's genre. What makes it difficult to see these two appropriations as similar, I would argue, is their placement in discourse as drastically different acts. It is the act of appropriation in the process of consuming and the subsequent use of pleasure to cathect boundaries within which ideological norms can be restructured, if only momentarily, that establishes these particular discursive genres as political. Such situations are political in that in the process women take pleasure into their own hands. They nominate, value, and regulate their own pleasure. I am suggesting that consumers can use the products of a consumer society, in this case television, in order to constitute acts of resistance while still remaining within the dominant economic order. This book is an attempt, in part, to create genres of discourse within which women can speak with full knowledge of and sympathy with the politically and socially subordinated position of women and yet seek to understand how women (and/or other sociocultural groups) can and do use what is available to them. Part of women's strength may be in the ability and effort to try to understand how women's daily lives are constructed and how aspects of popular culture like television function in this context. The other part is obviously in the power to speak, both to each other and publicly.

Chapter Notes and References

See Bibliography (p.223) for full bibliographic citations under name of author or editor(s).

Chapter 1

1. Women's Studies Group (eds) 1978.
2. Mulvey, L. 1975.
3. Althusser, L. 1978.
4. Gramsci, A. 1971.
5. Fiske, J. and Hartley, J. 1978, p.16.
6. *Ibid*. p.19.
7. Bowlby, R. 1985.

Chapter 2

1. Gallop, J. 1982.
2, 3, 4. *See Sydney Morning Herald*, 9 February 1987, 'The Guide', pp.1-2.
5. *See* Tulloch, J. and Moran, A. 1986.
6. *See Sydney Morning Herald*, 9 February, 1987, 'The Guide', p.1.
7, 8, 9. *Ibid*.
10. *See* Tulloch, J. and Moran, A. 1986.
11. Gallop, J. 1982, p.79.
12. McRobbie, A. 1981[a], p.6.
13. Gross, E. 1986, p.190.

211

14. Bowlby, R. 1985, p.4.
15. *Ibid*. p.19.
16. *Ibid*. p.16.
17. *Ibid*. p.18.
18. *Ibid*. p.32.
19. *Ibid*.
20. *See* Smythe, D. 1981.
21. *See* Modleski, T. 1982; Morley, D. 1986.
22. Leiss, W. et al, 1986, p.89.
23. *See* Ellis, J. 1982.
24. *See* Morley, D. 1986; Gray, A. 1986.
25. Jones, A.R., 1986, p.198.
26. *See* Hobson, D. 1982; Ang, 1985; Tulloch, J. and Moran, A. 1986.
27. Walkerdine, V. 1986.
28. *See* Morley, D. 1986; Gray, A. 1986.
29. *See* Radway, J. 1984.
30. Turner, V. 1977, p.34.
31. *Ibid*. p.49.
32. Hobson, D. 1982, pp.130-131.

Chapter 3

1. Wolf, C. 1986, p.100.
2. De Beauvoir, S. 1977, p.352.
3. Woolf, V. 1929, p.114.
4. *Ibid*. p.35.
5. *Ibid*. pp.77-78.
6. DuPlessis, R. 1985, p.43.
7. The concept of hegemony developed by Gramsci is central to cultural studies, where it refers to the ability of dominant classes to exercise social and cultural leadership (as opposed to coercion) to maintain economic, political, and cultural leadership. 'Hegemony naturalises what is historically a class ideology, and renders it into the form of common sense' (O'Sullivan *et al*, 1983, pp.102-104). Hegemony is never complete; it is always 'leaky.' The potential for opposition always exists because conflicts of interest between dominant classes and subordinate classes exist, and because there are voices to introduce opposition into the symbolic order. Art is seen as a privileged area, in which gaps in the symbolic order are most likely to

occur (Ecker, 1986, p.20); and critical analysis is a site where gaps are identified and moments of opposition described.

8. Woolf, V. 1929, p.28.
9. Ecker, G. (ed), 1986, p.22.
10. *See* Weigel, S. 1986, p.79.
11. Eisenstein, H. 1983, p.xii, citing Gordon, 1979, p.107n.
12. De Beauvoir, S. 1977, p.343.
13. Ang, I. 1985, pp.36-37.
14. Moi, T. 1985, p.46.
15. Fiske, J. and Hartley, J. 1978, p.88.
16. *Ibid.* p.89.
17. *Ibid.* p.86. Quoting Barthes, 1977.
18. Woolf, V. 1929, p.79.
19. Fiske, J. and Hartley, J. 1978, p.86.
20. *See* Seiter, E. (in press).
21. *See* Newcomb, H. and Alley, R.S. 1983.
22. Moi, T. 1985, p.8.
23. *See* Chatman, S. 1978.
24. *See* Ang, I. 1985; Allen, R.C. 1985.
25. *See* Schramm, W. and Roberts, D.F. (eds) 1971.
26. Said, E.W. 1983, p.133.
27. Ecker, G. (ed) 1986, p.47.
28. *See* Moi, T. 1985, pp.155-156, citing Volosinov, 1973 and Kristeva, 1980.
29. Ang, I. 1985, pp.64-66.
30. Ecker, G. (ed) 1986, p.38.
31. The philosophical influence behind most reader-oriented approaches is phenomenology . . . While autonomous objects have immanent (i.e. indwelling, inherent) properties only, heteronomous ones are characterised by a combination of immanent properties and properties attributed to them by consciousness. Thus heteronomous objects do not have a full existence without the participation of consciousness, without the activation of a subject-object relationship (Rimmon-Kenon, 1983, p.118).
32. Batsleer, J. *et al*, 1985, p.112.
33. Rimmon-Kenon, S. 1983, p.119; *see also* Chatman, S. 1978.
34. Koch, G. in Ecker, G. (ed) 1986, p.115.
35. *Ibid.* p.112.
36. Kermode, F. 1981, p.89.
37. Said, E.W. 1983, p.53.
38. Belsey, C. 1980, p.138.

39. Ellis, J. 1982, p.154.
40. *See* Thorburn, D. 1982 and Ang, I. 1985, for example.
41. Radway, J.A. 1984, p.207.
42. Brooks, P. 1976, p.54.
43. *See* Ang, I. 1985, pp.35-37.
44. *Ibid.* p.45.
45. *Ibid.* p.46.
46. *Ibid.* p.80.
47. Gilligan, C. 1982, p.19.
48. Allen, R.C. 1985, p.74.
49. Radway, J.A. 1984, p.139.
50. Allen, R.C. 1985, p.92.
51. DuPlessis identifies the moment of narrative closure as one place where trans-individual assumptions and values are most clearly visible, and where the word 'convention' is found resonating between its literary and its social meanings (1983, p.3).
52. Radway, J.A. 1984, p.65.
53. Rimmon-Kenon, S. 1983, pp.122-123.
54. Thorburn, D. 1982, pp.533-535.
55. DuPlessis, R.B. 1985, p.41.
56. *Ibid.* pp.32-33.
57. Brunsdon, C. 1983, p.70.
58. DuPlessis, R.B. 1985, pp.34-46 *passim.*
59. Batsleer, J. *et al*, 1985, p.142.

Chapter 5

1. *See* D'Acci, L. 1987; also Chapter 8 of this book.
2. *See* Olson, S.R. 1987.
3. At one point, Sue Ellen decided to become a businesswoman — and with great success. However, even this major structural change in her life was motivated by a wish to mess up J.R.'s schemes and plans. She started her business (Valentine Lingerie) as a shrewd tactic to get rid of J.R.'s mistress.
4. *See* Ang, I, 1985.
5. These figures come from a survey of the Department of Viewing and Listening Research, NOS, Hilversum, May 1982.
6. *See* Herzog, H. 1987.
7. It should be noted, however, that watching a television program does not necessarily involve identification with only one character. On the contrary, numerous subject positions can be

taken up by viewers while reading a television text. Consequently, a *Dallas* viewer may alternate between positions of identification and positions of distance and thus inhabit several, sometimes contradictory imaginary structures at the same time.

8. *See* Allen, R.C. 1985.
9. *See* Ang, I. 1985; Feuer, J. 1984; also for melodrama in general *see* Brooks, P. 1976; Gledhill, C. 1987.
10. Brunsdon, C. 1981, p.34.
11. The moment a soap opera becomes self-conscious about its own excess, which is sometimes the case with *Dynasty*, and no longer takes its own story seriously, it presents itself as a parody of the genre, as it were, accentuating its status as discourse through stylisation and formalism (such as slow motion techniques). Sections of the *Dynasty* audience that read the show as a form of camp, for instance, are responding to this aspect of the *Dynasty* text.
12. Modleski, T. 1985, p.107.
13. Mulvey, L. 1978, p.30.
14. Newcomb, H. 1974, p.178.
15. Moi, T. 1986; Rakow, L.F. 1986.
16. Walkerdine, V. 1983, p.168; *see also* Cowie, E. 1984; Kaplan, C. 1986.
17. Stern, L. 1982, p.56.
18. *See* Weedon, C. 1987.
19. Dyer, G. 1987, p.10.

Chapter 6

1. Hudson, B. 1984.
2. I use this term loosely, as have other feminist critics, to designate an institutionalised system of male privilege and female subordination under capitalism, and not as a strict anthropological description.
3. McRobbie, A. 1981b.
4. McRobbie, A. and Garber, J. 1976, p.213.
5. McRobbie, A. 1981b.
6. *See* Brake, M. 1985, Ch.7; Frith, S. 1981; McRobbie, A. 1985; Griffin, C. 1985.
7. *See* Feuer, J. 1984.
8. The initial impetus for these two categories of sign types was

derived from Nava's (1984) discussion of youth service provision to girls.

9. McRobbie, A. 1981b, p.119.
10. *See* Brown, M.E. and Fiske, J. 1987; and Lewis, L.A. 1987, for elaborations on Madonna's video tapes.
11. *See* Stone, G.P. 1965, pp.216-245; Vener, A.M. and Hoffer, C. 1965, pp.76-81.
12. Griffin, C. 1986, p.61.
13. Hudson, B. 1984, p.35.
14. *Ibid*. p.42.
15. Brownmiller, S. 1984, p.14.
16. Stanton, H.D. 1985, p.60.
17. Hudson, B. 1984, p.39.
18. Jerome, J. 1984, pp.82-93.
19. Miller, J. *et al*, 1985, pp.45-57.
20. *See* Carter, E. 1984, for discussion of assumptions in the work of Hoggart, 1958, Cohen, 1972, Hall and Jefferson, 1976, Hebdige, 1979, and Willis, 1977; McRobbie, A. 1981b, focuses on Willis, 1977, and Hebdige, 1979.
21. Carter, E. 1984, p.186.
22. *See* Gardiner, J. 1979; Weinbaum, B. and Bridges, A. 1979, pp.190-205; Harris, S. and Young, K. 1981, pp.109-147.
23. *See* Gramsci, A. 1971.
24. Leach, W. 1984, pp.338-339.
25. Matthews, G. 1985, p.8.

Chapter 7

1. Mulvey, L. 1975.
2. Hebdige, D. 1979; Grossberg, L. 1984; McRobbie, A. 1981b and 1984.
3. Feuer, J. 1982.
4. Cixous, H. 1981.
5. Penley, C. 1985.
6. *Ibid*. p.54.
7. Kaplan, E.A. 1987, p.89.
8. *Ibid*. p.115.
9. Goodwin, A. 1987, p.53.
10. *Ibid*. p.48.
11. Grossberg, L. 1984, p.2.
12. Marsh, P. 1977, p.113.
13. *See* Lewis, L.A. 1987 and Chapter 6.

14. *See* Neale, S. 1986, p.12.
15. Morse, M. 1983.
16. *Ibid*. p.57.
17. Dyer, R. 1982, p.68; *see also* Morse, M. 1983.
18. *Countdown* Magazine, Feb. 1986, p.69.
19. *Ibid*., November 1985, p.70.
20. Weeks, J. 1986, p.27.
21. Kaplan, E.A. 1987, p.111.
22. *See* Steward, S. and Garratt, S. 1984.

Chapter 8

1. *American Film*, July-August 1985, pp.11-12.
2. O'Connor, J. 1984.
3. Farber, S. 1984.
4. Reilly, S. 1985, p.14.
5. McHenry, S. 1984, p.23.
6. Modleski, T. 1983, p.68.
7. *Ibid*. p.71.
8. The fact that the target viewers of *Cagney & Lacey* (women from ages 18 to 35) are also the target consumers for traditionally 'feminine' products indicates the terrain of feminist struggle. *See also* White, M. 1987, p.158.
9. Modleski, T. 1983, p.70.
10. Brunsdon, C. 1983, p.81.
11, 12. White, M. 1987, p.158.
13. Kuhn, A. 1982, p.34.
14. Tompkins, J. 1987, p.169. This quotation occurs slightly out of context. Tompkins is referring to the public-private dichotomy within the academy that berates women for combining emotionality (personal response) with rationality (scholarly discourse). This said, I would add that the form this paper takes, and the positive reading of the text that I argue for here, emerges out of my own 'fierce identification' with and sense of empowerment by *Cagney & Lacey*.
15, 16. White, M. 1987, p.156.
17. Harvey, S. 1980, p.23.
18. *Ibid*. p.25.
19. DeLauretis, T. 1985, pp.167-168.
20. White, M. 1987, p.156.
21. Gledhill, C. 1980, p.16.
22. Mulvey, L. 1975, p.17.

23. Susan Brower notes that the producers of *Cagney & Lacey* consulted with rape crisis professionals in making this episode (p.29). In addition, several CBS affiliates followed this episode with a news segment on date rape. The seriousness and sensitivity with which this episode/issue was treated (and this is not the only example) suggests ways in which the power of *Cagney & Lacey*'s message extends beyond the text.
24. Doane, M.A. 1980, p.41.
25. *Ibid*. p.49.
26. Doane, M.A. 1982, p.83.
27. Brower states that *Cagney & Lacey* is 'by no means a radical show', even though its aesthetic and political marginalisation has been equated with 'quality' (i.e. progressive) television programming (p.28).
28. D'Acci, 1987, p.222.
29. *Ibid*. p.205.

Chapter 9

1. De Certeau, M. 1984.
2. *See* Williamson, J. 1986; Fiske, J. *et al*, 1987; Nava, M. 1987.
3. Bakhtin, M. 1968.
4. *See* Bowlby, R. 1987; Fiske, J. forthcoming; *also* Chapters 1 and 6 of this book.
5. *See* Mills, A. and Rice, P. 1982.
6. *See* Hall, S. 1981.
7. *See* Fiske, J. 1987.

Chapter 10

1. Jacko scored the role of a 'crew-cut, buffoonish character', Jetto, in a 1988 NBC action drama series, *The Highwayman*. But poor ratings meant it was axed from its prime time slot after eight episodes.
2. The routine sexualisation of mateship in early Australian society has been much commented on: see Robert Hughes, 1988. Hughes claims that: 'buggery . . . was as utterly pervasive in the world of hulks and penal settlement as it is in modern penitentiaries' (p.265), but that it was no less prevalent out in the bush: 'Bishop Ullathorne believed that sodomy was less frequent among the shepherds, who tended to live alone, than among stockmen, "a much more dissolute set" who practised

"a great deal of that crime" and even taught it to the formerly innocent Aborigines. And if the Man from Snowy River's convict forebear was not content with the brusque embraces of Jacky-Jacky, there were always sheep' (p.267).

3. Since this great write-up, of course, the ABC (Australian Broadcasting Corporation) has cancelled the program.
4. The media's favourite footnote to the match was that both teams played barefoot.

Chapter 11

1. *See* Parkin, F. 1979, for a good introduction to the Marxist and Weberian theories of class and the differences between them.
2. *See* Dahrendorf, R. 1959.
3. Bottomore, T. *et al*, (eds) 1983, pp.74-77.
4. Parkin, P. 1979, p.4.
5. *Ibid*. p.17.
6. Wright, E.O. 1978, p.31.
7. Parkin, F. 1979, pp.14-15.
8. Giddens, A. 1973, p.288.
9. Felson, M. and Knoke, D. 1974.
10. Oakley, A. 1974a, pp.34-39.
11. *See* Hacker, H. 1951.
12. Millett, K. 1971, p.26.
13. Hartmann, H. and Bridges, A. 1974, p.76; Middleton, C. 1974, pp.180-181.
14. *See* Rubin (1976), Milkman (1986 and 1987), and also Judith Stacey's recent work on working-class women of the Silicon Valley (Stacey 1987).
15. Sudman, S. 1976; Sudman, S. and Bradburn, N. 1983.
16. Rubin, L.B. 1976, p.11.
17. *See* Press, A.L., *Women Watching Television*, University of Pennsylvania Press (forthcoming) for further detail on the methodology of this study.
18. *See* Feuer (1986) for further information on the basics of the show, as well as some contextual information about its place within the melodramatic genre.
19. Wolfenstein, M. and Leites, N. 1977.
20. *See* Ang, I. 1985.
21. *See* Gitlin, T. 1979.
22. Horkheimer, M. and Adorno, T.W. 1972, p.167.
23. Radway, J. 1984b.

24. Other women in my sample bring up the fact that their husbands decide what they will watch and that rather than cause disagreement, they go along, even when they would clearly prefer some other choice. This brings up the interesting issue of how families who watch television together decide which shows to watch. Unfortunately, a full discussion of this issue would require research of a slightly different nature than my own; this would perhaps involve more extensive participant observation of television watching as it occurs in the family setting.

25. In this sense, my study differs from some former works. Ang (1985), for example, solicited forty-two mail responses to an advertisement she placed in a Dutch women's magazine asking for reasons viewers either liked or disliked watching *Dallas*, another prime-time soap. She found that those respondents who liked *Dallas* seemed more involved with the characters themselves, as well as more likely to judge the show to be 'realistic', than did viewers who disliked the show. Ang unfortunately solicited little sociological data describing her respondents. In addition, the self-selected nature of her sample makes it difficult to evaluate her findings.

Liebes (1984) and Liebes and Katz (1986) have produced some remarkably interesting cross-cultural studies of the reception of *Dallas*, which provide an interesting supplement to the work I present here.

26. *See* Feuer, J. 1986.

Chapter 12

1. *See* Jordan, R.A. and De Caro, F. 1986.
2. Fiske, J. and Hartley, J. 1978.
3. *See* Barwick, L. 1985, for extensive discussion of these points.
4. Brown, M.E. 1986; Brown, M.E. and Barwick, L. 1988.
5. Ong, W.J. 1982.
6. Allen, R. 1985, p.14. *See also* Modleski, 1982.
7. *Ibid.* p.138.
8. LaGuardia, R. 1977, p.41.
9. Gilbert, A. 1976, p.10.
10. Soares, M. 1978, p.23.
11. *Ibid.* p.17.
12. Gilbert, A. 1976, p.17.
13. Cantor, M. and Pingree, S. 1983, p.60.

14. Allen, R. 1985, p.104.
15. Cantor, M. and Pingree, S. 1983, p.55.
16. *Chambers Twentieth Century Dictionary*, 1966.
17. Bakhtin, M. 1965, p.4.
18. *Ibid*. p.7.
19. *Ibid*. p.7.
20. *See* Bakhtin, M. 1981, pp.271-273; White, A. 1984.
21. *See* Barwick, L. 1985, pp.250-251; Spender, D. 1980.
22. Taylor, S. 1987.
23. *See* Gluckman, M. 1965.
24. Bakhtin, M. 1965, p.10.
25. *Ibid*. p.11.
26. *Ibid*. p.11.
27. *See* Fiske, J. 1987.
28. Bakhtin, M. 1965, pp.11-12.
29. *Ibid*. p.19.

Recorded conversations cited in Chapter 12

Brown, M.E. Interview with American fans of *Days of Our Lives* (six women aged 18 to 80. Audiotape. Recorded July, 1985. Private collection.

Brown, M.E. Interview with British fan of *Coronation Street* (woman aged 29). Audiotape. Recorded September, 1986. Private collection.

Brown, M.E. Interview with Australian fans of *Sons and Daughters* (three women aged 15 to 18). Audiotape. Recorded October, 1986. Private collection.

Quin, R. Interview with Australian fan of *Days of Our Lives* (woman aged 36). Audiotape. Recorded June, 1987. Private collection.

Chapter 13

1. *See* Loach, L. 1987; Baehr, H. and Spindler-Brown, A. 1987; or any issue of *Media Report to Women*.
2. *See*, for example, Morley, D. 1986; Gray, A. 1987.
3. Comstock, G. *et al*, 1978.
4. Oakley, A. 1974b, p.25.
5. Mattelart, M. 1986, p.15.
6. *See* Hudson, B. 1984; Taylor, S. 1987.
7. Pendergast, S. and Prout, A. 1980.
8. Byars, J. 1987.

9. *See* Brown, M.E. 1987; Brown, M.E. and Barwick, L. 1985.
10. *In* Wright, E. 1984.
11. Gramsci, A. 1971.
12. Fiske, J. 1985.
13. Foucault, M. 1982, p.225.
14. *Ibid.* 1980, pp.100-102.
15. Jones, D. 1980, p.184.
16. Grossberg, L. 1984a, p.227.
17. Gray, A. 1987, p.42.
18. *Ibid.* p.50.
19. *Ibid.* p.49.
20. *See* Frow, J. 1985.
21. Frazer, E. 1987, p.413.
22. McRobbie, A. 1978.
23. Pendergast, S. and Prout, A. 1980.
24. *See* Oakley, A. 1979.
25. *In* Frazer, E. 1987, p.421.
26. *See* Ang, I. 1985; Buckingham, D. 1987.
27. Grossberg, L. 1984b.
28. *Ibid.* p.15.

Bibliography

ACKER, J. 'Women and Social Stratification: A Case of Intellectual Sexism'. *American Journal of Sociology.* 78, 1973: pp.936-945.

ALLEN, R. *Speaking of Soap Operas.* University of North Carolina Press, Chapel Hill. 1985.

ALTHUSSER, L. 'Ideology and Ideological State Apparatuses'. *Essays on Ideology.* Verso, London. 1978.

ALTMAN, R. 'Television/Sound'. *Studies in Entertainment: Critical Approaches to Mass Culture.* Tania Modleski (ed). Indiana University Press, Bloomington and Indianapolis. 1986.

American Film, 'Dialogue on Film'. July-August 1985: pp.11-12.

ANG, I. *Watching* Dallas: *Soap Opera and the Melodramatic Imagination.* Couling, D. (trans). Methuen, London and New York. 1985.

ARNOLD, M. 'Sweetness and Light' in *Matthew Arnold: Selected Prose.* P.J. Keating (ed). Harmondsworth, Penguin. 1970.

BAEHR, H. and DYER, G. (eds) *Boxed In: Women and Television.* Pandora Press, London. 1987.

BAKHTIN, M. *Rabelais and His World,* Iswoy. H. (trans), M.I.T. Press, Cambridge, Massachusetts. 1965.

BAKHTIN, M. *The Dialogic Imagination,* M. Holquist (ed). Emerson, C. and Holquist, M. (trans), University of Texas, Austin. 1981.

BARTHES, R. *Elements of Semiology.* Cape, London. 1968.

BARTHES, R. *Mythologies.* Hill and Wang, New York. 1972.

BARTHES, R. *Image-Music Text.* Fontana, London. 1977.

BARWICK, L. 'Critical Perspectives on Oral Song in Performance: The Case

223

of Donna Lombarda'. PhD Diss. Flinders University of South Australia, Adelaide. 1985.

BATSLEER, J., DAVIES, I, O'ROURKE, R., and WEEDON, C. *Rewriting English: Cultural Politics of Gender and Class.* Methuen, London. 1985.

BAUDRILLARD, J. *In the Shadow of the Silent Majorities and Other Essays.* Foss, P., Patton, P., and Johnston, J. (trans). Semiotexte, New York. 1983.

BEGO, M. *Madonna!* Pinnacle Books, New York. 1985.

BELSEY, C. *Critical Practice.* Methuen, London. 1980.

BENN, S.I., and GAUS, G.F. *Public and Private in Social Life.* St Martin's Press, New York. 1985.

BLAU, Z. 'Maternal Aspirations, Socialization and Achievement of Boys and Girls in the White Working Class'. *Journal of Youth and Adolescence* 1, 1972: pp.35-57.

BOTTOMORE, T. et al. (eds) *A Dictionary of Marxist Thought.* Harvard University Press, Cambridge, Massachusetts. 1983.

BOVENSCHEN, S. 'Is There a Feminine Aesthetic?' B. Weckmuller (trans). In *Feminist Aesthetics.* Ecker, G. (ed). Beacon Press, Boston. 1986.

BOWLBY, R. 'Modes of Modern Shopping: Mallarmé at the Bon Marché.' *The Ideology of Conduct.* Armstrong, N., and Tennenhouse, L. (eds). Methuen, New York and London. 1987: pp.185-205.

BOWLBY, R. *Just Looking.* Methuen, New York and London. 1985.

BRAKE, M. *Comparative Youth Culture.* Routledge & Kegan Paul, London. 1985.

BROCKREIDE, W. 'Rhetorical Criticism as Argument'. *Quarterly Journal of Speech* 60 1974: pp.165-174.

BROOKS, P. *The Melodramatic Imagination: Balzac, Henry James, Melodrama, and the Mode of Excess.* Yale University Press, New Haven: 1976.

BROWER, S. 'TV "Trash" and "Treasure": Marketing *Dallas* and *Cagney & Lacey*', *Wide Angle* 11.1, 1989: pp.18-31.

BROWN, M.E. 'The Politics of Soaps: Pleasure and Feminine Empowerment', *Australian Journal of Cultural Studies* 4.2, 1986: pp.1-25.

BROWN, M.E. and BARWICK, L. 'Fables and Endless Genealogies: Soap Opera and Women's Culture', *Continuum: An Australian Journal of the Media* 1.2, 1988: pp.71-82.

BROWN, M.E. and FISKE, J. 'Romancing the Rock: Romance and Representation in Popular Music Videos'. *OneTwoThreeFour: A Rock and Roll Quarterly.* 5, 1987: pp.61-73.

BROWNMILLER, S. *Femininity.* Fawcett Columbine, New York. 1984.

BRUNSDON, C. '*Crossroads:* Notes on Soap Opera.' *Regarding Television: Critical Approaches — An Anthology.* Kaplan, E.A., (ed). University Publications of America, Frederick, Maryland. 1983.

BRUNSDON, C. '*Crossroads:* Notes on Soap Opera'. *Screen* 22.4 1981: pp.32-37.

BUCKINGHAM, D. *Public Secrets:* Eastenders *and its Audience*, British Film Institute, London. 1987.

BYARS, J. 'Reading Feminine Discourse: Prime-Time Television in the U.S.', *Communication* 9. 3-4, 1987: pp.289-303.

CANTOR, M. and PINGREE, S. *The Soap Opera*. Sage, London. 1983.

CARTER, E. 'Alice in the Consumer Wonderland'. *Gender and Generation*. McRobbie, A. and Nava, M. (eds). Macmillan, London. 1984.

Chambers Twentieth Century Dictionary, Geddie, W. (ed) 1966.

CHATMAN, S. *Story and Discourse: Narrative Structure in Fiction and Film*. Cornell University Press, Ithaca, NY. 1978.

CHESLER, P. *Women and Madness*. Avon Books, New York, 1972.

CHODOROW, N. *The Reproduction of Mothering: Psychoanalysis and the Sociology of Gender*. University of California Press, Berkeley, 1978.

CIXOUS, H. 'The Laugh of Medusa'. 1976. *New French Feminisms*. Marks, E. and de Courtivion, I. (eds). Schocken, New York. 1980.

COHEN, P. 'Subcultural Conflict and Working-Class Community'. *Working Papers in Cultural Studies* 2. Spring 1972.

COOK, P. *The Cinema Book*. British Film Institute, London. 1985.

COMSTOCK, G., CHAFFE, S., KATZMAN, N., MCCOMBS, M., ROBERTS, D. *Television and Human Behaviour*, Columbia University Press, New York. 1978.

COWIE, E. 'Fantasia'. *m/f* 9, 1984: pp.71-105.

CULLER, J. *On Deconstruction: Theory and Criticism After Structuralism*. Cornell University Press, Ithaca, New York. 1982.

D'ACCI, J. 'The Case of Cagney and Lacey'. *Boxed In: Women and Television*. Baehr, H., and Dyer, G. (eds). Pandora Press, London. 1987.

DAHRENDORF, R. *Class and Class Conflict in Industrial Society*. Stanford University Press, Stanford, California. 1959.

DE BEAUVOIR, S. *The Second Sex*. Parshley, H.M. (trans), 1952. Excerpted in Agonito, R. (ed), *History of Ideas on Women: A Source Book*. G.P. Putnam's Sons, New York. 1977.

DE CERTEAU, M. *The Practice of Everyday Life*. University of California Press, Berkeley. 1986.

DE LAURETIS, T. *Alice Doesn't: Feminism, Semiotics, Cinema*. University of Indiana Press, Bloomington. 1984.

DE LAURETIS, T. 'Aesthetic and Feminist Theory: Rethinking Women's Cinema'. *New German Critique*. 34. Winter 1985, pp.154-175.

DE LAURETIS, T. 'Through the Looking-Glass'. *The Cinematic Apparatus*, De Lauretis and Heath (eds). Macmillan, London. 1985.

DEMING, C.J. 'Hill Street Blues as Narrative'. *Critical Studies in Mass Communication* 2. 1985: pp.1-22.

DEMING, C.J. and BECKER, S.L. (eds), *Media in Society: Readings in Mass Communication*. Scott, Foresman, Glenview, Illinois. 1988.

DOANE, M.A. 'Film and the Masquerade: Theorising the Female Spectator'. *Screen* 23, 3-4, 1982, pp.74-88.

DOANE, M.A. 'The Voice in the Cinema: The Articulation of Body and Space'. *Yale French Studies* 60, 1980: pp.33-50.

DOCKER, J. 'In Defence of Popular TV: Carnivalesque v. Left Pessimism', *Continuum: An Australian Journal of the Media* 1.2, 1988: pp.83-99.

DRUMMOND, P., and PATERSON, R. (eds), *Television in Transition*, British Film Institute, London. 1985.

DUPLESSIS, R.B. *Writing Beyond the Ending: Narrative Strategies of Twentieth-Century Women Writers*. Indiana University Press, Bloomington. 1985.

DYER, R. 'Don't Look Now — The Male Pin-Up'. *Screen* 23. 3-4. September-October, 1982: pp.61-73.

DYER, G. 'Women and Television: An Overview'. *Boxed In: Women and Television*. H. Baehr and G. Dyer (eds). Pandora Press, London. 1987.

DYER, R., GERAGHTY, C., JORDAN, M., LOVELL, T., PATERSON, R., STEWART, J. (eds) *Coronation Street*. BFI, London. 1981.

ECKER, G. (ed) *Feminist Aesthetics*. Anderson, H. (trans). Beacon Press, Boston. 1986.

ECO, U. *A Theory of Semiotics*. Indiana University Press, Bloomington, 1976.

EDMUNDSON, M. 'Father Still Knows Best'. *Channels* 6.3. 1986: pp.71-72.

EISENSTEIN, H. *Contemporary Feminist Thought*. G.K. Hall, Boston. 1983.

ELIOT, T.S. *Selected Prose*. Penguin, Harmondsworth. 1958.

ELLIS, J. *Visible Fictions: Cinema: Television: Video*. Routledge & Kegan Paul, London. 1982.

EPSTEIN, C.F. *Woman's Place*. University of California Press, Berkeley. 1970.

FARBER, STEPHEN. 'A New Chance for *Cagney & Lacey*'. *New York Times* 14 March 1984, Sec. C: 26.

FEIBLEMAN, J.K. *The Theory of Human Culture*. Duell, Sloan, and Pearce, New York. 1946.

FELSON, M. and KNOKE, D. 'Social Status and the Married Woman'. *Journal of Marriage and the Family* 36. 1974: pp.516-521.

FEUER, J. *The Hollywood Musical*. Macmillan, London, 1982.

FEUER, J. 'MTM Enterprises: An Overview.' *MTM: 'Quality Television'*. Feuer, J., Kerr, P., and Vahimagi, T.(eds). BFI, London. 1984.

FEUER, J. 'Melodrama, Serial Form and Television Today'. *Screen* 25.1. 1984: pp.4-16.

FEUER, J. 'Narrative Form in American Network Television'. *High Theory/ Low Culture*. C. McCabe (ed). St. Martin's Press, New York. 1986.

FISKE, J., and HARTLEY, J. *Reading Television*. Methuen, London. 1978.

FISKE, J. *Introduction to Communication Studies*. Methuen, London. 1982.

FISKE, J. 'The problem of the popular: how to read a woman's magazine'. A.C. Baird Lecture, University of Iowa Communication Studies Department, Iowa City. 1985.

FISKE, J. 'Television and Popular Culture: Reflections on British and

Australian Critical Practice'. *Critical Studies in Mass Communication* 3. 1986: pp.200-216.

FISKE, J. 'News, History, and Undisciplined Events', unpublished paper delivered to the Television and History Symposium, Chapel Hill, North Carolina. 1987.

FISKE, J. *Television Culture.* Methuen, London and New York. 1987.

FISKE, J., HODGE, R., TURNER, G. *Myths of Oz: Readings in Australian Popular Culture.* Allen & Unwin, Sydney. 1987.

FISKE, J. *Reading the Popular.* Routledge, London and New York, forthcoming.

FLITTERMAN, S. 'Thighs and Whiskers: The Fascination of *Magnum P.I.'* *Screen* 26.2.1985: pp.42-58.

FOUCAULT, M. 'Nietzsche, Genealogy, History'. *Language, Counter-Memory, Practice: Selected Essays and Interviews.* D. Bouchard (ed). Blackwell, Oxford. 1977.

FOUCAULT, M. *The History of Sexuality, Volume I: An Introduction,* Random House, New York. 1980.

FRAZER, E. 'Teenage Girls Reading *Jackie*', *Media, Culture and Society* 9. 4. 1987: pp.407-25.

FREUD, S. *The Standard Edition of the Complete Psychological Works* (24 vols.) The Hogarth Press and the Institute of Psychoanalysis, London. 1953.

FRITH, S. *Sound Effects: Youth, Leisure, and the Politics of Rock 'n' Roll.* Pantheon Books, New York. 1981.

FROW, J. 'Discourse and Power', *Economy and Society* 14. 2. 1985: pp.193-214.

GALLOP, J. *Feminism and Psychoanalysis: the Daughter's Seduction.* Macmillan, London and Basingstoke. 1982.

GARDINER, J. 'Women's Domestic Labor'. *Capitalist Patriarchy and the Case for Socialist Feminism.* Z.R. Eisenstein (ed). Monthly Review Press, New York. 1979.

GERAGHTY, C. 'The Continuous Serial: A Definition'. *Coronation Street.* R. Dyer et al. (eds). British Film Institute, London. 1981.

GIDDENS, A. *The Class Structure of the Advanced Societies.* Hutchinson, London. 1973.

GILLIGAN, C. *In a Different Voice: Psychological Theory and Women's Development.* Harvard University Press, Cambridge, Massachusetts. 1982.

GITLIN, T. 'Prime Time Ideology: The Hegemonic Process in Television Entertainment'. *Social Problems* 26.3, 1979: pp.251-266.

GITLIN, T. *Inside Prime Time.* Pantheon, New York. 1983.

GLEDHILL, C. '*Klute* 1: A Contemporary Film Noir and Feminist Criticism'. *Women in Film Noir.* C. Gledhill (ed). British Film Institute, London. 1980.

GLEDHILL, C. (ed). *Home is Where the Heart Is.* BFI, London. 1987.

GLUCKMAN, M. 'Gossip and Scandal', *Current Anthropology* 3. 1965: pp.307-16.

GOODWIN, A. 'Music Video in the (Post) Modern World', *Screen* 28. 3. 1987: pp.36-55.

GORDON, L. 'The Struggle for Reproductive Freedom: Three Stages of Feminism', *Capitalist Patriarchy and the Case for Socialist Feminism.* Eisenstein Z.R. (ed). Monthly Review Press, New York. 1979.

GRAMSCI, A. *Selections from the Prison Notebooks.* Hoare, Q. and Nowell-Smith, G. (ed and trans). Lawrence and Wishart, London. 1971.

GRAY, A. 'Behind Closed Doors: Video Recorders in the Home'. Baehr, H., and Dyer, G. (eds). *Boxed In: Women and Television*, Pandora, London. 1986.

GRIFFIN, C. 'Leisure: Getting Out and Having a Laugh'. *Typical Girls? Young Women From School to the Job Market.* Routledge & Kegan Paul, London. 1986.

GROSS, E. 'What is Feminist Theory?' *Feminist Challenges.* Pateman, C. and Gross, E. (eds). Allen & Unwin, Sydney. 1986.

GROSSBERG, L. 'Another Boring Day in Paradise: Rock and Roll and the Empowerment of Everyday Life', *Popular Music* 4. 1984a: pp.225-258.

GROSSBERG, L. 'I'd Rather Feel Bad Than Not Feel Anything at All (Rock and Roll: Pleasure and Power)', *Enclitic* 8. 1-3. 1984b: pp.1-33.

HABERMAS, J. *Strukturwandel der Offentlichkeit.* Luchterhand Verlag, Berlin. 1962.

HACKER, H. 'Women as a Minority Group'. *Social Forces* 30. 1951: pp.60-69.

HALL, S. 'The Narrative Construction of Reality', *Southern Review* 17. 1984: pp.1-17.

HALL, S. 'Notes on Deconstructing The Popular'. Samuel, R. (ed). *People's History and Socialist Theory.* Routledge & Kegan Paul, London. 1981.

HALL S., and JEFFERSON, T. (eds) *Resistance Through Rituals: Youth Sub-cultures in Post-War Britain.* Hutchinson, London. 1976.

HARRIS, O., and YOUNG, K. 'Engendered Structures: Some Problems in the Analysis of Reproduction'. *The Anthropology of Pre-Capitalist Societies.* Kahn, J.S., and Llobera, J.R. Humanities Press, Atlantic Highlands, New Jersey. 1981.

HARTLEY, J. 'Invisible Fictions: Television Audiences, Paedocracy, Pleasure'. *Textual Practice* 1.2, Summer 1987. pp.121-138.

HARTLEY, J. *Understanding News.* Methuen, London. 1982.

HARTMANN, H., and BRIDGES, A. 'Pedagogy by the Oppressed'. *Review of Radical Political Economics* 6, 1974. pp.75-79.

HARVEY, S. 'Woman's Place: The Absent Family in Film Noir'. *Women in Film Noir.* Gledhill, C. (ed). British Film Institute, London. 1980.

HEBDIGE, D. *Subcultures: The Meaning of Style.* Methuen, London. 1979.

HENLEY, N. *Body Politics.* Prentice Hall, Englewood Cliffs. 1977.

HERZOG, M. H. 'Decoding *Dallas*: Comparing American and German

Viewers'. *Television in Society*. A.A. Berger (ed). Transaction Books, New Brunswick, New Jersey, 1987. pp.95-103.

HOBSON, D. 'Housewives and the Mass Media', *Culture, Media, Language*. Hutchinson, London. 1980.

HOBSON, D. 'Housewives: Isolation as Oppression': *Women Take Issue*, Women's Studies Group (eds). Hutchinson, London. 1978.

HOBSON, D. Crossroads: *The Drama of a Soap Opera*. Methuen, London. 1982.

HOBSON, D. *Channel 4* (in press).

HOGGART, R. *Uses of Literacy: Changing Patterns in English Mass Culture*. Essential Books, Fair Lawn, New Jersey. 1957.

HORKHEIMER, M., and ADORNO, T.W. *Dialectic of Enlightenment*, Cumming, John (trans). Seabury Press, New York. 1972.

HUDSON, B. 'Femininity and Adolescence' *Gender and Generation*, McRobbie, A., and Nava, M. (eds). Macmillan, London. 1984.

HUGHES, R. *The Fatal Shore: A History of the Transportation of Convicts to Australia 1787-1868*. Pan Books, London. 1988.

IRIGARAY, L. 'Ce sexe qui n'en est pas un'. Marks, E., de Courtviron, I. (eds) *New French Feminisms*. University of Massachusetts Press, Amherst. 1980.

JEROME, J. 'Cyndi Lauper'. *People Weekly* 17 Sept. 1984. pp.82-93.

JOHNSTON, C. 'Women's Cinema as Counter Cinema'. *Notes on Women's Cinema*: London, Society for Education in Film and Television, 1973. pp.24-31.

JONES, A.R. 'Mills and Boon Meets Feminism'. *The Progress of Romance*. Radford, J. (ed). Routledge & Kegan Paul, London. 1986.

JONES, D. 'Gossip: Notes on Women's Oral Culture', *Women's Studies International Quarterly* 3. 1980. pp.193-8.

JORDAN, A., and DE CARO, F. 'Women and the Study of Folklore'. *Signs* 11.3. 1986. pp.500-18.

JORDON, M. 'Character Types and the Individual', *Coronation Street*. Dyer, R. et al. (eds). BFI, London. 1982.

KAPLAN, E.A. *Rocking Around the Clock: Music Television, Postmodernism and Consumer Culture*. Methuen, London. 1987.

KAPLAN, C. 'The Thornbirds: Fiction, Fantasy, Femininity', *Formations of Fantasy*. Burgin, V., Donald, J., and Kaplan, C. (eds). Methuen, London and New York. 1986.

KERMODE, F. 'Secrets and Narrative Sequence'. *On Narrative*. Mitchell, W.J.T. (ed). University of Chicago, Chicago Press. 1981.

KOCH, G. 'Why Women Go to Men's Films'. *Feminist Aesthetics*. Ecker, G. (ed), Anderson, H. (trans). Beacon Press, Boston. 1984.

KRAMARAE, C., and TREICHLER, P.A. *A Feminist Dictionary*. Pandora Press, Boston. 1985.

KRISTEVA, J. 'Woman's Time'. Keshane, O., Rosaldo, M., and Yelpi, B.

Feminist Theory: A Critique of Ideology. University of Chicago Press, Chicago. 1979.

KRISTEVA, J. *Desire in Language: A Semiotic Approach to Literature and Art.* Roudiez, L.S. (ed), Jardin, A., Gora, T., and Roudiez, L. (trans). Blackwell, Oxford. 1980.

KUHN, A. *Women's Pictures: Feminism and Cinema.* Routledge & Kegan Paul, London. 1982.

LACAN, J. *Ecrits: A Selection*, Sheridan, A. (trans.), 1966. Norton, New York. 1977.

LAGUARDIA, R. *Ma Perkins to Mary Hartman: The Illustrated History of Soap Operas.* Ballantine, New York. 1977.

LEACH, W.R. 'Transformations in a Culture of Consumption: Women and Department Stores, 1890-1925'. *Journal of American History* 71.2, 1984. pp.319-342.

LEISS, W. *et al. Social Communication in Advertising.* Methuen, New York and London. 1986.

LEWIS, L.A. 'Female Address in Music Video: The Emergence of a Contradictory Cultural Discourse'. Dissertation, University of Texas, Austin. 1987.

LIEBES, T. 'Ethnocentricism: Israelis of Moroccan Ethnicity Negotiate the Meaning of *Dallas*'. *Studies in Visual Communication.* 10.30, 1984. pp.46-72.

LIEBES, T., and KATZ, E. 'Patterns of Involvement in Television Fiction: A Comparative Analysis'. *European Journal of Communication* 1, 1980. pp. 151-171.

LOACH, L. 'Campaigning for change', in Baehr, H. and Dyer, G. (eds), *Boxed In: Women and Television*, Pandora, London. 1987.

LOEVENGER, L. 'The Ambiguous Mirror: The Reflective-Projective Theory of Broadcasting'. *Mass Media: Forces in Our Society.* Voelker, F., and Voelker, L. (eds). Harcourt Brace Jovanovich, San Francisco. 1978. (Rpt. from *Journal of Broadcasting* 12. 1968. pp.97-116.)

MCHENRY, S. 'The Rise and Fall — And Rise of TV's *Cagney & Lacey*'. *Ms*, April 1984. pp.23-26.

MCROBBIE, A., and GARBER, J. 'Girls and Subcultures'. *Resistance Through Rituals: Youth Subcultures in Post War Britain.* Hall, S., and Jefferson, T. (eds). Hutchinson, London. 1976.

MCROBBIE, A. 'Working Class Girls and the Culture of Femininity'. Unpublished thesis, Centre for Contemporary Cultural Studies, Birmingham. 1977.

MCROBBIE, A. 'Working Class Girls and the Culture of Femininity'. *Women Take Issue.* Women's Studies Group (eds). Hutchinson, London. 1978.

MCROBBIE, A. 'Just Like a *Jackie* Story'. *Feminism for Girls.* Robbie, A., and McCabe, T. (eds). Routledge & Kegan Paul, London. 1981a.

MCROBBIE, A. 'Settling Accounts with Subcultures: A Feminist Critique'. *Culture, Ideology and Social Process.* Bennett, T., Martin, S, Mercer, C, and Woollacott, J. (eds). Batsford Academic and Educational Ltd. in association with The Open University Press, London. 1981b.

MCROBBIE, A. 'Dance and Social Fantasy'. *Gender and Generation.* McRobbie, A., and Nava, M. (eds). Macmillan, London. 1985.

MANDER, J. *Four Arguments for the Elimination of Television.* William Morrow, New York. 1978.

MARKS, E., and DE COURTIVRON, I. (eds) *New French Feminisms.* Amherst, Massachusetts. 1980.

MARSH, P. 'Dole-queue rock'. *New Society.* January, 1977. pp.112-114.

MATTELART, M. *Women, Media and Crisis: Femininity and Disorder,* Comedia, London. 1986.

MATTHEWS, G. *Madonna.* Wanderer Books/Simon and Schuster, New York. 1985.

MAYERLE, J. 'Character Shaping Genre in *Cagney & Lacey'. Journal of Broadcasting and Electronic Media* 31. 1987. pp.133-151.

Media Report to Women, Women's Institute for Freedom of the Press, Washington, DC.

METZ, C. *The Imaginary Signifier: Psychoanalysis and the Cinema.* Indiana University Press, Bloomington. 1982.

MIDDLETON, C. 'Sexual Inequality and Stratification Theory'. In *The Social Analysis of Class Structure.* Frank Parkin, (ed). Tavistock, London. 1974.

MILKMAN, R. 'Women's History and the Sears Case'. *Feminist Studies* 12.2. 1986. pp.375-400.

MILKMAN, R. *Gender at Work: The Dynamics of Job Segregation by Sex During World War II.* University of Illinois Press, Chicago. 1987.

MILLER, J., MCGUIGAN, C., UEHLING, D., HUCK, J., and MCALEVERY, P. 'Rock's New Women'. *Newsweek* 4 March 1985. pp.45-57.

MILLETT, K. *Sexual Politics.* Avon, New York. 1971.

MILLS, A., and RICE, P. 'Quizzing the Popular'. *Screen Education* 41. Winter/Spring, 1982. pp.15-25.

MODLESKI, T. *Loving with a Vengeance: Mass-Produced Fantasies for Women.* Methuen, New York. 1982.

MODLESKI, T. 'The Rhythms of Reception: Daytime Television and Women's Work'. *Regarding Television.* Kaplan, E.A. (ed). American Film Institute, Los Angeles. 1983.

MODLESKI, T. *Studies in Entertainment: Critical Approaches to Mass Culture.* Indiana University Press, Bloomington and Indianapolis. 1986.

MOI, T. *Sexual/Textual Politics: Feminist Literary Theory.* Methuen, London. 1985.

MONTRELAY, M. 'Inquiry into Femininity'. *m/f* 1. 1978. pp.83-101.

MORLEY, D. *Family Television: Cultural Power and Domestic Leisure.* Comedia, London. 1986.

MORSE, M. 'Sport on Television: Replay and Display', *Regarding Television,* Kaplan, E.A. (ed). AFI, Los Angeles. 1983.

MULVEY, L. 'Notes on Sirk and Melodrama'. *Movie* 25. 1978.

MULVEY, L. 'The Image and Desire'. *ICA on Desire*. London. 1983.

MULVEY, L. 'Visual Pleasure and Narrative Cinema'. *Screen* 16. 3. Autumn 1975. pp.6-18.

NAVA, M. 'Consumerism and its Contradictions. *Cultural Studies* 1: 2. 1987. pp.204-210.

NAVA, M. 'Youth Service Provision, Social Order and the Question of Girls'. *Gender and Generation*. McRobbie, A., and Nava, N. (eds). Macmillan, London. 1984.

NEALE, S. 'Masculinity as Spectacle'. *Screen* 24. 6. November-December 1983. pp.2-16.

NEALE, S. 'Sexual Difference in Cinema — Issues of Fantasy, Narrative and the Look'. *Oxford Literary Review*. 8.1-2. 1986. pp.123-131.

NEWCOMB, H., and ALLEY, R.S. *The Producer's Medium: Conversations with Creators of American TV*. Oxford University Press, New York. 1983.

NEWCOMB, H. *TV: The Most Popular Art*. Anchor Books, New York. 1974.

NOVAK, M. 'Television Shapes the Soul'. *Understanding Television*. Adler, R. P. (ed). Praeger, New York. 1981.

O'CONNOR, J. *Cagney & Lacey*, Police Series on CBS. *New York Times* 2 July 1984.

O'SULLIVAN, T., HARTLEY, J., SAUNDERS, D., and FISKE, J. *Key Concepts in Communication*. Methuen, London. 1983.

OAKLEY, A. *Women's Work: The Housewife, Past and Present*. Vintage, New York. 1974a.

OAKLEY, A. *The Sociology of Housework*. Vintage, New York. 1974b.

OAKLEY, A. *Becoming a Mother*. Martin Robertson, Oxford. 1979.

OLSON, S.R. 'Meta-television: Popular Postmodernism'. *Critical Studies in Mass Communication*. 4. 1987. pp.284-300.

ONG, W.J. *Orality and Literacy: The Technologizing of the World*. Methuen, London. 1982.

PARKIN, F. *Marxism and Class Theory: A Bourgeois Critique*. Columbia University Press, New York. 1979.

PARKIN, F. *Class, Inequality and Political Order*. Praeger, New York. 1971.

PENDERGAST, S., and PROUT, A. ' "What will I do . . .?" Teenage Girls and the Construction of Motherhood'. *Sociological Review*. 28. 3. 1980.

PENLEY, C. 'Feminism, Film theory and the Bachelor Machines'. *m/f*. 10. 1985. pp.39-59.

PICCIRILLO, M.S. 'On the Authenticity of Televisual Experience: A Critical Exploration of Para-Social Closure'. *Critical Studies in Mass Communication* 3. 1986. pp.337-355.

POSTMAN, N. *Amusing Ourselves to Death*. Penguin, New York. 1985.

POULANTZAS, N. *Classes in Contemporary Capitalism*, D. Fernbach (trans), New Left Books, London. 1975.

POULANTZAS, N. *Political Power and Social Classes*, T. O'Hagen (trans), New Left Books, London. 1973.

PRESS, A. 'Deconstructing the Audience: Class Differences in Women's Interpretations of Television Narrative and Characters'. PhD Diss. University of California at Berkeley, 1987.

RADWAY, J.A. 'Interpretive Communities and Variable Literacies: The Functions of Romance Reading'. *Daedalus* 113.3, 1984a. pp.49-73.

RADWAY, J.A. *Reading the Romance: Women, Patriarchy and Popular Literature*. University of North Carolina Press, Chapel Hill. 1984b.

RAKOW, L.F. 'Feminist Approaches to Popular Culture: Giving Patriarchy Its Due'. *Communication* 9. 1986. pp.19-41.

REILLY, S. 'The Double Lives of Cagney and Lacey'. *McCall's*. April 1985: pp.14,204.

REITER, R.R. 'Men and Women in the South of France: Public and Private Domains'. *Toward an Anthropology of Women*. Reiter, R.R. (ed), Monthly Review Press, New York. 1975.

RICH, A. 'Compulsory Heterosexuality and Lesbian Experience'. *Powers of Desire: The Politics of Sexuality*. Snitow, A., Stansell, C., and Thompson, S. (eds). Monthly Review Press, New York. 1983.

RIMMON-KENON, S. *Narrative Fiction: Contemporary Poetics*. Methuen, London. 1983.

ROSALDO, M., and LAMPHERE, L. (eds). *Women, Culture and Society*. Stanford University Press, Stanford, California. 1974.

ROSEN, R. 'Search for Yesterday'. *Watching Television*. Gitlin, T. (ed). Pantheon, New York. 1986.

RUBIN, G. 'The Traffic In Women: Notes on the Political Economy of Sex'. *Toward an Anthropology of Women*. Reiter, R.R. (ed). Monthly Review Press, New York. 1975: pp.157-210.

RUBIN, L.B. *Worlds of Pain: Life in the Working-Class Family*. Basic Books, New York. 1976.

RYAN, M.P. 'Femininity and Capitalism in Antebellum America'. *Capitalist Patriarchy and the Case for Socialist Feminism*. Eisenstein, Z.R. (ed). Monthly Review Press, New York. 1979.

SAID, E.W. *The World, the Text, and the Critic*. Harvard University Press, Cambridge, Massachusetts. 1983.

SAUSSURE, F. DE. *Course in General Linguistics*. 1915. Fontana, London. 1974.

SCHRAMM, W., and ROBERTS, D.F. (eds). *The Process and Effects of Mass Communication*. Rev.ed. University of Illinois, Urbana, Illinois. 1971.

SEITER, E. 'Stereotypes: Notes on Research and Pedagogy'. *Journal of Communication*, in press.

Seventeen. 'Funky Frills take centre stage in Cyndi Lauper and Madonna-inspired Extras', July 1985. p.34.

SHARISTANIAN, J. (ed.) *Beyond the Public/Private Dichotomy: Contemporary Perspectives on Women's Public Lives*. University of North Carolina Press, Greenwood, forthcoming.

SHARISTANIAN, J. (ed). *Gender, Ideology and Action: Historical Perspectives on Women's Public Lives.* University of North Carolina Press, Greenwood. 1986.

SILVERMAN, K. *The Subject of Semiotics.* Oxford University Press, New York. 1983.

SMYTHE, D. *Dependency Road.* Ablex, Norwood, New Jersey. 1981.

SOARES, M. *The Soap Opera Book.* Harmony, New York. 1978.

SPENDER, D. *Man Made Language.* Routledge & Kegan Paul, London, 1980.

STACEY, J. 'Sexism By a Subtler Name? Postindustrial Conditions and Post-femininist Consciousness in the Silicon Valley'. *Socialist Review* 17.6. 1987. pp.7-28.

STANTON, H.D. *Interview.* December 1985. pp.56-68.

STERN, L. 'The Body as Evidence'. *Screen* 23.5. 1982. pp.38-60.

STEWARD, S., and GARRATT, S. *Signed, Sealed and Delivered: True Life Stories of Women in Pop.* Pluto Press, London. 1984.

STONE, G.P. 'Appearance and the Self'. *Dress, Adornment and the Social Order.* Roach, M.E., and Bubolz Eicher, J. (eds). John Wiley, New York. 1965.

SUDMAN, S. *Applied Sampling.* Academic Press, New York. 1976.

SUDMAN, S., and BRADBURN, N.M. *Asking Questions: A Practical Guide to Questionnaire Design.* Jossey-Bass, San Francisco. 1983.

TAYLOR, S. 'The Tender Trap: Teenage Girls, Romantic Ideology, and Schooling', unpublished paper, Educational Studies Department, Brisbane College of Advanced Education, Kelvin Grove Campus, Brisbane. 1987.

THORBURN, D. 'Television Melodrama'. *Television: The Critical View.* 3rd ed. Newcomb, H. (ed). Oxford, New York. 1982.

TOMPKINS, J. 'Me and My Shadow'. *New Literary History* 19. 1. Autumn 1987. pp.169-78.

TULLOCH, J., and MORAN, A. A Country Practice: *Quality Soap.* Currency Press, Sydney. 1986.

TURNER, V. 'Frame, Flow and Reflection: Ritual and Drama as Public Liminality'. *Performance in Postmodern Culture.* Benamou, M., and Carmello, C. (eds). Coda Press, Madison, Wisconsin. 1977.

VENER, A.M., and HOFFER, C. 'Adolescent Orientations to Clothing'. *Dress, Adornment and the Social Order.* Roach, M.E., and Eicher, J.B. (eds). John Wiley, New York. 1965.

Village Voice Advertisement. 'JRs! Desperately Seeking Madonna Look-Alikes'. 1985. 30: p.24.

VOLOSINOV, N.V. *Marxism and the Philosophy of Language.* 1929. Matejka, L., and Titunik, I.R. (trans). Seminar Press, New York. 1973.

WALKERDINE, V. 'Some Day My Prince Will Come: Young Girls and the Preparation for Adolescent Sexuality'. *Gender and Generation.* McRobbie, A., and Nava, M. (eds). Macmillan, London, 1983.

WALKERDINE, V. 'Video Replay: Families, Films and Fantasy'. Burgin, V. et al. *Formations of Fantasy*. Methuen, London, 1986.

WEEDON, C. *Feminist Practice and Poststructuralist Theory*. Basil Blackwell, Oxford, 1987.

WEEKS. J. 'Masculinity and the Science of Desire'. *Oxford Literary Review* 8. 1-2. 1986.

WEIGEL, S. 'Double Focus: On the History of Women's Writing'. *Feminist Aesthetics*. Ecker, G. (ed), Anderson, H. (trans). Beacon Press, Boston. 1986.

WEINBAUM, B., and BRIDGES, A. 'The Other Side of the Paycheck: Monopoly Capital and the Structure of Consumption'. *Capitalist Patriarchy and the Case for Socialist Feminism*. Eistenstein, Z.R. (ed). Monthly Review Press, New York. 1979.

WHITE, A. 'Bakhtin, Sociolinguistics and Deconstruction'. *Theory of Reading*. Gloversmith, F. (ed). Harvester Press, Sussex. 1984.

WHITE, M. 'Ideological Analysis and Television'. *Channels of Discourse*. Allen, R. C. (ed). University of North Carolina Press, Chapel Hill. 1987.

WILLEMAN, P. 'Anthony Mann: Looking at the Male'. *Framework*. 15/16/17. Summer 1981.

WILLIAMS, R. *Television: Technology and Cultural Form*. Fontana, London. 1984.

WILLIAMS, R. *Keywords: A Vocabulary of Culture and Society*. Fontana, London, 1983.

WILLIAMS, R. *Marxism and Literature*. Fontana, London, 1977.

WILLIAMSON, J. *Consuming Passions*. Marion Boyars, London. 1986.

WILLIS, P. *Learning To Labour: How Working Class Kids Get Working Class Jobs*. Saxon House, London. 1977.

WITTIG, M. *Les guérillères*. Le Vay, D. (trans), 1969. Avon, New York. 1971.

WOLF, C. 'A Letter About Unequivocal and Ambiguous Meaning, Definiteness and Indefiniteness; About Ancient Conditions and New View-Scopes; About Objectivity'. *Feminist Aesthetics*. Ecker, G. (ed), Anderson, H. (trans). Beacon, Boston. 1986.

WOLFENSTEIN, M., and LEITES, N. *Movies: A Psychological Study*. 1950; Atheneum, New York, 1977.

WOLLHEIN, R. *Freud*. Fontana, London. 1971.

WOMEN'S STUDIES GROUP, (eds). *Women Take Issue*. Hutchinson, London. 1978.

WOOD, P. 'Television as Dream'. *Television*. Adler, R. (ed). Praeger, New York. 1981.

WOOLF, V. *A Room of One's Own*. Harcourt, Brace & World, New York. 1929.

WRIGHT, E. *Psychoanalytic Criticism: Theory in Practice*, Methuen, London. 1984.

WRIGHT, E.O. *Class, Crisis and the State*. New Left Books, London. 1978.

The Contributors

IEN ANG is currently a lecturer at the Department of Communication, University of Amsterdam, where she teaches theories of culture and ideology. Apart from *Watching Dallas*, her English publications include a contribution to *Television in Transition*. She has published widely in Dutch about television, popular culture and feminist cultural politics.

MARY ELLEN BROWN has taught courses on women and the media since 1975. Until recently she taught media studies and women's studies at the Western Australian College of Advanced Education and has now joined the Department of Communication faculty of the State University of New York at Brockport, New York. Her work has appeared in *The Australian Journal of Cultural Studies*, *Communication*, *Continuum*, and *OneTwoThreeFour* and is forthcoming in *Doing Research on Women's Communication*. She is currently completing a dissertation on soap opera.

DANAE CLARK teaches media students at the University of Pittsburgh. In addition to her work in feminist criticism, she is currently completing a study of actors' labour history.

CAREN J. DEMING is Professor and head of the Department of Media Arts at the University of Arizona in Tucson. She has published in numerous communication and literary journals in the United States. She is co-editor with Samuel L. Becker of *Media in Society: Readings in Mass Communication*.

JOHN FISKE teaches in the Department of Communication Arts at the University of Wisconsin, Madison. He has held academic appointments in the UK, the US and Australia. He is author or co-author of *Reading Television, Introduction to Communication Studies, Key Concepts in Communication, Myths of Oz* and *Television Culture*.

JOHN HARTLEY is author or co-author of *Reading Television, Understanding News, Key Concepts in Communication* and *Making Sense of the Media*. He is currently teaching in the School of Humanities, Murdoch Campus, University of Western Australia.

DOROTHY HOBSON is the author of *Crossroads: The Drama of a Soap Opera* and has written, lectured and broadcast extensively on women. Her latest book (in press) is *Channel 4 1982-87*. She is a contributor to *Women Take Issue* (1980), to *Feminism for Girls: An Adventure Story*, and is joint author of *Culture, Media, Language*. She has been involved in teaching and research at the Centre for Contemporary Cultural Studies at the University of Birmingham, UK. She now works as a full-time writer.

LISA A. LEWIS completed a dissertation on the subject of female address in music video at the University of Texas at Austin in 1987. She has published articles from her research in *Communication, The Journal of Communication Inquiry* and *OneTwoThreeFour*. She is conducting fieldwork on film and video productions involving the female musicians she has studied.

VIRGINIA NIGHTINGALE co-ordinates media studies teaching at the University of Western Sydney-Nepean, Sydney, Australia. She completed post-graduate studies and a research project for Prix Jeunesse at C.M.C.R., Leicester University, UK, in 1980 and has published widely in Australian journals.

BEVERLEY POYNTON is a graduate of Murdoch University, Perth, Western Australia, with a major in Communication Studies. She is a fan of Australian Rules Football through family commitments and maintains an interest in popular culture by working in community video production and independent film-making.

ANDREA L. PRESS teaches at the University of Michigan at Ann Arbor having completed her PhD at The University of California, Berkeley on women audiences. She has been a Visiting Fellow at the University of Kentucky in Lexington and has published internationally.

SALLY STOCKBRIDGE teaches film, television and cultural studies at Curtin University of Technology, Western Australia. She has taught sociology and film in Sydney, Melbourne and England and has worked at various international film festivals. Her PhD dissertation is on the Australian music video industry. Recently her articles have been published in *Media Information Australia* and *Cultural Studies*.

Index